COMMUNICATING WAR

"In an era of sustained military operations by western nations in Afghanistan and Iraq, continued conflict and crisis in countries such as Sudan, and a 'global war on terror', this volume provides an important contribution to our understanding of the interaction between media, governments and those caught up in contemporary war. Combining insights from academia, journalists and practitioners, this volume provides a particularly diverse and illuminating study of the conflicting pressures confronting media when reporting 21st century conflict."
Piers Robinson,
Lecturer in International Politics, University of Manchester

"The editors of *Communicating War* have assembled essays by leading figures writing on war and media today. Through an impressive range of case studies, the volume covers many of the most pressing issues facing journalists, militaries and civilians, offering insights and analysis that will prove valuable to students and practitioners alike."
Dr Ben O'Loughlin,
War Studies, Kings College London

COMMUNICATING WAR:
MEMORY, MEDIA AND MILITARY

Edited by

Sarah Maltby

Richard Keeble

Published 2007 by arima publishing

www.arimapublishing.com

ISBN 978-1-84549-197-0

© Richard Keeble & Sarah Maltby 2007

All rights reserved

This book is copyright. Subject to statutory exception and to provisions of relevant collective licensing agreements, no part of this publication may be reproduced, stored in a retrieval system, or transmitted in any form or by any means, without the prior written permission of the author.

Printed and bound in the United Kingdom

Typeset in Garamond 10/16

This book is sold subject to the conditions that it shall not, by way of trade or otherwise, be lent, re-sold, hired out, or otherwise circulated without the publisher's prior consent in any form of binding or cover other than that which it is published and without a similar condition including this condition being imposed on the subsequent purchaser.

Abramis is an imprint of arima publishing
arima publishing
ASK House, Northgate Avenue
Bury St Edmunds, Suffolk IP32 6BB
t: (+44) 01284 700321

www.arimapublishing.com

Dedicated to all those who are suffering from wars across the globe

Table of Contents

List of Illustrations ix

Acknowledgements x

Editors xi

Contributors xii

Introduction

Communicating War: Strategies and Implications
Sarah Maltby 1

PART I: Remembering and Forgetting Communicated War

1. Ghost in the Machine: Television and Wars' Past(s)
   Andrew Hoskins 18

2. Exploring Legal Black Holes: Extraordinary Rendition, Investigative Journalism and the Moral Imagination
   John Tulloch 29

3. Reporting Africa's Unknown Wars
   Lara Pawson 42

4. Unreported Mass Killings of Civilians
   Jeremy Tunstall 55

PART II: Communicating War through Media Institutions and Practices

5. Information War: Encountering a Chaotic Information Environment
   Howard Tumber and Frank Webster 62

6. Truth in a War Zone: The Role of Warblogs in Iraq
   Donald Matheson and Stuart Allan 75

7. Positioning the News Audience as Idiot
   Oliver Boyd-Barrett 90

8. Fighting Discourses: Discourse Theory, War and Representations of
the 2003 Iraqi War
Nico Carpentier 103

9. Keeping the Peace: Media Representations of the Anti-Gulf War
Movement in the British Press
Chris Atton 117

PART III: Military Communication of War

10. Western and Terrorist Ways of War
Martin Shaw 130

11. Dimensions of Perception: Shaping the British Approach to Information
Strategy During Military Operations
Angus Taverner 141

12. A Century of Psyops: Psychological Warfare from the First World War
to Lebanon
Ron Schleifer 151

13. Kidnap Videos: Setting the Power Relations of New Media
Makram Khoury-Machool 163

14. Pat Tillman and The Military-Media Complex
David Altheide 177

15. The Military, the Media and Mimesis
Neal Curtis 188

16. The Necessary Spectacular 'Victories': New Militarism,
the Mainstream Media and the Manufacture of the Two Gulf
Conflicts 1991 and 2003
Richard Keeble 200

Index 213

LIST OF ILLUSTRATIONS

Figure 8-1: The Ideological Model of War 108

Figure 11-1: DIME Model versus the DME Model 142

Figure 11-2: An Effects-Based Approach to Measuring the
Effectiveness of Information Strategy: 'A Conceptual Model' 144

Acknowledgements

Sarah Maltby would like to thank members of the War and Media Network; her colleagues at the University of Surrey, particularly Martin Innes for his intellectual counsel; Bryan Maltby for his encouragement and Kevin McSorley for his support and academic inspiration.

Richard Keeble would like to thank his colleagues and students at the University of Lincoln for the challenges they have set him; John Pilger and Phillip Knightley for inspiring him over the years and his partner Maryline Gagnere for her constant support.

EDITORS

Dr Sarah Maltby is founder and co-ordinator of the War and Media Network (www.warandmedia.org). Her core academic interests centre upon the intersection between war and terrorism and contemporary military and media practice. This includes the tactical and strategic role of mediated information in the implementation of security provision, institutional information management in conflict, and the impact of mediated information on social behavior in conflict scenarios.

Richard Keeble is Professor of Journalism at the University of Lincoln. Before that he taught for 19 years at City University, London. His publications include *Secret State, Silent Press* (John Libbey, 1997), *The Newspapers Handbook* (4th edition, Routledge 2005) *Ethics for Journalists* (Routledge 2001) and he jointly edited *The Journalistic Imagination: Literary Journalists from Defoe to Capote and Carter* (Routledge 2007). He is the joint-editor of *Ethical Space: The International Journal of Communication Ethics* and editor of *Print Journalism: A critical Introduction* (Routledge 2005) and *Communication Ethics Today* (Troubador 2005)

CONTRIBUTORS

Stuart Allan is Professor of Journalism at Bournemouth University, UK. He is the author of *News Culture* (1999, second edition, 2004), *Media, Risk and Science* (2002) and *Online News: Journalism and the Internet* (2006). His edited collections include *Journalism After September 11* (2002) and *Reporting War: Journalism in Wartime* (2004), both co-edited with Barbie Zelizer, and *Journalism: Critical Issues* (2005). His current work focuses on the online reporting of war and conflict, with a special interest in blogging and citizen journalism.

Professor David Altheide is Regents Professor at the School of Justice and Social Inquiry, Arizona State University. His research interests include mass communication, qualitative research methods, propaganda and official information and social control. His publications include *Terrorism and the Politics of Fear* (Altamira Press, 2006); *Creating Fear: News and the Construction of Crisis* (Aldine de Gruyter, 2002), *An Ecology of Communication: Cultural Formats of Control* (Aldine de Gruyter, 1995) and *Media Worlds in the Postjournalism Era* (with Robert P. Snow, Aldine de Gruyter 1991).

Dr Chris Atton is Reader in Journalism at the School of Communication Arts, Napier University, Edinburgh, Scotland. He is one of the leading international scholars in the study of alternative and radical media, on which he has published extensively. His books include *Alternative Literature* (Gower, 1996), *Alternative Media* (Sage, 2002) and *An Alternative Internet* (Edinburgh University Press, 2004). He has edited special issues on alternative media for *Journalism: Theory, Practice and Criticism* and *Media, Culture and Society* (both 2003). He is currently writing *Alternative Journalism* (Sage, 2008) with James Hamilton.

Dr Oliver Boyd-Barrett is Director of the School of Communication Studies, and holds a joint professorship in the departments of Journalism and Telecommunications at Bowling Green State University, Ohio. He has written and published extensively on international media. His books include *The International News Agencies* (1980), *Le Trafic Des Nouvelles* (with Michael Palmer, 1981), *Contra-Flow in Global News* (with Daya Thussu, 1992), *The Globalization of News* (1998), *The Media Book* (with Chris Newbold and Hilde Van Den Bulck, 2002), *Globalization, Media and Empire* (ed, 2006). He is currently working on *Media and the War on Terrorism*, for Marquette publications.

Dr Nico Carpentier is a media sociologist working at the Communication Studies Departments of the Free University of Brussels (VUB) and the Catholic University of Brussels (KUB). He is co-director of the VUB research centre CEMESO and a board member of the European Communication Research and Education Association (ECREA formerly ECCR). His theoretical focus is on discourse theory; his research interests are situated in the relationship between media, journalism, politics and culture, especially towards social domains as war and conflict, ideology, participation and democracy.

Neal Curtis is lecturer in the Department of Cultural Studies at the University of Nottingham. He is the author of *Against Autonomy: Lyotard, Judgement and Action* (Ashgate, 2001), and *War and Social Theory: World, Value and Identity* (Palgrave, 2005).

Andrew Hoskins is Associate Professor in the Department of Sociology, University of Warwick. He is founding Editor-in-Chief of a new Sage interdisciplinary journal of *Memory Studies* (www.sagepub.co.uk/ms), founding Co-editor of the new Sage journal of *Media, War and Conflict* (www.sagepub.co.uk/mwc) and Principal Investigator of an AHRC funded three-year research project 'Conflicts of Memory: Mediating and Commemorating the 2005 London Bombings' (www.media-memory.com). Recent relevant publications include: *Televising War: From Vietnam to Iraq* (Continuum, 2004). Relevant forthcoming publications include: *Media and Memory* (Routledge, 2007), *Television and Terror: Conflicting Times and the Crisis of News Discourse* (with Ben O'Loughlin, Palgrave Macmillan, 2007), and *Media, War and Conflict* (with Ben O'Loughlin, Polity, 2008).

Dr Makram Khoury-Machool (SOAS, London) is the journalist who announced the outbreak of the first Palestinian Intifada in 1987. He is the author of the first academic textbook on Arab media in English, titled: *Arab Media: From the first press to New Media* (Routledge). He has taught at the Universities of London, Bedfordshire and Cambridge and is leading Media Studies at Anglia Ruskin University, Cambridge.

Donald Matheson is Senior Lecturer in Mass Communication at Canterbury University, New Zealand. He is the author of *Media Discourses* (Open University Press, 2005) and co-editor of the journal *Ethical Space*. He writes on journalism practices, with particular emphasis on news language and the communicative ethics of the news, interests which have led him to study weblogs and other online media. He previously worked at Cardiff and Strathclyde universities in the UK and as a journalist in New Zealand.

Lara Pawson is a freelance journalist specializing in African affairs. Between 1997 to 2005 she worked for the BBC World Service Africa section. During that time she spent two years in Angola covering the conflict; she also lived and worked in Ivory Coast during the conflict there in 2004 and in the same year, reported from Mali. Lara has worked mainly in radio and print (including Reuters, the *Economist*, IRIN, the *Irish Times*, the *Independent*) but has also done small amounts of reporting for BBC television. She has traveled extensively in Africa since studying African politics at the School of Oriental and African Studies at the University of London.

Dr Ron Schleifer lectures at Ariel College, Bar Ilan University and the IDF Command College in Israel. His research field is information warfare including cyberwar, psychological warfare, military-media interface, and its applications in the Arab-Israeli conflict. His book on the psychological warfare perspective of the first Intifada was published by Sussex Academic Press in January 2007.

Professor Martin Shaw is a sociologist of war and global politics and holds the Chair of International Relations and Politics at the University of Sussex. His research interests include war and military power; genocide and political violence; media, civil society and intervention; state and global political change; historical sociology and international relations. His publications include: *What is Genocide?* (Polity, 2007), *The New Western Way of War* (Polity, 2005), *War and Genocide: Organised Killing in Modern Society* (Polity, 2003), *Civil Society and Media in global Crises: Representing Distant Violence* (Pinter, 1996) and *Dialectics of War: an Essay in the Social Theory of War and Peace, London* (Pluto, 1988). His website is martinshaw.org.

Angus Taverner is a strategic analyst and communications consultant who advises the UK Ministry of Defence, overseas governments and commercial organizations on Information Strategy, Media Relations and Crisis Communication. A former soldier, he developed the current UK doctrine for military media operations and subsequently initiated a fresh approach to measuring the effectiveness of military information campaigns and conducted a year-long study to assess the impact of perception in the development of general military strategy. He is a frequent speaker, both in the UK and overseas, and he has recently completed a Masters on 'The Relationship between Terrorism and Public Relations'.

Professor John Tulloch is head of the School of Journalism at the University of Lincoln. He is an active researcher and publisher in a number of areas including media ethics, popular journalism, media representations of grief, official news management, the development of 'spin' and press regulation. He co-edited *Tabloid Tales: The Global Debates on Media Standards* (Rowan and Littlefield, 2000) and is currently researching the journalism of Charles Dickens.

Professor Howard Tumber is Professor of Sociology and Dean of the School of Social and Human Sciences. He was previously Head of the Department of Sociology for three years. Before joining City University full time in 1988 he held research positions at the Universities of Greenwich, Stirling, Kent and at the Broadcasting Research Unit at the BFI. His research interests are in the sociology of news and journalism and he is co-founder and co-editor of the academic journal: *Journalism – Theory Practice and Criticism*.

Professor Jeremy Tunstall pioneered the teaching of media studies at City University from 1974 onwards. He held research posts at the University of Essex and the London School of Economics and led the sociology discipline in the early years of the Open University. He is the author of ten books (including *The Fishermen, Journalists at Work, The Media are American, The Media in Britain*) and the co-author of three books including *Media Moguls*. His latest books are *Television Producers* (Routledge, 1993), *Newspaper Power* (Oxford, 1996) and *The Anglo-American Media Connection* (Oxford, 2001)

Professor Frank Webster is Professor of Sociology at City University, London. He has held chairs at Oxford Brookes University and the University of Birmingham. He is author and editor of many books. Recent publications include: *Culture and Politics in the Information Age* (2001); *Theories of the Information Society*, 2nd edition (2002), *The Virtual University* (with Kevin Robins, 2002); *The Intensification of Surveillance* (with Kirstie Ball, 2003); *Manuel Castells*, 3 volumes (with Basil Dimitriou, 2004), and *The Information Society Reader* (2004).

Introduction

Communicating War:
Strategies and Implications

Sarah Maltby

The vast body of literature dedicated to the subject of warfare reflects the difficulties of analyzing war with any generality, particularly regarding its causes, conditions and effects. Whilst the term 'war' is used to describe a myriad of ambiguous and fractious social situations in which organized violence occurs, the structural factors involved in its cause and execution vary greatly. For example, 'limited war' is markedly different from 'total war'[1] and modern regular warfare from irregular combat, guerrilla warfare and terrorism. To consider war within a singular concept, therefore, disables an analysis of the constituent factors apparent in specific wars. At the same time, to consider each war as entirely distinct undermines an attempt to examine common factors in all wars, particularly the varied contributions that technological, political and economic development have made to the practice of war and the role of media in its prosecution. This conundrum presents the scholar of war and media with the unenviable task of, on the one hand, grappling with the general principles associated with war, the ways in which they might be understood and how the media may impact upon them whilst, on the other, identifying specific factors apparent in different conflicts.

Such a conundrum reflects the degree to which the study of the convergence of war and its reportage is essentially a cross-disciplinary activity requiring contributions from scholars within war studies, international relations, sociology, and media and cultural studies to offer a more comprehensive understanding of the issues involved. Similarly, and in an effort to fully interrogate the implications of war conduct and its reportage, it is increasingly important to engage practitioners in the study of war and media including politicians, military members and journalists. *Communicating War* is an attempt to bring together such contributions in both accessible and thought-provoking ways whilst offering some insights into the diverse array of issues relevant to the study of war and media.

'Western' warfare in the 21st century

During the later half of the twentieth century, involvement in war for Western states was generally limited to strategies of policing and peacekeeping under the auspices of the UN and NATO, often in countries fighting for democracy, independence or control of resources. By 2007, such interventions were continuing, reflecting an increasing 'doctrinal' element to war operations in an attempt to preserve international alliances and universal principles such as human rights (see Wight 1979).

Concurrently, in response to more recent terrorist activities, and certainly since 9/11, we appear to be witnessing a return to a war of fear and rivalry politics reminiscent of the Cold War era. The US administration's declaration of a 'global war on terror' in response to 9/11 is indicative of this, framed by the rational apprehension of the threat to security that terrorism, particularly Islamic fundamentalist ideologies and 'rogue' states are believed to pose to the stability of global governance and democracy. As President Bush stated in 2002: 'New deadly challenges have emerged from rogue states and terrorists...the nature and motivations of these new adversaries, their determination to obtain destructive powers hitherto available only to the world's strongest states, and the greater likelihood that they will use weapons of mass destruction against us, make today's security environment more complex and dangerous.'[2]

Since this declaration, the global fight for liberal democracy seems to have extended beyond doctrinal-based. international police-keeping strategies to encompass more aggressive war campaigns such as those in Afghanistan and Iraq. Yet, despite the rhetoric of fear, motivation for these wars remains unclear. They can, and have been, variously positioned in accordance with the notions of fear, doctrine or gain by those involved in their execution. The 2003 Iraq War, in particular, was simultaneously defined as a war of liberation for Iraqi civilians, a war of protection from Weapons of Mass Destruction (WMD) and terrorist cells, and a war of gain for economic and commercial interests.[3] By 2007, none of these apparent motivations had been realized. Evidence of WMD had yet to be found,[4] and political and economic stability seemed increasingly elusive as Iraq collapsed further into civil conflict, uncontained by international policing efforts. Instead, terrorist and insurgency activity appeared to be on the increase in both Iraq and potentially elsewhere, and the conduct of war, terrorism or international paramilitary threats were becoming increasingly indivisible from the media discourses that surround them.

It is within this context that the execution of war or terrorist acts can be seen to contain a critical informational component. Of course, successful war strategies are not merely restricted to information flows. The dominant system of warfare used by Western states is also distinguishable by its orientation towards flexibility, mobility and rapid reaction; as reflected in the US aspiration to overpower Iraqi forces in 2003 through military stealth and speed. Yet, reliant on information and communication technologies such as computers, electronic communication and global communication structures – often referred to as the 'Revolution in Military Affairs' (RMA) – such a system of warfare is contingent on the effective use and protection of information (Hirst 2001; Molander 1996).

Yet the notion of RMA has been criticized for paying little heed to the political, economic and social dynamics that have reshaped the organization of war to one that is fundamentally information-based, especially with the blurring of traditional boundaries between nations, governments, and private and public interests (Robins and Webster 1999; Molander 1996). Others contend that the notion of Information Warfare misrepresents the 'newness of information' in conflict, arguing that information and communication technologies have long been in existence in the organization of warfare, albeit in a more primitive guise.[5]

For Webster (2003), the informational component of war has much wider scope, extending beyond the technologically focused Revolution in Military Affairs. Whilst

RMA includes the evolution of weapons and information technology (particularly precision weaponry, the increased use of intelligence, and the implementation of command, control and communications warfare), Webster argues that 'Information War' is additionally discernable by its use of propaganda, deception and perception management. Increasingly, these are an integral element of warfare needed to generate and sustain the vital support of the public and to pursue a competitive advantage over an enemy. Given that modern war no longer requires the direct mass mobilization of citizens in its conduct, the provision and management of information that offers citizens an experience of war, albeit vicarious, is key to the effective mobilization of popular and political support (Ignatieff 2001; Tumber and Webster 2006). However, when all parties to a conflict are engaged in the exploitation of information as a means with which to engender support for their respective cause, the 'truth' becomes ever more elusive.

Certainly the multiple and diverse means of disseminating information in the public sphere have undermined the means by which states are able to control what is revealed, or concealed, about their activities. Indeed, the emergence during April 2004 of photographs showing the abuse and torture of prisoners by US troops in Abu Ghraib prison, Baghdad, and the rape and killing of Iraq civilians by US soldiers in Mahmudiya[6] are testimony to how information cannot be completely controlled by even the most powerful states. Ultimately, the ability to produce information for mass dissemination is no longer restricted to those in power, nor limited to those who own the means of media production.

Consequently, there is mounting pressure for Western states to engage in information-based strategies such as 'perception management' when conducting military campaigns. In particular, operations must be seen to be conducted efficiently and without incurring casualties if states are to avoid undermining the legitimacy of a war campaign in the public sphere. In this way, aerial bombardments that avoid land engagements and transfer the risk of casualties to enemy targets – such as those witnessed in Iraq (1991 to the present), Kosovo (1999) and Somalia (1992-1993) – provide one of the key ways Western military organizations try to conduct operations whilst attempting to appease the public desire for them to be 'clean' and 'efficient' (Shaw 2003). Certainly images of hi-tech aerial bombardments broadcast during the 1991 Gulf War were successful at distancing the notion of death from the destruction of the war, an issue that subsequently generated much criticism (Taylor 1992; Norris 1994; Jeffords 1994). Sixteen years on, the conflict in Iraq and its continued land engagement have challenged military attempts to exploit aerial bombardments as a means of promoting campaigns as clean and cost free.

In addition, the growth of alternative media outlets including the Internet and Arab networks that amplify civilian deaths or military failures have culminated in the progressive undermining of military efforts to conceal the horror of war. In particular, the Arabic television network Al Jazeera's consistent focus on civilian casualties rather than precision weaponry was considered especially detrimental to the US media campaign during the 2003 Iraq War. In addition, parties to a conflict are acutely aware of the value of facilitating journalistic opportunities to report on such events to destabilize an adversary's propaganda machine. It is not surprising, therefore, that in retaliation to Al Jazeera's reportage the US government accused Al Jazeera of acting as a conduit for Iraqi propaganda (Iskandar and el-Nawaway 2004). Certainly, Al Jazeera's reporting highlighted the degree to which US/UK government and military media management could no longer restrict the flow or content of information about their operations.

Media and military

Given that media representations of war can have a defining impact on the maintenance or weakening of civilian morale and public support for war, the relationship between how war is conducted and how it is portrayed is of crucial importance. The shift from the explicit censorship of the Falklands War of 1982 to the apparent transparency of the 2003 Iraq War is indicative of how militaries are increasingly concerned with developing highly sophisticated mechanisms to sell and justify war operations to the public. As a result, some commentators stress that military-media relations are now fundamentally oriented to co-operation (rather than censorship), an open information policy and a strict differentiation between media information and disinformation (Badsey 1994; Taylor 2000).

These principles may be characteristic of a critical shift in military thinking from a position of hostile censorship to one of public relations, driven by governmental recognition that a more sophisticated approach is needed (Dandeker 2000). Such an approach includes protecting a media campaign from both enemy exploitation and preventing the critical implications that result from the collapse of tactical and strategic decision-making in war reportage (Badsey 2001). As Freedman states: 'By and large, when officials claim that they have been bounced off course by media pressure they often mean that their opponents have used their media contacts more effectively' (2001: 140). Hence, whilst there remains a traditionalist military reticence towards the media – evident in the inhibition of free discussion over national security issues – some contend that the current state of military-media relations now shows elements of a 'new' openness (Blackwell 2003).

This is regularly contested by those who argue that current systems of media management are fundamentally founded on minimizing journalistic access to the battle space (and hence information) whilst maximizing the control of information through other means (Thompson 1992; Thrall 2000). The growth of military operations employing brief and spectacular manoeuvres that are difficult for the media to verify independently but potentially satisfy a demand for the spectacular (such as air bombardments and 'shock and awe' tactics) can thus be seen to have an increasingly strategic element in perception management terms. Similarly, the seductiveness of facilities like 'embedding' may provide journalists with unprecedented access to the front lines but are accompanied by contractual obligations, an encouragement to identify with military goals and censorship regulations. Combined, this permits militaries a level of control regarding what they wish to keep concealed whilst revealing those activities that will detract attention from the wider political and moral context of the war (Keeble 2004; Schechter 2003; Tumber and Palmer 2004).

Of course, technological advances in media communication systems have permitted a degree of journalistic autonomy in recent years. Indeed, the rise of unilateral reporting is testimony to the degree to which these developments have been embraced by the media to seek out alternative, unofficial information. Despite this, and particularly in the shadow of the 2003 Iraq War, the safety implications for those reporting independent of the military have served to heighten the debates regarding military and government information control. Some 17 journalists were killed during the first six weeks of the invasion – an unprecedented figure according to the International Federation of Journalists (cited in Tumber and Palmer 2004: 36). Amongst those killed by Coalition forces were ITN reporter Terry Lloyd, whose car was fired upon by US Marines, a Reuters correspondent and Spanish television reporter who were resident in Baghdad's Palestine Hotel when it was fired upon by US forces and the BBC's Kurdish translator, Kamaran Abdurrazak Mohammed, the victim of a US 'friendly fire' attack. These incidents caused BBC's John Simpson to state that the death of journalists was the 'ultimate form of censorship' (ibid: 37). As a result, accusations continue to be leveled at the US military that they deliberately targeted unilateral journalists – or certainly disregarded their safety – in an effort to control media reportage.[7]

Yet if journalistic access to information about war is contingent on geographical, technological and political access, the use of military and government institutions as news sources remains fundamental to the production of war news. Consequently, whilst governments and militaries are accused of controlling information, the mainstream media are accused of disseminating the same information in a manner that is devoid of critical engagement or context. Dependent on governments and closed to alternative viewpoints, news journalism is believed to propagate state-endorsed information considered to be in the 'national interest' (Herman 1982). Oliver Boyd Barrett (2004) suggests that as a distinct category of journalism, war journalism in particular conforms to this 'propaganda model' because of its failure to identify the meta-narratives and grand strategies of war by focusing – almost exclusively – on action. He argues that with consistent alignment to official sources the media fail to engage the multiplicity of other information sources available – including humanitarian organizations, anti-war groups and ordinary civilians – thereby rendering themselves vulnerable to manipulation (see also Schechter 2003). Robinson (2004) suggests that this may be, in part, due to reinforced media management strategies employed by states. At the same time, Robinson contends that media relations with the state during wartime remain continually deferential despite the significant growth in transnational media and advances in media technologies that have heightened media autonomy and the potential to challenge government discourses.

In light of these arguments, the management of information about war can be seen to be strategically important to governments and militaries (who wish to promote events as news) *and* the media (who produce news), particularly if they perceive it to be crucial to their political processes and outcomes (Tiffin 1989). Certainly, during the 2003 Iraq War, the Iraqi regime permitted a large number of unilateral reporters to cover the war from Baghdad. Despite this, few commentators have engaged with a critical assessment of journalists' relations with the Iraqi regime or considered in any depth the conditions under which these journalists were reporting – a factor that is critical if we are to assess the degree to which unilateral coverage is, indeed, independent (see Burns 1996).

In journalistic terms, independence is synonymous with objectivity, and maintaining a balance between objectivity and diverse coverage can be difficult when warring parties facilitate reporting opportunities that attempt to overshadow an adversary's perspective. In fact, concern with these issues has been more recently expressed by journalists themselves who are increasingly conscious of the cumulative effect news can have on the course of a conflict. They insist that in the process of devising media strategies militaries make it increasingly difficult for journalists to report 'facts', not least because they adapt their behavior for presentational purposes. Each subsequent media report then 'adds another layer to the collective understanding of how reporters are likely to report the story in the future' which in turn feeds back in to the actions of those in the conflict (Lynch 2002). Gurevitch (1991:185) presents a similar argument with regard to television reportage suggesting that television is no longer an observer or witness but 'an active participant in the events it purportedly covers' especially when it acts as a channel of communication between hostile governments. Nash (1998) cites evidence of this phenomenon during the NATO peacekeeping mission in Bosnia where media observance of warring factions became pivotal to promoting their compliance with the Dayton Accords of 1995.

Similarly, by accompanying military convoys through checkpoints television crews helped ensure the protection of troops and the aid they were attempting to deliver (see also Gowing 1996). In this sense, contrary to notions of divergent military and media objectives, there may be times when military and media objectives run in parallel or converge, especially in peacekeeping missions where the media can play a critical role in furthering the peacekeeping process (Badsey 1994). Indeed, tacit agreements were frequently made between the military and the media in Bosnia although, according to Badsey (1996), commanders failed to fully realize the value of the media in furthering peacekeeping. Despite these examples, media involvement in peace processes remains relatively unacknowledged, partly because armed forces – acting under the auspices of the UN – are not permitted to facilitate or exploit the media in case it may imply bias or compromise their role of neutrality. Nevertheless, they raise key issues regarding the 'observer' or 'participant' role of the war journalist in conflict scenarios.

Media and terrorism

Issues of journalistic involvement are also increasingly relevant to debates regarding media coverage of terrorism. Certainly, some consider that the media provide motivation for the commission of violent acts by terrorists (see Schmid and De Graaf 1982). Proponents of such a view are united in their shared assumption that coverage of terrorist acts benefits terrorists through 'amplifying and inspiring' terror (Nossek 1985). Others suggest the media are complicit in defining of acts as 'terrorist' in a manner that exaggerates their threat to serve the interests of the government officials, private security firms and analysts (Herman and O'Sullivan 1989).

In some ways primitive, but no less effective than 'Western ways of war', terrorist acts are distinctly guerrilla in their use of asymmetric warfare. Guerrilla warfare, favored by separatist or minority groups and usually motivated by religion, patriotism or nationalism – particularly against occupying forces – has traditionally utilized local populations to hide combatants whilst exploiting an enemy's unfamiliarity with difficult terrain (Lacquer 1997). Those activities collectively categorized as 'terrorism' – including hijacking, suicide bombing, small arms and the global dispersal of combatants – mirror these tactics in an attempt to exploit a technologically superior 'enemy' by attacking their vulnerabilities.

For Downey and Murdock (2003: 71) the increasing use of guerilla and terrorist activity represents an emerging globalization of guerrilla warfare, where low technology weaponry is used to combat the advanced weaponry and communication systems of dominant European and Western states. For Tumber and Webster (2006) the intensification of guerrilla warfare and terrorism is best understood as resulting from the exclusionary processes of globalization where those opposing its universal principles – including democracy and secular capitalism – illustrate a propensity to becoming what Giddens (1994) terms 'enemies without states'.

If, as Castells (1999) identifies, media provide the essential space of politics, then there is growing recognition amongst these 'enemies' that the media can be harnessed for political effect. Those excluded from or resistant to global processes or powerful political alliances therefore utilize information to avoid political marginality and generate a presence in the wider global sphere. Of course, this point is not necessarily new. In his definitive study of guerrilla warfare and terrorism, Laqueur (1997) suggests that obtaining support for and legitimating war and terrorism through information dissemination and propaganda is fundamental to the efficient execution of guerrilla warfare and terrorism: 'The success of a terrorist operation depends almost entirely on the amount of publicity it receives' (ibid: 109). However, this creates particular vulnerabilities for those involved in the execution of information warfare when global information infrastructures present a new frontier for terrorist warfare activity and where paramilitary and terrorist groups are able to manipulate information for perception management purposes (Molander 1996). As Tumber and Webster (2006) highlight, the use of perception management is no longer the monopoly of one side in a conflict.

For those devoid of modes of production or access to the media, particularly the less powerful, coverage can be secured through the organization of 'disruptive' or shocking terrorist events, partly arranged for the convenience of the mass media (Molotch and Lester 1974). These models of habitual and disruptive access render visible the processes through which terrorists may secure news coverage of particular events as part of a campaign. This is perhaps most evident in the filming of terrorist acts, such as the Moscow theatre siege by Chechen rebels in October 2002, or the beheading of hostages by various terrorist organizations including Tawhid Wal Jihad.[8] These acts are executed in a manner that makes them distributable in simple, accessible formats whilst galvanizing media attention to ensure their communication.

It is noteworthy that these type of events place particular burdens on the media to devise standards for dealing with such reportage. However, these tend to be balanced by the 'logic of the media' that exploits the need for dramatic and newsworthy reportage (see Altheide and Snow 1979; Livingstone 1986). Consequently we have witnessed a growing visibility of 'terrorist' activity in the media, particularly 'terrorist' videos whose content appears to be specifically designed for media dissemination. This is suggestive of how terrorists appreciate the value of engaging the media in the communication of particular definitions about their activities to bring attention to their actions and legitimate the ideologies behind them. Moreover, the planning of such 'pseudo events' – particularly for the purpose of being reported – can become self-fulfilling in the sense that they will suggest 'this is a significant event' with the aim that it will become one, whilst also generating a tendency to spawn other, subsequent pseudo-events (Boorstin 1961). In this sense, there is a potential collapse between the execution of terrorist activity and its media reportage; the media thus become participants, rather than mere observers of the terrorism they cover (Wardlaw 1982).

Forgotten wars

Concurrently, there are those who have no means to produce or secure the dissemination of information for public consumption. As a result, there are a number of conflicts and political acts that remain invisible in terms of a global profile, such as those in Chad, Somalia, the Democratic Republic of Congo, Laos and Georgia. As Castells (1999) argues, globalization reaches out to the whole planet but does not include the whole planet. Those prohibited from joining the global political and economic alliances as a result of these exclusionary global processes have been the more likely to engage in conflict in the later half of the last century, especially African and Eastern European states. With underdeveloped institutional structures unable to contain political tensions, and with an inability to resolve conflict through diplomatic negotiation and consensus, these 'excluded' states have tended to descend into civil conflict, often motivated by identity politics that disregard national boundaries (Freedman 1993).

For Kaldor (2001) these 'new wars' arise from both the collapse of the state and its monopoly of legitimized, organized violence and the implosion of traditional distinctions, particularly between public and private spheres of activity in war (including the privacy of economic activity and the public state activities) and civil and military matters (where the non-legitimate bearer of arms is deemed criminal). Moreover, devoid of technologically superior means through which to conduct war in the same manner as Western states, these conflicts are predominantly executed with the aim of expelling civilians through irregular, guerrilla or insurgency tactics and as such reflect a tendency towards 'degenerate war' in which combat increasingly incorporates the targeting of civilians (ibid; Shaw 2003). Certainly the ongoing conflicts in the Caucasus region and some African states adhere to these characteristics.

International intervention in these wars, often justified on the grounds of doctrinal principles, is inconsistent. For every humanitarian crisis that has elicited an international policing response, there is one that has not. Indeed, Freedman (1993) contends that violence emerging within such 'weak' states only induces Western intervention when it is seen to threaten the Western state system and only then when intervention can be limited to containment rather than resolution (see also Wight 1979). Others suggest that doctrinal principles of involvement are displaced by other more strategic based motivations such as US attempts to safeguard their own interests in regions of economic importance, especially those with mineral resources (Downing and Murdock 2003). Yet, as Tumber and Webster (2006) argue, strategic or territorial interests cannot satisfactorily explain some examples of intervention for example the 1999 Kosovo intervention and the 2000 British-led peacekeeping mission in Sierra Leone. Instead, they conclude that warfare is now centrally concerned with more than strategic or territorial interests precisely because the informational dimension of organized violence is critical and hard to contain (ibid: 40).

Despite these assertions it still remains that the majority of these wars receive little, if any journalistic coverage. When they do it is sparse and often founded on the geo-political importance of a conflict event and the degree to which policy implications are evident (Shaw 1996). In this sense, and given the domestication of foreign news, it is unlikely that these conflict events will be covered unless there is some national involvement. Moreover, once defined as 'newsworthy' there tends to be a global uniformity regarding how these wars are defined deriving from the media's collective reliance on new agencies for information (Golding and Eliot 1979). Indeed, sending reporters to cover foreign events is usually contingent on initial agency selection of the event as 'newsworthy'; such is the solipsistic world of news media (Rock 1973).

Accordingly, coverage of these conflicts is erratic and disproportionately focused on the spectacular or the disastrous generating an environment where war events compete with each other in tragedy in order to maintain their newsworthiness. Even then, anticipated events are not newsworthy until tragedy, or certainly tragedy that can be filmed, has occurred (Moeller 1999).[9] In these instances, devoid of context, war reportage becomes focused on human-interest stories, suffering and victims, creating an essential 'sameness' to all suffering that debilitates constructive analysis regarding causes (Ignatieff 1998; see also Brauman 1993). It may be, as some suggest, that this is related to an absence of clear journalistic frameworks for interpreting and explaining conflict in the post Cold War era (Robinson 2004; McLaughlin 2002). Instead of the predictable patterns and narrative outcomes of the bi-polar relations of East versus West, capitalism versus communism apparent during the Cold War period, the conceptually different 'New World Order' has failed to provide an adequate means with which to explain world conflict, particularly 'genocide' and 'ethnic conflict', or global terrorism, in an accessible manner.

For McLaughlin (ibid), journalism continues to struggle with this issue, tending to interpret events narrowly, personalize them or draw upon the simple dichotomies of 'good versus evil' for the sake of viewers' understandings. Undoubtedly war news avoids discussion regarding the complex structural factors of war through personification and metonymy. This reduces conflict events to stories about people constructing a reality through the actions and reactions of the individuals involved (Galtung and Ruge 1973; Fiske 1987; see also Levi-Strauss 1987). In so doing, the social and political origins of a conflict become lost in characterization as individual motivations appear to be the origin of action or individuals such as Saddam Hussein, President of Iraq, Osama Bin Laden, Al Qaeda leader, or Robert Mugabe, President of Zimbabwe, come to embody specific social and political values. As a result, and particularly in broadcast media, opportunities to focus on the subtle nuances and processes of political events are restricted (Bourdieu 1996). Conflict events are reduced to their elements, cut off from the antecedents and consequences to the point where all conflict news stories begin to look the same.

All of these factors are crucial to understanding how media agents negotiate and manage their role as 'story tellers' of war. As Brown (2003: 87) states: 'The way in which the mass media represent the conflict is part of the conflict.' Thus, ideas regarding media representations and news selection of conflicts are increasingly important to an analysis of the relationship between war and media. Moreover, given that the international media can play a central role in constituting incidents as 'global crises' or defining an event as 'conflict', the ways in which these events are represented becomes intrinsic to global understandings and the actions of those involved (Allen and Seaton 1996).

The chapters: an overview

In response to these issues and the perceptible increase in the visibility of war in recent years *Communicating War* draws together a selection of authors interested in exploring critically the ways the media represent conflict *and* how militaries manage information for the media. These contributors comprise practitioners from within the journalistic and military communities and scholars from a broad range of social sciences. Many of the papers were first presented at the launch conference of the War and Media Network (see www.warandmedia.org). Each chapter is sensitive to the complexities of conflict and terrorism and the wider social, political and historical aspects of 'communicating war'.

Part One: Remembering and Forgetting Communicated War

Part one of *Communicating War* locates the centrality of memory to the contemporary and historical understanding of war. It explores the contributions of the media and cultures of collective memory to the framing of war and the political, social and ethical implications of both remembering and forgetting war. Andrew Hoskins's chapter 'Ghost in the Machine: Television and Wars' Past(s)' explores the mediatization of memory to the contemporary and historical understanding of war. He argues that the modern media age marks a crisis of memory. He considers not only the rapid consumption and re-consumption of past events, with anniversaries commemorated almost to oblivion, but also the pre-emption of history-in-the-making, as conflict and catastrophe are tracked by the second through highly portable and ubiquitous audio-visual recording and broadcast technologies.

In John Tulloch's chapter 'Exploring Legal Black Holes: Extraordinary Rendition, Investigate Journalism and the Moral Imagination', the strengths and limitations of contemporary journalism are discussed in relation to the CIA's programme of 'extraordinary rendition'. He compares the strengths and weaknesses of investigate journalism as a tool with which to uncover acts of political violence or criminality that powerful institutions would rather were concealed and forgotten. Through an analysis of British press coverage of the rendition issue in 2005, Tulloch argues that, contrary to contentions that investigative journalism is in decline, there is evidence to suggest that global investigative journalism, and its incalculable impacts, may be emerging as a direct result of the necessary networking that developed to cover the rendition story.

The notion of 'forgetting war' is explored in chapters three and four. Lara Pawson's 'Reporting Africa's Unknown Wars' is a detailed and candid account of the failures of journalism to cover those conflicts in Africa that are so deserving of our attention. Drawing on her experiences as a broadcast journalist in Angola, she highlights how the structural and cultural practices of journalism result in the superficial reportage of the African continent, culminating in a portrayal of African wars as savage, anarchical and unique to Africa. In her plea to end the misrepresentation of Africa, Pawson draws attention to significant Western geo-political, economic and social links with African states such as Angola and the Congo, which demand greater media analysis if we are to have a sophisticated understanding the African continent and our relationship to it.

Lastly, Jeremy Tunstall's short but important chapter 'Unreported Mass Killings of Civilians' considers the degree to which the mass killing of civilians has been largely, and consistently ignored by the media. Utilizing eight case studies to illustrate his point, Tunstall concludes by highlighting the retrospective nature of mass killing reportage, usually as a result of political change or advances in forensic technology.

Part Two: Communicating War through Media Institutions and Practices

Part two considers the organization, newsgathering and production practices of both traditional and online media, and how these may structure the style and content of war reportage. Howard Tumber and Frank Webster's chapter 'Information War: Encountering a Chaotic Information Environment' locates the importance of these issues within the spread of 'Information War'. By focusing on the changing information environment of Information War, Tumber and Webster highlight the tensions between increased efforts to manipulate and control information with tendencies for openness and proliferation of information from and about conflict situations. Drawing on their own empirical analysis, they consider the position of reporters, their practices and motivations within this information environment and the contribution they make to the conditions of Information War.

In 'Truth in a War Zone: The Role of Warblogs in Iraq', Donald Matheson and Stuart Allan examine the emergence of war blogging and its implications for traditional war journalism through an analysis of Iraq War blogs posted by major news organizations, freelance journalists and citizens. They argue that the multiple perspectives of war blogging coupled with the immediacy and subjectivity of postings are its most celebrated aspects, an issue that presents distinct challenges to the dominant model of the war correspondent. They conclude by arguing that whilst blogging is not necessarily a substitute for traditional journalism, its emphasis on daily experience is testimony to the cultural mode of 'real virtuality' that continually shapes and orients social life around media representations.

Oliver Boyd-Barrett's 'Positioning the News Audience as Idiot' considers how new reportage of war and terrorism consistently privileges certain readings over others in a manner that positions the audience as 'innocents and idiots'. He contrasts this with the ways in which audiences are positioned in relation to fictional texts about war and terrorism arguing that factual news media continue to be framed within a project of propaganda. In 'Fighting Discourses: Discourse Theory, War and Representations of the 2003 Iraqi War', Nico Carpentier utilizes Laclau and Mouffe's (1985) discourse theory to analyze the hegemonic discourses apparent in the transformation of the adversary into an enemy in representations of the Iraq War. He argues that such a transformation is critical to the legitimation of war campaigns. Carpentier suggests that Laclau and Mouffe's theory offers a unique tool to improve our understanding of the interconnectedness of discourses emanating from state and media and the powerlessness of media to escape the ideological model of war.

The final chapter in this section is Chris Atton's 'Keeping the Peace: Media Representations of the Anti-Gulf War Movement in the British Press'. He explores the degree to which media representations of protest activity have adapted to accommodate the shift from potential criminality and deviance to the togetherness of the 'rainbow coalition'. Through a comparative examination of British national press coverage of anti-Iraq war protests in 2003 and 2006 he assesses whether activists were portrayed through the frames of marginalization, demonization and deviance or through normative depictions of protest that emphasize consensus and normalization.

Part Three: Military Communication of War

Part three of *Communicating War* is concerned with the strategic importance of media communication to military and terrorist organizations. Contributors explore the current contours of information strategies that attempt to legitimate or make visible military and terrorist activities through a range of media technologies. In his consideration of the 'Western and Terrorist Ways of War', Martin Shaw considers how terrorists and Western militaries have responded to the changing conditions of warfare, arguing that the terrorists' way is better adapted to the global surveillance mode of warfare. At the centre of his discussion Shaw raises the critical question regarding whether the notion of 'global war on terror' and its 'Western way' of war was the most appropriate and realistic response to terrorism under such global surveillance conditions.

Angus Taverner's chapter 'Dimensions of Perception: Shaping the British Approach to Information Strategy During Military Operations' offers an important insight into the British Military's Information Strategy. Utilizing the 'effects-based model', Taverner locates the importance of perception management to the achievement of military goals at both a tactical and strategic level, whilst incorporating a multitude of audience groups for military effect. In a similar vein, Ron Schleifer's chapter 'A Century of Psyops: Psychological Warfare from the First World War to Lebanon' considers the historical and contemporary use of psychological warfare as a weapon of war. He argues that despite minimal changes in the basic principles of psychological warfare from 1939 to the present date, technological advances have led to considerable developments in the communication of psyops messages culminating in psyops becoming a critical aspect of any war campaign.

Makram Khoury-Machool's chapter 'Kidnap Videos: Setting the Power Relations of New Media' argues that with the development of information communication technologies, resistant groups are able to acquire a media presence that undermines the dominance of Western discourses regarding war actions. He examines the use of low-cost video productions by kidnappers and resistance groups, and their dissemination via the new media in the Arab and Islamic worlds especially the Internet and satellite television. He pays particular attention to *mise en scène*, rhetoric and target audiences to argue that all political communication should be considered within broader political, cultural-linguistic and socio-religious contexts.

Chapters five and six are centrally concerned with the relationship between military propaganda and the entertainment media industries, including the news media. In 'Pat Tillman and The Military-Media Complex', David Altheide draws upon his previous work regarding the 'military-media complex' and explores this relationship through the celebration of Pat Tillman as a US military poster-boy, and the subsequent cover up of his death as a result of 'friendly fire'. Through Tillman's story, Altheide highlights the broader context in which the growing relationship between the military propaganda and media industries is located.

Using the work of Paul Virilio, Jean Baudrillard and James Der Derian's claims regarding the Military-Industrial-Media-Entertainment-Network (MIME-net), Neal Curtis's chapter 'The Military, the Media and Mimesis' argues that war propaganda is increasingly akin to public relations. He suggests that the media have been correspondingly co-opted by the military as part of their Command, Control, Communications and Intelligence (CCCI) matrix. As such they are becoming an essential component in the perception management of information war. Curtis examines how both news media, and the 'soft' media of the entertainment industries are thus being deployed to further a militarist view of the world.

To conclude, Richard Keeble's chapter 'The Necessary Spectacular "Victories": New Militarism, the Mainstream Media and the Manufacture of the Two Gulf Conflicts 1991 and 2003' focuses on the myth of war. Keeble argues that post Cold War conflicts executed by the US/UK can be best understood as 'New Militarist' ventures, manufactured to provide the necessary spectacular victories required to legitimize US imperialism and the military-industrial complex. He concludes by suggesting that central to the manufacture of New Militarism is the dissemination of disinformation to legitimize the permanent war economy. Whilst Keeble highlights a media complicity with state propaganda either through journalistic ignorance or a reticence to challenge official sources, he optimistically states that journalists are increasingly willing to contest official assertions in a manner that will eventually lay bare the 'big lies' that comprise manufactured wars.

Notes

[1] Total War was defined by Ludendorff (1935) as the complete mobilization of all resources, including policy and social systems, to the winning of war

[2] National Security Strategy of the United States of America, President George W. Bush, the White House (17 September 2002). Available online at:
http://www.whitehouse.gov/nsc/nss.pdf, accessed on 14 October 2006

[3] The US Deputy Defense Secretary, Paul Wolfowitz, claimed the real motive for the Iraq War was that Iraq was 'swimming' in oil. See the *Guardian*, 4 June 2003

[4] On 30 September 2004, the Iraq Study Group released the Duelfer Report, on Iraq's WMD programmes. It concluded that Iraq had no deployable WMD of any kind as of March 2003 and had no production since 1991. Available on line at http://www.lib.umich.edu/govdocs/duelfer.html, accessed 14 October 2006

[5] See Downing and Murdock (2003: 72) who cite the use of the maps, the telegraph and strategic planning and Hirst (2001: 93) who cites the use of electronic communications in the Second World War

[6] In the alleged Mahmudiya attack, four US troops alleged repeatedly raped an Iraqi girl in her home, later killing her and her three family members. See BBC http://news.bbc.co.uk/1/hi/world/middle_east/5253160.stm, accessed on 14 October 2006

[7] See the *Independent*, 9 April 2003, Robert Fisk: Did the US murder these journalists? Available online at http://news.independent.co.uk/world/fisk/article116701.ece; BBC News 30 October 2003. Available online at:
http://news.bbc.co.uk/1/hi/world/middle_east/3227819.stm; FAIR (Fairness and Accuracy In Reporting) Media Advisory: Is Killing Part of Pentagon Press Policy? 10 April 2003. Available online at http://www.fair.org/press-releases/iraq-journalists.html, accessed 14 October 2006

[8] Tawhid Wal Jihad, under the leadership of Jordanian Abu Musab al-Zarqawi, were responsible for the beheading of Kenneth Bigley, along with Jack Hensley and Eugene Armstrong in 2004. Videos of the killings were posted on Islamist websites and on at least one US-based website

specializing in violence and pornography. Before the beheadings, video footage of their captivity was released and distributed through the media

[9] Moeller (1999) highlights this with particular reference to famine where, despite being pre-warned, media attention fails (as it did in Ethiopia in 1983) to focus on the issue of famine until images of starving women and children become available, thereby turning it into a newsworthy event

References

Allan, Stuart and Zelizer, Barbie (2004) Rules of Engagement: Journalism and War, in Allan, Stuart and Zelizer, Barbie (eds) *Reporting War: Journalism in Wartime*, London: Routledge pp 3-21

Allen, Tim and Seaton, Jean (eds) (1999) *The Media of Conflict: War Reporting and Representations of Ethnic Violence*, London: Zed Books

Altheide, David, and Snow, Robert (1979). *Media Logic*. California: Sage Publications

Badsey, Stephen (1994) Modern Military Operations and the Media, *Camberley: Strategic and Combat Studies,* occasional paper Vol. 8

— (1996) The Influence of the Media on Recent British Military operations, in Stewart, Ian and Carruthers, Susan (eds) *War, Culture and the Media: Representations of the Military in 20th Century Britain*, Wiltshire: Flick Books pp 5-21

— (2001) Guarding the Media Flank, *JSCSC: Advanced Command Staff Course*, No 5. September 2001 to July 2002

Bell, Martin (1995) *In Harm's Way*, London: Penguin

Blackwell, Stephen (2003) Conference Paper: A Spirit of Mutual Antagonism? Military Media Relations and the Defence Establishment in Britain. Presented at: The Role of Media in Public Scrutiny and Democratic Oversight of the Security Sector, Budapest, 6-9 February 2003

Boorstin, Daniel (1961) *The Image*, New York: Athenaeum.

Bourdieu, Pierre (1996) *Television and Journalism*, London: Pluto

Boyd-Barrett, Oliver (2004) Understanding: The Second Casualty, in Allan, S. and Zelizer, B. (eds) *Reporting War: Journalism in Wartime*, London: Routledge pp 24-42

Brauman, Rony (1993) When Suffering Makes a Good Story, in M. s. Frontières (ed.), *Life, Death and Aid*, London: Routledge and Hachette

Burns, John (1996) Media as Impartial Observers or Protagonists, in Gow, James, Paterson Richard and Preston, Alison (eds) *Bosnia by Television*, London: BFI pp 92-100

Castells, Manuel (1999) An Introduction to the Information Age, in Mackay, Hugh and O'Sullivan, Tim (eds) *The Media Reader: Continuity and Transformation*, London: Sage pp 398-410

Dandeker, Christopher (2000) The United Kingdom: The Overstretched Military, in Moskos, Charles, Williams, John and Segal, David (eds) *The Postmodern Military. Armed Forces After the Cold War*, Oxford: Oxford University Press pp 32-50

Downey, John and Murdock, Graham (2003) The Counter-Revolution in Military Affairs: The Globalization of Guerrilla Warfare, in Thussu, Daya Kishan and Freedman, Des (eds) *War and the Media*, London: Sage pp 70-86

Fiske, John (1987) *Television Culture*, London: Routledge

Freedman, Lawrence. (1993) Weak States and the West: the Future Surveyed, the *Economist*, 11 September pp 42-44

Galtung, Johan, and Ruge, Mari (1973) Structuring and selecting news, in Cohen, Stan. and Young, Jock (eds) *The Manufacture of the News: Social Problems, Deviance and the Mass Media*, London: Constable pp 62-71

Gerbner, George, Gross, Larry, Signorielli, Nancy, Morgan, Michael and Jackson-Beeck, Marilyn (1979) The Demonstration of Power: Violence Profile No. 10, *Journal of Communication*, 3 pp 117-196

Giddens, Anthony (1994) *Beyond Left and Right*. Cambridge: Polity Press

Golding, Peter and Elliot, Philip (1979) *Making the News*, London: Longman

Gowing, Nik (1996) Real-Time TV Coverage from War: Does it Make or Break Government Policy? in Gow, J. Paterson, R. Preston, A. (eds), *Bosnia by Television*, London: BFI Publishing pp 81-91

Gurevitch, Michael (1991) The Globalisation of Electronic Journalism, in Curran, James and Gurevitch, Michael (eds) *Mass Media and Society*, London: Edward Arnold pp 178-193

Herman, Edward (1982) *The Real Terror Network: Terrorism is Fact and Propaganda*, Boston: South End

Herman, Edward and O'Sullivan, Gerry (1989) The 'Terrorism' Industry: The Experts and Institutions that shape our view of terror, New York: Pantheon

Hirst, Paul. (2001) *War and Power in the 21st Century*, Cambridge: Polity

Ignatieff, Michael (1998) *Warriors Honor: Ethnic War and the Modern Conscience*, London: Chatto and Windus

— (2001) *Virtual War: Kosovo and Beyond*, London: Vintage

Iskandar, Adel and El-Nawawy, Mohammed (2004) Al-Jazeera and War Coverage in Iraq: The media's quest for contextual objectivity, in Allan, Stuart and Zelizer, Barbie (eds) *Reporting War: Journalism in Wartime*, London: Routledge pp 315-332

Jeffords, Susan (1994) Afterword: Bringing the Death-World Home, in Jeffords, Susan. and Rabinovitz, Lauren. (eds) *Seeing Through the Media: The Persian Gulf War*, New Jersey: Rutgers University Press pp 301-306

Kaldor, Mary (2001) *New and Old Wars: Organised Violence in a Global Era* (2nd ed.) Cambridge: Polity Press

Keeble, Richard (2004). Information Warfare in an Age of Hyper-Militarism, in Allan, Stuart and Zelizer, Barbie (eds) *Reporting War: Journalism in Wartime*, London: Routledge pp 43-58

Laqueur, Walter (1977) *Guerrilla: A Historical and Critical Study*, London: Weidenfeld and Nicolson

Levi-Strauss, Claude (1978) *Myth and Meaning*, London: Routledge and Kegan Paul

Ludendorff, Erich (1935) *Der Totale Krieg (The Total War)*: Munich

Lynch, Jake (2002) *Reporting the World: A Practical Checklist for the Ethical Reporting of Conflicts in the 21st Century, Produced by Journalists for Journalists*, Berkshire: Conflict and Peace Forums

McLaughlin, Greg (2002) *The War Correspondent*, London: Pluto Press

Moeller, Susan (1999) *Compassion Fatigue: How the media sell disease, famine, war and death*, New York: Routledge

Molander, Roger. Riddile, Andrew and Wilson, Peter (1996) *Strategic Information Warfare: A New Face of War*, RAND Report MR-601, California: RAND Corporation.

Molotch, Harvey, and Lester, Marilyn (1974) News as Purposive Behaviour, *American Sociological Review*, Vol. 39 pp 101-112

Nash, William (1998) The Military and the Media in Bosnia, *Harvard International Journal Press/Politics*, Vol. 3, No. 4 pp 131-135

Norris, Margot (1994) Only Guns Have Eyes: Military Censorship and the Body Count, in Jeffords, Susan and Rabinovitz, Lauren (eds) *Seeing Through the Media: The Persian Gulf War*, New Jersey: Rutgers University Press pp 285-300

Nossek, H. (1985) The Impact of Mass Media on Terrorists, Supporters and the Public at Large, in Merari, A. (ed.) *On Terrorism and Combating Terrorism*, Frederick MD: University Publications of America pp 87-94

Robins, Kevin and Webster, Frank (1999) Cyberwars: the military information revolution, in Robins, Kevin and Webster, Frank (eds) *Times of the Technoculture: From Information Society to the Virtual Life*, London: Routledge pp 149-167

Robinson, Piers (2004) Researching US Media-State Relations and Twenty-first Century Wars, in Allan, Stuart and Zelizer, Barbie (eds) *Reporting War: Journalism in Wartime*, London: Routledge pp 96-112

Rock, Paul. (1973) News as Eternal Recurrance, in Cohen, Stan and Young, Jock (eds) *The Manufacture of the News: Deviance, Social Problems and the Mass Media*, London: Constable and Co Ltd pp 73-80

Schechter, Danny (2003) *Embedded: Weapons of Mass Deception: How the Media Failed to Cover the War in Iraq*, New York: News Dissector/Mediachannel.org

Schmid, Alex and De Graaf, Janny (1982) *Violence as Communication: Insurgent Terrorism and the Western News Media*, Beverly Hills, CA: Sage

Shaw, Martin (1996) *Civil Society and Media in a Global Crisis: Representing Distant Violence*, London: Pinter

— (2003) *War and Genocide*, Cambridge: Polity Press

Part I:

Remembering and Forgetting Communicated War

CHAPTER ONE

GHOST IN THE MACHINE:
TELEVISION AND WARS' PAST(S)

ANDREW HOSKINS

The convergence of media/memory

Memory is almost by definition part of the past. Yet in significant ways it is a central resource for making sense of the present and thus for extending the continuous present out to edges of the personal and collective horizons of time/space. Television, and TV news in particular (the focus of this chapter), functions in a similar way, mixing and messing with the synchronic and the diachronic, powerfully shaping and reshaping past, present and projections of the future through its audio/visual scopic regimes. In fact, the electronic and now digital media have become the ultimate constituents of what I am setting out here as the contradictions of contemporary memory: ephemeral, fleeting and artificial in one sense (e.g. the rapid and continuous circulation of news and images) but also explicit, enduring and authentic in another (e.g. the potentially depthless storage capacity of archives from which 'original' footage can be retrieved and 're-lived' by new generations for a first time).

In response to these often technologically-influenced shifts affecting how, what and why we remember, and evidenced in, for example, the renaissance of the heritage, monument, and museum industry, there now appears to be much more social, political, religious and cultural conflict than consensus about the nature of our relationship with a past that is increasingly intertwined with, and reliant on, media data (language, image, sound): a problem of 'new memory' (Hoskins 2004). Despite the inexorable trend in media convergence, the medium of television still bears the closest resemblance to the temporality of memory in its real-time unending flow within which it selectively edits and reassembles the past, notably a 'past that becomes it'.

For example, television news self-consciously reveals and promotes itself in the actual production of that which it documents, reflexively scripting and re-scripting the moment-by-moment trajectory of events, and thus constantly adding to its archive, its own repertoire of memory. It selectively sustains and reframes the past through the highly selective repeating of video footage and still images. Thus a key function in television's relationship with the past, today, is in its *renewal* of memory (Hoskins 2007). However, any process of renewal inevitably involves obsolescence, displacement and discarding. Thus the amnesiac effects of the process of television's renewal of memory are crucial to any critical understanding of how modern societies in particular come to live with, deny, and transform their pasts, notably in ways that are deemed appropriate for, and reveal much about, the present.

It is not a coincidence that the memory obsession (and memory boom) of late modern societies is that which fills the dominant media of the age: television, namely conflict, catastrophe and warfare. The past quarter of a century is marked by an extraordinary *convergence*, aggregation, and interpenetration, of a new, more immediate, proximate and visual media coverage of current and ongoing conflict, with a wholesale marking, commemorating, and commodifying of past wars and catastrophes. Television is a primary medium of new memory in this way as it routinely effects a simultaneity between pasts and presents, re-combining and renewing them into a converged present, and soon-to-be more recent past.

For instance, frequent repetition and re-framing of key television images and discourses extends the past into the present in new ways, through the creation of 'media templates' (Kitzinger 2000) with which to measure and interpret and reinterpret the present, imposing one on top of another to create an 'extended present' (cf. Nowotny 1992) from the past into the future. The convergence of media/memory is not, however, a random nor neutral process. So, in the same way that social memory should not be treated as merely the recollections of our past, but also as the history which we 'expect' for the present (Connerton 1989), the convergence of media/memory involves the representing and the reshaping of past conflict (and the emotions attached or presumed to be attached to those representations) for potentially multiple political and/or commercial ends. To briefly mention two examples:

Firstly, a Vietnam media template was employed extensively in the US media (and even in the UK) to inject new interest into the diminishing news value of the ongoing 'aftermath' of the 2003 Iraq War. The resonances of the military and political failure in Vietnam in the US collective and journalistic psyche have been carried since by and through the same media deemed to have been partly responsible for this 'defeat'.[1] However, following the cathartic convergence of the media/memory of the Vietnam War with the media representing and legitimizing of the US-led 1991 Gulf War, this media/memory re-converged in renewed critical discourses on US foreign military interventions with the casualties of US forces sustained in Iraq from 2003. Furthermore, this is also an example of a 'speculative' template as a means to provoke debate and action to respond to the discursive prospects of the repetition of past 'mistakes' having potentially the same or similar outcomes, in this case the political and military humbling of a superpower. Secondly, in the UK, the widespread deployment of the 'Blitz spirit' media template in response to the 7 July 2005 London bombings, is indicative of what Paul Gilroy (2004) calls 'post-colonial melancholia'. A nostalgic 'pathology' of greatness is employed to assuage the insecurities of present-day anxieties and insecurities, that, paradoxically, the media themselves are compelled to 'amplify' in the first place (Hoskins and O'Loughlin 2007).

So, to position the medium of television in the convergence of media/memory in the wider transformations in the relationship between war and media, I now turn to explore the idea that memory itself may be 'mediatized' (after Jameson 1999) in the sense that memory processes are increasingly embedded in a self-reflexive and self-accumulative 'media logic'.

The mediatization of memory

The era of 'new memory' is marked or even defined by an extensive re-narrativizing and commemoration of particularly twentieth and early twenty-first century conflicts and catastrophes (i.e. events that traditionally are seen as 'nodal' points or ruptures in social memory) and the related rise in public discourses on this past. Why have these events become such a dominant feature of our memory landscape and why have they significantly shaped how we conceptualize memory today? One can point to two key explanations. Firstly, the mass-mediated insecurities of today are often contrasted with the historical certainties of the survival of societies and the continuities of the past. For instance, the relative finality of past conflicts through the defeat of knowable and tangible embodiments of evil, provide markers if not 'lessons' that promote a reassurance in an environment lacking such absolutes and temporal horizons, particularly compared with the horizon-less 'war on terror'.

Secondly, the ever-accumulating technologies of the electronic and digital media shape and direct the mass representing and archiving of all-things-past through a near-obsessive commemoration of events. These are derived from a collecting of the individual, personal, and wherever possible, emotional accounts of eyewitnesses to, and survivors of, past wars and catastrophes. To some extent, the first explanation has been displaced by the second. The cycle of mass-mediated commemoration has shifted in recent years to envelop the much more recent past, the past still intimately connected with the present. Partly, this is owing to the mass and immediate availability of witness testimony to the catastrophes and conflicts of recent times.

However, the doubly-authenticating mass and immediate availability of audio-visual footage that is bonded with the personal testimony of these events has created a seemingly compulsive environment of mediatized memory, propelled via a cycle of commemoration that spins ever closer to the present. Just as with the idea that intense mass media coverage 'amplifies' certain kinds of behavior or, more seriously, that there is a reflexivity to real-time news reporting of events, we also need to consider the impact of the extension of this media logic into the nature of and the formation and reformation of memory. I will shortly examine some examples of these trends, but firstly, will provide a more detailed conceptualizing of this term 'mediatization'.

Mediatization refers to the impact of the media upon processes of social change so that everyday life is increasingly embedded in the mediascape. This is not just a question of the ubiquity of both new and old media in that today we can observe the satiation of electronic media (images, sounds, and events) as our surround, but that there is a self-reflexive and self-accumulative 'media logic'. That is to say, as the presentational modes and production routines of the media shift, an awareness of the perceived impact of these (upon audiences' consciousness-in-the-world) feeds back to affirm and/or to develop these modes and routines.

Let us consider then the mediatization of time in respect of the medium of television. For a long 'time' it has been considered to shape and reflect the daily temporal rhythms and routines as in the viewing habits of audiences, as with radio. The evening news or nightly bulletins are examples from a programming genre that is particularly cognizant with a particular (24-hour) temporal cycle (in terms of news gathering, editing, and broadcast). Electronic newsgathering of the 1970s followed by the advent of satellite news gathering from the 1980s are developments or stages of the mediatization of time. A pivotal point in this process is that which CNN is practically synonymous with the round-the-clock television coverage of the 1991 Gulf War, remediated via local and national networks around the world. This apparent global simultaneity – the feeling that previously disparate audiences were unified in time and global space with the event – the Gulf War – unfolding at it was being watched (by audiences, the White House, and Saddam Hussein, President of Iraq) ushered in a new and compelling mediatized axis of audiences-broadcasters-event. But, this compulsion for the (potential) drama of the temporally connected places of the same event was, thereafter, pursued through the presentational modes and production routines of the electronic media, demonstrating the mediatization of time and what today we might call an 'economy of liveness'. It is the logic of the media that is triumphant.

More generally, the idea of the development of mediatization is one advanced by Scott Lash (2005). He argues that there are 'two modernities': 'The second modernity is one in which the media spread like a disease. The first modernity describes a process of rationalization. And the second modernity describes one of mediatization.' And, to return to Jameson's influential definition in his writing on the spatial turn of post-modernism:

> the traditional fine arts are *mediatized*: that is, they now come to consciousness of themselves as various media within a mediatic system in which their own internal production also constitutes a symbolic message and the taking of a position on the status of the medium in question (1991: 162).

New memory is not only directed and made visible through new technologies but it is also reflexively formed through media cultures and practices – very much part of the schemata of modern memory. This includes the rhetorical structures of journalists, programme makers and editors who make assumptions about the knowledge of other professionals and their audiences (cf. Schudson 1990). The phenomenon of mediatization then is not just a question of the uses of media technology, but, as Philip Auslander (1999: 32) argues, it is also a matter of 'media epistemology'.

Living and post-memory

So let us return then to this idea of the dual-authenticating role of the mass media and particularly television news and other programming. Television's real-time wholesale consumption of the present affords it the dual capability of reflexively 'creating' events as narrator, and in later authoring their (re) construction and import as media witness. So, on the one hand the media prevent human memory from evolving, but on the other, may also enable future generations to engage with events that would once have been difficult, if not impossible, outside of the living memory frame of those events. Yet it is this period of living memory – or what one might also call generational memory – that is now the most intensive engagement with a past that seems to dominate our present. Television mixes and matches the present with the past through its enhanced scopic versatility. Past images and sound-bytes are used to direct unfolding interpretations or 'frames' of the present whilst, simultaneously, re-shaping the past record through these new juxtapositions. The nature of this reflexive relationship between past and present as effected through television is relatively under-explored in accounts of modern memory.

Television's siege of the late twentieth and early twenty-first century is, then, partly attributable to the advances in audio-visual recording technology of this period and partly owing to the proximity of witnesses (including journalists) to those events. However, a great proportion of the electronic media's accumulating archives of the past involve the insertion of the testimony of co-present witness to events being remembered or commemorated that serves to authenticate film or video footage on television. More broadly, considerable authority and legitimacy is conveyed upon those who were witness to past events, when the value of memory is defined in relation to personal testimony.

In relation to those events beyond – or soon to be beyond – the direct living memory, the testimony of those who do survive as witnesses of, or participants in, particularly catastrophic events are afforded greater significance as they inevitably continue to diminish in number. For example, the BBC screened a documentary in November 2005 entitled The Last Tommy, which showed the last few surviving British veterans of World War One narrating their experiences and stories to camera, embedded in film clips and photographic stills from the time. Though the series took almost two years to research and produce, it was done with some urgency given the state of health of the handful of the British veterans of the Great War, some of whom died before the programmes were broadcast.

In this respect, as time goes on, the less survivors or witnesses there are to an event, the more precious their accounts become (to programme makers, at least) but also the less accurate. So, to trace a history of recordings of World War One veterans over the period since the end of the war would reveal, no doubt, a series of accounts that have transformed with each retelling. Where then does a 'collective memory' of the Great War lie? Without the living memory of the storytellers of events, what function and value do their mediated ghosts have? Living memory, according to Paul Gilroy, involves negotiating 'the living memory of the changing same' (1993: 198). That is to say, the telling and retelling of stories 'serve[s] a mnemonic function: directing the consciousness of the group back to significant, nodal points in its common history and its social memory' (ibid). Does the mnemonic function of the mass media then become much more significant as events recede and disappear altogether in living memory?

'Remembering' the Holocaust

Recent work has begun to deal with the nature and substance of post-living memory, or 'post-memory'. This is particularly the case amongst scholars of the Holocaust, one of the most documented and nodal events in twentieth century history. James E. Young (2000: 3-4) for example, points to the inevitably 'mediated' nature of this memory:

As the survivors have testified to *their* experiences of the Holocaust, their children and their children's children will now testify to their experiences of the Holocaust. And what are *their* experiences of the Holocaust? Photographs, film, histories, novels, poems, plays, survivors' testimonies. It is necessarily mediated experience, the afterlife of memory, represented in history's after-images: the impressions retained in the mind's eye of a vivid sensation long after the original, external cause has been removed.

Yet, in an era of post-memory, some claim there is a real dissatisfaction with these 'secondary' forms and experiences of relating to the Holocaust. Gary Weissman (2004: 4) goes even further in his exploration of what he calls 'fantasies of witnessing' which 'express a desire for the Holocaust to feel *more real* than it does in American culture'.

This is the actualizing of fantasies in an attempt to 'gain access' and 'remember' the Holocaust as a personal experience that eludes us, according to Weissman.

One way to characterize the shifting experience and record of an event over time is through separating out the role of historians and the nature of 'history', from that of 'memory'. In respect of scholarly treatments of the Holocaust, Weissman highlights Langer's work and his identifying of a 'second stage of Holocaust response': 'The first stage appears to have been dominated by historians and their project of determining, through archival research, our historical knowledge of the event, while the second stage involves moving from "what we know" to "how we remember it"' (2004: 103-104). In other words, the latter stage extends beyond the limits of Holocaust knowledge, and involves "remembering" the Holocaust 'not as a distinct historic event, but as an immediate, personal experience' (ibid: 107).

There is a growing body of work to support this claim. Alison Landsberg (2004), for example, identifies what she calls 'prosthetic memory' which is produced 'at the interface between a person and a historical narrative about the past, at an experiential site such as a movie theatre or museum' (ibid: 2). She claims that the individual does not merely engage with historical knowledge, 'but takes on a more personal, deeply felt memory of a past event through which he or she did not live' (ibid). Landsberg's concept of prosthetic memory is, thus, liberating in its apparent transgression of the exclusivity carried by generational or living memory (and with historical knowledge, for that matter) in enabling new experiential connections with the past. In this way she moves beyond some of the more pessimistic discourses on modern memory.

'Re-imaging' past events

In addition to television's heavily trailed events and its anniversary schisms that feed the current culture of commemoration, the mediatization of memory involves the 're-imagining' of past events in much less contrived ways. The tenth anniversary of the 1995 massacre at Srebrenica, where more than 8,000 Bosniak men and boys were murdered by Serbian military, was widely covered by the international media. A more acute example of the media re-imagining of this atrocity, however, began on the 1 June 2005 with the showing of video evidence to the Hague war crimes tribunal where President Milosevic was on trial, and which was then broadcast on a number of Serbian and Bosnian TV stations later that evening. The video shows what are alleged to be Serbian paramilitaries leading six unarmed Bosnian Muslim prisoners to their deaths, four being shot at close range. The footage also contains scenes of their torture, but these have not been publicly broadcast.

It is the families of the victims that are faced with a new witnessing of atrocities, with at least two of the dead having been identified by the families as missing following the fall of Srebrenica in July 1995. One mother watches her teenage son murdered in cold blood, in color, on Bosnian television, which is then broadcast as a news story, in the UK, the US and around the world. So this constitutes a new, mediated and globally documented form of witnessing by the mother of the execution of her son. This is a much more random, but no less powerful, layering and accumulation of new memory; the public document becomes fused with personal testimony which is then re-mediated in a new form of public record.

It is important to implicate the mass media in forcing communities of the victims, and the perpetrators, of atrocities to confront events anew. The emergence of the video of the executions of Bosniak Muslims near the village of Trnovo in 1995 is an effective illustration of the power of the visual media to re-shape and re-define past events for those personally involved, and for the shifting historical record. The electronic media, in particular, increasingly fuse personal and public memory. And it is these interventions that disturb and disrupt, but ultimately which shape the remembering process, that should be more explicitly acknowledged and employed to contribute to the coming to terms with difficult pasts.

This example points to a key corollary of the mediatization of memory, and that is in television's immediate visual capacity to affect the potential for the individual and personal imagination or re-imagination of past and present events. The neurobiologist, Steven Rose (1992), for example, contrasts the memory-keeping of early human societies with the memorial processes of today. In the oral cultures of the former, memories needed to be constantly trained and renewed, with select individuals afforded the considerable responsibility of 're-telling' the stories which preserved the common culture. Rose (ibid: 60) argues: 'People's memories, internal records of their own experiences, must have been their most treasured – but also fragile – possessions.' But also, the moment of each storytelling was unrepeatable. 'Then, each time a tale was told it was unique, the product of a particular interaction of the teller, his or her memories of past stories told, and the present audience' (ibid: 61). In contrast, Rose argues, new technologies actually challenge both the uniqueness and dynamic of human memory: 'A videotape or audiotape, a written record, do more than just reinforce memory; they freeze it, and in imposing a fixed, linear sequence upon it, they simultaneously preserve it and prevent it from evolving and transforming itself with time' (ibid).

Twenty-first century memory

Yet, today's media-processing of events effect, if not always-fixed 'artificial memory' in Rose's terms, but an often-instantaneous memory-schema of events which are a powerfully explicit part of a dialectical relationship between the media and human memory. Furthermore, since the media (journalists, photojournalists, and the news programmes themselves) are increasingly co-present and connected with the 'production' of the original event, they are to some extent inevitably involved in the production and re-production of the memory of that event. The accumulation of audio-visual records of some media events are so intensively and extensively mediated, it becomes difficult to imagine a history of them that is not already inscribed and visually imprinted on social memory.

For instance, there seems little point in being a historian of the attacks on the US of 9/11 when there has already occurred such an explicit rendering of oral testimony, combined with the seemingly endless archive of audio-visual material and, notably, the fusion and re-fusion of the two. For example, a commemorative programme In Memoriam: New York City 9/11/01 (Channel 4, 11 September 2002) re-narrativised events through the oral and visual contributions from 16 news organizations and 118 survivors and onlookers, and declared that the attack on the World Trade Center was 'the most documented event in history' (Hoskins 2004). One year on, this appeared to be an extraordinary claim, but one that demonstrates, albeit at one end of a spectrum of media news events, a certain shrinking of media-historical time. That is to say the historical time-lag of events of which the electronic media are tied up in the first and often immediate dissemination – or production – of, is compressed through that same media.

Almost four years later, another layer of the record of the attacks of 11 September was made public on 12 August 2005. Following a lawsuit brought principally by *The New York Times*, the New York Fire Department released 15 hours of radio transmissions in addition to 12,000 pages of the transcripts of the oral histories of firefighters, paramedics and frontline medical technicians, which were recorded over the months that followed the terrorist attacks. The recording, accumulation, and legal challenges over the tapes, are an example of the contested nature of the new memory of events that are reflexively authored (rather than just 'filtered') through and by the mass media.

On the day of their release, all main national evening news bulletins in the US (ABC, CBS, and NBC) carried the tapes as their lead story. All these programmes played extracts from the audio recordings of the radio transmissions over video footage of the attacks and aftermath from their archives. Some even mapped the timing of the audio extracts to the timing of the videotape, synchronizing the audio from both sources, the visuals from the video, and a transcript of the audio across the screen, into a new news frame (a 'new' memory). ABC's World News Tonight provided narration over archival video in the form of a voice-over reading of extracts from oral history transcripts, and the words themselves were shown as captions on screen.

All three news programmes played an extract taken from the same recording of an unidentified civilian calling for help over a firetruck radio on 11 September, as well as putting the transcript on screen: 'I'm trapped inside one of your firetrucks underneath the collapse that just happened. I can't breathe much longer, save me. I'm in the cab of your truck' (NBC Evening News, 12 August 2005). At the same time, the footage of the scene at the foot of the Twin Towers is played, effectively matching the call for help with the visuals of the unfolding catastrophe, bringing the viewer in to almost hearing distance of the person trapped. This provides one illustration of how the vivid multiple personal testimonies of 11 September are fused with the archival data of the mass media and demonstrates the capacity of television to keep selective memories alive and dynamic though the merging of texts from different sources. In this way television re-imagines events, and reconnects new fragments as they become available with the already familiar, to produce ever more ubiquitous views of the past.

The US evening television news broadcasts of the 12 August 2005 combined what may be defined as an episodic or event-driven memory with a schematic form of narrative memory. For example, Bob Woodruff, anchor of ABC's World News Tonight, describes the impact of the release of the '9/11 tapes': 'The horror came rushing back today when the city of New York released new recordings made that day of firefighters and civilians caught up in the chaos. They are a significant addition to what we know about that day and also a reminder, nearly four years later, of how fresh the tragedy still is' (12 August 2005). The media 'flashframe' (Hoskins 2007) is tied to a notion of a sudden intervention of the past – a 'rushing back' – in this case the repetition of the now-iconic images and sounds of the planes hitting the Twin Towers and the ensuing chaos (people fleeing for their lives through dust clouds, sounds of emergency sirens etc.) At the same time, the news reports build upon a number of narrative frames that evoke the day through using the same or similar images and sounds that first (and later) defined that day in American collective, or rather collected, consciousness.

What is interesting here is the idea of the 'freshness' of an event, or the memory of that event, as prompted or sustained through televisual sounds and images. The addressees of the news anchor – the real or implied programme audience – are routinely and discursively constructed as part of this memory group. They are presumed to possess a certain shared knowledge of the event(s) of 9/11 and its televisual and other mass media signifiers. The visual icons of the remnants of the structure of the Twin Towers, of the after-event, are counterposed with video replays of the actual unfolding day, and the newly available personal testimonies (as above). These temporally separate bits of media data are made simultaneous via the televisual frame, which routinely subverts chronological narratives in gathering and disordering past and present fragments into an instantaneous mix. A 'rushing back' is an appropriate description here, but it is a rushing back of key iconic elements of an established media narrative of 9/11 to date, promoted with the immediacy of the news value-oriented 'latest' information released that day.

More than 400 relatives of those killed in the attacks on the World Trade Center had requested copies of the recordings of the radio transmissions (sent to them on 23 CDs) and the transcripts of the oral histories. However, although only extracts of the '9/11 tapes' were broadcast on news programmes in August 2005, the entire collection of dispatches were made available online as mp3 audio files on news sites on their public release.[2] In this way, television programming functions as a directional media and gateway into the vast archives of the Internet (and the net also directs audiences back to television programming, including that increasingly available online). This is a relatively simple example of the vast and complex phenomenon of 're-mediation' (Bolter and Grusin 1999) in terms of the growing inter-dependence of different media, and the circulating images and sounds that inhabit our network society. But, for the purposes of this chapter, it can be seen as an example of the re-mediatization of memory.

The shrinking of the commemorative cycle of new memory, however, may actually afford a more intensive dialectic between news publics and the mass-mediating of the unfolding histories of those new publics, in other words a greater reflexivity of memory. This is particularly so when, as I have suggested, living memory is so bound up with the initial representation (as well as later re-representations) of events through the media.

For example, on the first anniversary of the March 2004 Madrid train bombing (Spain's so-called '3-11'), the Spanish Prime Minister, under pressure from families of the victims, urged media outlets not to broadcast grisly footage and photos of the train bombings. And, the Spanish media responded by effectively sanitizing this event, seen as a demonstration of the country's resilience through its move to 'normality' in the aftermath of the bombing.

For instance, Spain's TVE television news coverage of the anniversary did not show images of the injured or dead, or even close-up shots of the train wreckage, but only some very fleeting distant aerial footage of the scene of the terrorist attack from one year earlier. As with many significant national and international events in the West, both the actual images of the bombing and the context of their experience for many become bound up in the electronic media that broke the story. In fact, it becomes difficult to imagine, or to remember, historic events of the modern age separate from the media that produced them more frequently on a global scale.

The sanitizing modes of representation of our age

Many contemporary events are already mitigated by the selectively sanitizing modes of representation of our age, and given the massively increased availability and portability of audio-visual recording equipment, the record of catastrophes and warfare – notably the primary obsession of modern memory – will be made, re-made, and contested increasingly through television, film, and the Internet. Whether this more intensive dialectic of the mediatization of memory and also the commemorative filter of the mass media will produce more, or less sanitized, pasts, remains to be seen. For instance, Jesús Martín-Barbero (2002) considers the role of the media in respect of Colombia's difficult past: 'Abundant today in the media are ways of remembering that actually erase the past by blurring it, diffusing it, rendering it painless…we do not get a living, wounding, conflictive memory, but rather a neutral, indifferent discourse.'

These tensions of representation and memory revolve around assumptions on the part of news organizations, editors and broadcasters as to what audiences will find palatable or, rather, what they will not. That this appears to change with time affords some optimism as to the redemptive potential of the mediatization of memory, although, as I have suggested, considerable power is tied up with the medium of the initial production of events, and considerable import afforded to those images connected with the initial media coverage of an event (being forged under and within the conditions of 'event time'; cf. Gitlin 1980).

Whether the dizzying circulation of increasingly recent-past discourses via the mass media creates a perpetual amnesiac present and that the documentation, storage, and re-assemblage of our past(s), of and through the mass media and their associated technologies, condemn human memory, or whether a more intense and visual experience of living memory affords us a more 'useable' past, remains to be seen. I have argued, however, that the mediatization of memory is increasingly a significant means through which we first and later experience that which becomes 'past'. Television news in particular increasingly enters into the memory trajectory of the events of which it reports, records, and selectively repeats. And, given that the availability and portability of modern broadcast and recording devices have ushered in a new immediacy, intensity, and intimacy to the coverage of today's and future conflicts and catastrophes, the cyclical convergence of media/memory is destined to accelerate and is critical to the mediated legitimizing or otherwise of wars present and past.

Notes

[1] On the myth of the U.S. television news coverage of casualties during the Vietnam War, see Daniel C. Hallin (1986) *The 'Uncensored' War: The Media and Vietnam*, Oxford: Oxford University Press
[2] See, for example, the CBS News web pages at:
www.cbsnews.com/stories/2005/08/12/terror/main773198.shtml, accessed 12 August 2005

References

Auslander, Philip (1999) *Liveness: Performance in a Mediatized Culture*, London: Routledge
Connerton, Paul (1989) *How Societies Remember*, Cambridge: Cambridge University Press
Gilroy, Paul (1993) *The Black Atlanti: Modernity and Double Consciousness*, London: Verso
— (2004) *After Empire: Melancholia or Convivial Culture?* London: Routledge
Gitlin, Todd (1980) *The Whole World is Watching: Mass Media and the Making and Unmaking of the New Left*, London: University of California Press
Hallin, Daniel C. (1986) *The 'Uncensored' War: The Media and Vietnam*, Oxford: Oxford University Press
Hoskins, Andrew (2004) *Televising War: From Vietnam to Iraq*, London: Continuum
— (2007) *Media and Memory*, London: Routledge
Hoskins, Andrew and O'Loughlin, Ben (2007) *Television and Terror: Conflicting Times and the Crisis of News Discourse*, Basingstoke: Palgrave Macmillan
Jameson, Fredric (1991) *Postmodernism, or the Cultural Logic of Late Capitalism*, London: Verso
Kitzinger, Jenny (2000) Media Templates: Patterns of Association and the (Re)Construction of Meaning over Time, *Media, Culture and Society*, Vol. 22, No. 1 pp 61-84
Landsberg, Alison (2004) *Prosthetic Memory: The Transformation of American Remembrance in the Age of Mass Culture*, New York: Columbia University Press
Lash, Scott (2005) *Intensive Media – Modernity and Algorithm* (draft). Available online at http://roundtable.kein.org/node/125, accessed 15 January 2006
Martín-Barbero, Jesús (2002) *The Media: Memory, Loss and Oblivion*, GSC Quarterly, 4, Spring. Available online at: http://www.ssrc.org/gsc/newsletter4/martinbarbero.htm, accessed 25 January 2005
Nowotny, Helga (1994) *Time: The Modern and Postmodern Experience*, Cambridge: Polity Press
Rose, Steven (1993) *The Making of Memory: From Molecules to Mind*, London: Bantam Books
Schudson, Michael (1990) Ronald Reagan Misremembered, in Middleton, David and Edwards, Derek (eds) *Collective Remembering*, London: Sage pp 109-119
Weissman, Gary (2004) *Fantasies of Witnessing: Post-war Efforts to Experience the Holocaust*, Ithaca: Cornell University Press
Young, James E. (2000) *At Memory's Edge: After-Images of the Holocaust in Contemporary Art and Architecture*, London: Yale University Press

Chapter Two

Exploring Legal Black Holes: Extraordinary Rendition, Investigative Journalism and the Moral Imagination

John Tulloch

A parallel universe of secret prisons, connected by phantom planes, into which people vanish from the street, to become ghosts in a global system of incarceration and torture. Such is the vision which has emerged from almost five years of work by investigative journalists and human rights organizations on both sides of the Atlantic. Since 2002, a large number of ugly facts about these human rights abuses have been revealed by the American and European press. The stories of individual rendees have been obtained (for example, see Deneen and Priest 2003; Grey 2004a, 2005a: Hirsh, Hosenball and Barry 2005; Van Natta Jr 2005). Agents and former agents of the state have testified, on and off the record (Priest and Gellman 2002; Mayer 2005; Laurin 2005).

Innovative sources, such as plane spotters, have been enlisted (Priest 2004; Dickey 2005). Aircraft used by the CIA have been exhaustively tracked by the painstaking use of flightlogs (Grey 2004b; Cobain, Grey, Norton-Taylor 2005b; Shane, Grey, Williams 2005; Crewdson and Hundley 2005; Edes 2005; Corera 2005). Key political actors have been held to some sort of account (Cobain et al 2005a, 2005b; Bright 2006; Marty 2006; Rennie 2006). A global network of prisons has been charted in part. (Grey 2004b, Burke 2004, Priest 2005b, Marty 2006). Pulitzer and other prizes have been awarded.

But what does the gradual uncovering of the CIA programme of 'extraordinary rendition' have to tell us about the strengths and limitations of contemporary investigative journalism?

A brief background to extraordinary rendition

Although disreputable methods are inseparably associated with the history of CIA activities (see, for example, Woodward 1987; Snepp 2001; Hersh 2004, 2005; Coll 2004; Danner 2004; McCoy 2005, 2006a), the US policy of abducting or 'rendering' suspects from foreign countries without an extradition process seems to have begun under President Reagan, when CIA and FBI snatch squads were encouraged to kidnap suspected drug dealers and terrorists from 'lawless states' and transport them to the US, where they would be put on trial (Center for Human Rights and Global Justice 2005: 9; Harding 2005).

The rendition programme was placed on a new basis in the mid-1990s, after the first World Trade Center (WTC) bombing, with a directive from President Clinton which stated that suspected terrorists, domiciled overseas and wanted for violations of US law, might be forcibly returned to the US, without the co-operation of the host government.[xii] Carlos 'the Jackal', accused of involvement in a string of terrorist outrages including the 1970 Munich massacre, was picked up in the Sudan in 1994 while Ramzi Yousef, who was convicted of the 1993 WTC bombing, in Pakistan in 1995 (Coll 2004: 272-274; Amnesty 2006). In Croatia, the CIA captured Talaat Fouad Qassem, an important figure in an Egyptian Islamist group, and handed him over to Cairo, torture and death in custody (Chandrasekaran and Finn 2002a).

According to ex-CIA sources, intelligence gathering was not an aim of the programme before 9/11. The former head of the CIA's Bin Laden Unit, Michael Scheuer, says:

> It was never intended to talk to any of these people. Success, at least as the Agency defined it, was to get someone, who was a danger to us or our allies 'off the street' (interview in Marty 2006: par. 31).

In July 1998, a CIA team snatched five Egyptian Islamists in a joint operation with Albania's secret police (Chandrasekeran and Finn 2002b). After the Albanians tortured them for three days, the Americans flew them by an unmarked US jet to Cairo – where all the men were tortured and two hanged.

This was a mere harbinger of what was to come. The programme expanded hugely after the 11 September attacks with new, classified directives from President Bush (Jehl and Johnston 2005; Risen 2006). The CIA gained additional powers (Hersh 2005: 16-17), and 'new importance was attached to the collection of intelligence' (Marty 2006: par. 35). With the capture of more than 3,000 suspects, officials were placed under tremendous pressure by the administration to deliver results. The process is described by Ron Suskind:

> …time and again, borders are stretched. The President, or Vice President, repeatedly expresses a desire, or need, to a senior official. It's clear that neither elected official wants to know too much…They just want it done, accomplished, to do something – as the President often said to top aides – 'you didn't think you were capable of' (Suskind 2006: 230-231).

The network of secret prisons in eight countries included at least two in Eastern Europe (Marty 2006: par 2.6).

As revelations mounted in 2004, driven by reports by a relatively small group of American and European investigative journalists, the global nature of the scandal was exposed. By November 2005 Spain, Sweden, Norway and the European Parliament had opened inquiries into CIA flights and criminal investigations were underway in Germany, Italy and the UK (Whitlock 2005; Tremlett 2005). Revelations were widespread about the direct or indirect involvement of European governments. For example, *Der Spiegel* revealed that after 9/11 the CIA flew to Germany 437 times, with the most intense period for flights in 2002-2003, making Germany a major hub for the covert trade (*Der Spiegel*, 4 December 2005). RTE, Ireland national television and radio station, reported that CIA aircraft had landed at Shannon on 38 occasions (Russell

2005). The *Guardian* revealed that a database of flight records showed that aircraft involved in the operations had made at least 210 flights into the UK since 9/11 – i.e. about once a week:

> The 26-strong fleet run by the CIA have used 19 British airports and RAF bases, including Heathrow, Gatwick, Birmingham, Luton, Bournemouth and Belfast. The favourite destination is Prestwick, which CIA aircraft have flown into and out from more than 75 times. Glasgow has seen 74 flights and RAF Northolt 33 (Cobain, Grey and Norton-Taylor 2005b).

A four-day visit to Berlin, Brussels and Ukraine, in December 2005, by US Secretary of State Condoleezza Rice saw her 'in a shift flagged by her diplomats as a major policy change', pledge that the US would follow obligations under the UN's Convention against Torture 1985 worldwide, although:

> ...officials traveling with Miss Rice emphasized that the change had not been triggered by European attacks...The timing of Miss Rice's words gave the appearance that Washington recognized the row was worsening its already damaged reputation among close allies (*Daily Telegraph* 2005).

ABC television was told by CIA officials that the agency had emptied two secret prisons in Eastern Europe of suspects in November 2005 'in a frantic effort to defuse the "rendition" controversy' before her visit, and moved the prisoners to North Africa (Russell and Connolly 2005). Poland and Romania denied hosting secret jails. On 15 December, President Bush agreed to the Detainee Treatment Act ('the McCain torture ban') banning the use of torture of terrorist suspects, while claiming that the US did not carry out such acts. But critics allege that the framing of the presidential assent engineered significant loopholes to allow the continuance of abuse (McCoy 2006b).

Extraordinary rendition and investigative journalism

In considering the reporting of the rendition controversy, there is a danger of creating a mythology around the confrontation between official or corporate power and journalism. Notoriously the Watergate controversy in the US (1972-1974) became the vehicle for a powerful narrative of journalistic virtue and persistence: foregrounding two journalists and one newspaper, and in the process marginalizing other journalists, and a range of political and institutional actors, crucial to the unfolding scandal and President Richard Nixon's resignation (Woodward and Bernstein 1974; Schudson 1992; de Burgh 2000: 78-79).

In essentials, the coverage of extraordinary rendition conformed to the well-established dynamics of the media political scandal, where 'private acts that disgrace or offend the idealized, dominant morality of a social community are made public and narrativized by the media, producing a range of effects from ideological and cultural retrenchment to disruption and change' (Lull and Hinermann 1997: 3). Media scandals are described by Cottle as 'struggles for symbolic power' that 'unfold[s] through time' (Cottle 2006). More precisely, the story falls within the framework of political 'power scandals' as defined by John Thompson:

...the purest form of political scandal, in the sense that the rules or conventions whose transgression lies at the heart of political scandal are the rules and conventions governing the form of power...which is constitutive of the political field (Thompson 2000: 196; see also Thompson 1997 and Tomlinson 1997).

The coverage – with newspapers, broadcasting organizations and Internet sites threading together a worldwide narrative over five years of a circuit of rendition, a 'spiders web' (Marty 2006: par 24) linking the US to Britain, Germany, Poland, Romania, Jordan, Egypt, Morocco, Spain – may be seen as representing the integration of the public sphere into the 'global network society', where received ideas of the distinction between 'home' and 'foreign' journalism have to be reviewed (Volkmer 2002 : 244-5). At one level the story represented a contest for symbolic power within US agencies – notably between the administration and former and serving CIA and FBI officials – and between sections of the US legal system, with human rights and international law NGOs prominent in exposing abuses.

It may also be seen as an ongoing moral drama at a global level. Ettema and Glasser observe: 'An investigative story...is always a call for the community to affirm that certain conduct is, in fact, a transgression of the moral order' (Ettema and Glasser 1998: 82). In this case, the call was both to US moral and legal values, but beyond that, to international law and universal human rights. At the core of this was the absolute prohibition of torture, seen by liberal theorists as one of the touchstones of the Enlightenment and modern democracy (see, for example, Ignatieff 2005: 136.) However, Parry (2005: 521-5) argues that torture is, in fact, 'the basis of the modern state': done to the 'other'; hidden or, at best, an 'open secret' and, therefore, deniable and enmeshing citizens in a collective hypocrisy in which 'we often look the other way while our government does what it must'.

British coverage of rendition

British press coverage of the rendition issue in 2005 was extensive but patchy. Investigative coverage was limited, and confined to a small group of newspapers – mainly the *Guardian*, the *Independent*, the *Observer*, and *The Sunday Times*; the *New Statesman*; radio and television programmes carried by the BBC (Radio 4: File on Four; BBC2: Newsnight) and television reports from Channel 4 (Dispatches; Channel 4 News). Within that framework, a number of experienced freelance investigative journalists contributed across several outlets – for example Stephen Grey and Andrew Gilligan.

British commentators were overwhelmingly hostile to the practice of extraordinary rendition, but the level of criticism of the United States varied considerably, from outright condemnation of the US political system to a sorrowful reproachfulness. The volume of coverage also varied markedly. For example, in a survey of coverage for December 2005, as interest in torture flights and secret prisons in Europe reached renewed heights, news items using the term 'rendition' and/or 'extraordinary rendition' were highest in the *Independent* (76 references to renditions and extraordinary renditions), closely followed by the *Guardian* (61 references), with *The Times* (43) and *Daily Mail* (39) affording substantial coverage in third and fourth place respectively (see Tulloch 2005). Most striking was the lack of coverage in popular News Corporation newspapers (owned by Rupert Murdoch) – notably the *Sun* and the *News of the World*, with both papers only notching up one reference to 'torture flights' and none to 'rendition', compared to the rival tabloid, the left-of-centre *Daily Mirror* (17 references to 'rendition', 5 'torture flights') and the right-of-centre *Daily Express* (11 references to 'rendition', 7 to 'torture flights') (Tulloch 2005).

Of the papers surveyed, none explicitly argued for the use of torture against terrorist suspects, although the *Sun*, *News of the World*, and the *Daily Express*, in varying ways, gave some support to the argument that the 'war on terror' required exceptional methods. Within the broadly consensual approach of the rest of the press, there were certain distinct positions – ranging from a stand on the absolute human rights enshrined in the UN Convention Against Torture and a total condemnation of torture under any circumstances, to a more nuanced, equivocal, utilitarian position – implying that, in certain circumstances, and in a changed world, it might be understandable, if regrettable, as a lesser evil to prevent a greater evil. The *Independent*'s editorial comment for 2 December 2005 is a good illustration of the absolutist human rights position:

> Britain and Europe must stand by their principles…
>
> The British political establishment has been demonstrating a *disgracefully equivocal attitude* on the subject of torture for some time…now we learn that our government has *sunk even lower into this immoral quagmire* than we previously imagined….Torture 'no matter how light' cannot be justified on any grounds. It is not too late for Britain to stand up to its ally and refuse to have any part in *this vile practice* whatsoever (*Independent* 2005, my italics).

Imagery associated with swamps – the treacherous territory of moral uncertainty, summoning up entrapment, dirt, and contamination – recurs frequently in the discussion by British leader writers. The animating idea is of the reduction of all moral certainties to a relativist morass in which all states, no matter what their human rights records, become equivalent.

The perils of naivety and the need for alertness to moral ambiguity also characterizes *The Times*'s David Aaronovitch comment piece, which adopts an uneasy, ambivalent rhetorical posture that moves confusingly between condemning torture and hinting that, in some circumstances, it is understandable:

> All right it can work – but let's keep the thumbscrews under lock and key…
>
> …*Good old-fashioned disastrous* realpolitik would suggest that we turn aside when torture happens. If, in the short term, we have a chance of extracting a few key names, places and plans, then lives may be saved and *we should let the renderers rend.* It is precisely the same logic that led us to trade smiles and Sandhurst places with Middle Eastern dictators for years (Aaronovitch 2005, my italics).

In this faux-jocular rhetoric, 'realpolitik' is both 'good' and 'disastrous'. Lives 'may be saved' if we let rendition continue and perhaps 'torture works' if a ticking bomb is involved. However, because 'we' are enlisted in a 'war of ideas', in which it is assumed 'we' have the moral high ground, 'we' must not become like the 'Middle Eastern' dictators who, of course, represent everything 'we' must not become. Torture itself is characterized in a jokey way as 'thumbscrews', summoning up Pythonesque images of the Spanish Inquisition, rather than the sophisticated repertoire of 21st century assaults on the nervous system and the integrity of the personality, developed by the former

USSR, the British and, with an investment that dwarfed all other players, the CIA (McCoy 2005 and 2006a). As Peters observes:

> Not only the traditional institutions, but the traditional methods of torture have been generally discarded; the strappado, the rack, thumbscrews, legsplints and fire now below to an age whose technology…has been surpassed by modernity (Peters 1996: 163).

This may be to subject a columnist's linguistic play to a more demanding interrogation than routine, diurnal wordsmithery should be asked to withstand. But Aaronovitch represents a key distinction within the anti-torture consensus between papers taking a broadly pro-American stance and those more critical of US policy. *The Sunday Times*, which provided the longest and most detailed analysis of rendition published by the weeklies (see 11 December 2005) ran a more-in-sorrow-than-in-anger leader which was both critical of torture but supportive of the US:

> A noble vision lost…
>
> The White House is *understandably irritated* by a *holier than thou attitude of Europeans* who would be the first to complain if suspects had knowledge of impending terrorist attacks in their cities which was not extracted from them. But we are *rarely if ever* talking about the 'ticking time bomb' threat beloved of apologists for brutality… [The US] was built on the enlightenment rejection of arbitrary justice. To tolerate torture betrays that *great republic's* founding fathers (my italics).

In its appeal to the myth of the Founding Fathers and the purity of their Enlightenment project – airbrushing slavery and the arbitrary justice meted out to native people from the picture (e.g. see Rose 2004: 138) – this accepts the main charge whilst being supportive of the US.

The *Observer*, along with the *Guardian*, also stood on an absolutist human rights position in rejecting torture and took a more explicitly anti-American line. A leader of 4 December declares 'the fact that this repugnant practice exists shames an administration…cavalier approach to human rights…undermine the very values that the War against Terror was supposed to encourage' (*Observer* 2005). The following Sunday, Henry Porter's long comment piece condemned US policy for sinking 'to the moral level of Saddam' and invoked World War Two as a touchstone of civilization:

> Are we Europeans content as long as the torture is not going on in our backyard? It would seem so, but in Britain we should remember that during the war, when we faced a greater threat than the one posed by Al Qaeda, we did not resort to torture (Porter 2005).

Ironically, Porter's piece was soon followed by revelations from *Guardian* investigative journalists about the torture of German prisoners of war in British detention camps (see Cobain 2005c).

Comparing investigative stories

Within this context British investigative stories on extraordinary rendition employed a variety of approaches, from a human-interest style focus on the experience of individual victims, through to the classic exposé structure employing a compelling density of named and unattributed sources, and leaked documents. There was a broad similarity of approach to comparable US investigative stories, although the US reporters were able to deploy notably more ex-intelligence officials and off-the-record serving officers. Comparing British and American stories, a crude typology of extraordinary rendition stories (with substantial overlaps) looks like this:

Victim-centered stories, their narrative dominated by accounts of rendees or their relatives in the first or third person focusing on the experience of rendition: e.g. Stephen Grey's America's Gulag, in the *New Statesman*, 17 May 2004. This starts:

> Over the Atlantic, at 30,000 feet, on board a Gulfstream jet, Maher Arar looked out through the portholes of the private plane at the clouds beneath and the red glow of dawn. Stretching out on the wide, upholstered leather seat, he glanced across at the large video screen on which was displayed the path of the plane from its departure point near New York, onwards to Washington, DC and then to its final refuelling point at Portland, Maine, before heading across the ocean (Grey 2004a).

System-centered stories, with their narrative typically dominated by former or current agents of the state e.g. Dana Priest's *Washington Post* story: CIA Holds Terror Suspects in Secret Prisons: Debate is Growing Within Agency About Legality and Morality of Overseas System Set Up After 9/1, of 2 November. This starts:

> The effort President Bush authorized shortly after 11 September 2001, to fight Al Qaeda has grown into the largest CIA covert action program since the height of the Cold War, expanding in size and ambition despite a growing outcry at home and abroad over its clandestine tactics, according to former and current intelligence officials and congressional and administration sources (Priest 2005b).

Human rights and legal process stories, with their narrative typically dominated by legal sources and human rights experts. For example, Stephen Grey's long piece in *Le Monde Diplomatique* of April 2005 :

> A Swedish immigration lawyer, Kjell Jonsson, was on the phone to a client, asylum seeker Mohammed al-Zery from Egypt, on the afternoon of 18 December 2001. 'Suddenly there was a voice coming in, saying to al-Zery to end the telephone conversation,' Jonsson recalls. 'It was the Swedish police, who had arrested him' (Grey 2005b).

Cover-up stories that focused on attempts by authorities to conceal wrong-doings e.g. Martin Bright's Rendition: the Cover-Up, in the *New Statesman*, 23 January 2006:

> At Foreign Office Questions recently the minister responsible for Middle East Affairs snapped. MPs from all sides were pressing for answers about 'extraordinary rendition' and were dissatisfied with the stock reply from Kim Howells…The truth is the Government is involved in a cover-up, not so much of what it knows about this shady business, but what it doesn't know (Bright 2006).

Stories that aspire to **comprehensive, quasi-historical exposition**, utilizing a balanced range of victim, state, and legal sources, e.g. Jane Mayer's magisterial Outsourcing Torture in the *New Yorker*, 14 February 2005:

On 27 January, President Bush, in an interview with *The Times*, assured the world that 'torture is never acceptable, nor do we hand over people to countries that do torture'. Maher Arar, a Canadian engineer who was born in Syria, was surprised to learn of Bush's statement. Two and a half years ago, American officials, suspecting Arar of being a terrorist, apprehended him in New York and sent him back to Syria, where he endured months of brutal interrogation, including torture. When Arar described his experience in a phone interview recently, he invoked an Arabic expression. The pain was so unbearable, he said, that 'you forget the milk that you have been fed from the breast of your mother' (Mayer 2005).

Reasons to be cheerful?

Pronouncing obsequies on the death of Anglo-American investigative journalism has been a growth area of contemporary media scholarship, conducted with eloquence and passion by scholars such as Robert McChesney (2003), Douglas Kellner (2003: 101), Alan Doig (1997: 189-205) and numerous distinguished journalists including John Pilger (2004). The main component of the undertaker's case is that, for media organizations, investigative journalism is literally a waste of space. First it costs too much, requiring time and journalistic expertise that can be more efficiently deployed on unproblematic stories. Second, it creates awkward conflicts with the powerful, against the commercial interests of the media organization. Third, in a politically disengaged, promotional, celebrity-driven media culture, audiences don't see the point.

The problem with these gloomy scenarios is their all-embracing, histrionic quality – they tend to ignore or explain away inconvenient instances where moral conviction, human ingenuity and the artful exploitation of opportunities within, and in the cracks between, media organizations, allows serious investigative journalism to flourish. For example, David Leigh, assistant editor of the *Guardian*, once a notorious pessimist, is now notably more hopeful about the prospects for investigative journalism. He finds that 'one of the most heartening developments in recent years, has been the growth in networking – especially cross-border networking – by investigative journalists' (Leigh 2006).

Examples of this networking involve annual conferences and get-togethers by journalists, such as the annual summer school at City University, London, funded by the Lorana Sullivan Foundation, regular European conferences run by VVOJ, the Flemish journalists organization; and the Washington-based International Consortium of Investigative Journalists, with a network of about 150 investigative journalists worldwide.

Undoubtedly a powerful impetus to networking and collaboration is given by a sense of shared moral outrage. Dorothy Byrne, head of news and current affairs for Channel 4, who commissioned a one-hour documentary on rendition in 2005 (see Gilligan 2005) as part of a season of programmes on torture, commented:

> The scandal...undermines the fundamental values which underpin our Western democracies. The so-called war on terror is justified by the need to preserve our liberal democratic systems of government. Abducting men and shipping them round the world for torture should form no part of what we do. This story was important and shocking in itself but it also symbolized the ethical error it is possible for a Western democracy to make when it is under pressure (Byrne 2006).

But this territory is a tricky one for journalists. Ettema and Glasser observe that, as a professional species, investigative journalists tend to avoid explicit moral statement, resorting to irony (Ettema and Glasser 1998: 12). On extraordinary rendition, moral statement tended to be near the surface and at times explicit. This lays the journalist open to the charge of partisanship, as Stephen Grey was acutely aware:

> The hardest thing was…trying to get hard information without becoming a campaigner. I wanted to tell the story from the inside and the hardest thing is penetrating a secret world: to get behind the walls and get people in the CIA to talk to me and tell me their story and to really handle them in a fair way, although you are writing a story that isn't going to suit their purposes because it's really damning (Grey 2006).

The longer term impact of the story is impossible to assess. Although renditions will no doubt continue, it seems clear that the revelations have made co-operation between US and European police and intelligence agencies more fraught, and limited its scope. For example, 'the Swedish police have been forced to issue regulations requiring that any prisoner transfer be conducted by Swedish officials' (Huq 2006: 30). In the UK, the civil rights group Liberty has pressured police forces to undertake criminal investigations of offences committed on British soil, including torture, aiding and abetting torture, false imprisonment and kidnap (Liberty 2005). Criminal investigations currently continue (February 2007) in a number of other European countries.

Conclusion

Robert McChesney defines investigative journalism as 'original research into public issues, not merely reporting on what people in power are talking about' and argues it is 'on the endangered species list' (McChesney 2003: 309). Against the optimistic account of rendition as a triumph of journalistic exposure, it can be argued that most of what passed for investigative journalism in the uncovering of extraordinary rendition was questionable in the originality of its research, and in its relation to powerholders. After all, it has taken nearly five years for the main elements of the system to be revealed and much still remains secret or ambiguous, including the precise number of victims. In fact, as Philippe Sands observes:

> Between 9/11 and the emergence of the scandals at Abu Ghraib there was a noticeable reluctance on the part of the press and TV to investigate critically the administration's misuses of legal arguments to justify everything from the indefinite detention of foreigners at Guantanamo to the legal basis for the war in Iraq (Sands 2006: 231).

In addition it can be argued that much journalism was:
- indebted to heavy and self-interested briefing by unnamed intelligence sources; looked investigative but was heavily dependent on the painstaking research of a large band of human rights NGOs, academics and lawyers;
- recycled the stories of a handful of 'innocent' rendees and the efforts of their defense lawyers;
- worked from the basis that the use of illegal methods and torture was essentially an 'extraordinary' departure by the authorities from civilised and legal forms of conduct.

Nevertheless, the development of the rendition story can also be seen to embody encouraging signs about the prospects for investigative journalism, both in relation to traditional news organizations and the emergent resources of the world wide web. Among these signs are: the use of computer based resources; enhanced networking and co-operation between journalists; and the emergence of a new model of professionalism.

References

Aaronovitch, David (2005) All right it can work – but let's keep the thumbscrews under lock and key, *The Times*, Features section, 6 December p. 24

Amnesty International (2006) Below the radar: Secret flights to torture and 'disappearance'. Available online at: http://web.amnesty.org/library/index/ENGAMR510512006, accessed 14 June 2006

Bright, Martin (2006) Rendition: the Cover-Up, *New Statesman,* 23 January 2006

Burke, Jason (2004) Terror Backlash: Global web of secret US prisons, the *Observer,* 13 June

Byrne, Dorothy (2006) Personal communication with author, 14 July

Center for Human Rights and Global Justice (2005) *Beyond Guantanamo: Transfers to Torture One Year After Raul v. Bush*, New York: NYU School of Law. Available online at http://www.nyuhr.org/beyondguantanamo.htm, accessed 14 June 2006

Chrandrasekan, Rajiv and Finn, Peter (2002a) US Behind Secret Transfer of Terror Suspect, *International Herald Tribune,* 11 March 2002

— (2002b) US Bypasses Law in Fight Against Terrorism, *International Herald Tribune,* 12 March 2002

Cobain, Ian, Grey, Stephen and Norton-Taylor, Richard (2005a) Evidence emerges of Britain's role in extraordinary rendition, the *Guardian* 12 September 2005

— (2005b) Destination Cairo: human rights fears over CIA flights, the *Guardian*, 12 September 2005

Cobain, Ian (2005c) Britain's Secret Torture Centre: The interrogation camp that turned prisoners into living skeletons, the *Guardian*, 17 December pp 8-9

Coll, Steve (2004) *Ghost Wars: The Secret History of the CIA, Afghanistan and Bin Laden, from the Soviet Invasion to September 10, 2001*, London: Penguin

Corera, Gordon (2005) Does UK Turn a Blind Eye to Torture? BBC News 5 April 2005. Available online at: http://www.news.bbc.co.uk/2/hi/uk_news/4414491.stm, accessed 14 June 2006

Cottle, Simon (2006) Mediatized Rituals: beyond manufacturing consent, *Media, Culture and Society*, Vol. 28, No. 3 pp 411-432

Crewdson, John and Tom Hundley (2005) Boston Red Sox Jet Tied to Secret Guantanamo Flights, *Chicago Tribune*, 20 March 2005

Daily Telegraph (2005) Editorial: Rice gives torture promise to quell terror flights row, 8 December

Danner, Mark (2004) *Torture and Truth: America, Abu Ghraib, and the War on Terror*, London: Granta Books 2005

de Burgh, Hugo (2000) *Investigative Journalism: Context and Practice*, London: Routledge

Deneen, L. Brown and Priest, Dana (2003) Deported Terror Suspect Details Torture in Syria, *Washington Post*, 5 November

Dickey, Christopher (2005) Plane Spotting. How aviation hobbyists put vital evidence about secret CIA flights on the Web – and provided evidence for lawsuits about detainee abuse, *Newsweek*, 14 December

Doig, Alan (1997) The Decline of Investigatory Journalism, in Bromley, Michael and O'Malley, Tom (eds) *A Journalism Reader*, London: Routledge pp 189-213

Edes, Gordon (2005) CIA uses jet, Red Sox partner confirms. 'Stunned' by report of controversial prisoner transfers, *Boston Globe*, 21 March. Available online at: http://www.boston.com/news/nation/articles/2005/03/21cia_uses_jet_red_sox_partner, accessed 31 July 2006

Ettema, James and Glasser, Theodore (1998) *Custodians of Conscience: Investigative Journalists and Public Virtue*, New York: Columbia University Press

Gilligan, Andrew (2005) Dispatches: Kidnap and Torture American Style, Channel 4, 23 November 2005

Grey, Stephen (2004a) America's Gulag, *New Statesman*, 17 May 2004

— (2004b) US accused of 'torture flights', *Sunday Times* (London), 14 November 2004

— (2005a) File on Four: Rendition, BBC Radio 4, 8 February 2005

— (2005b) United States: trade in torture, *Le Monde Diplomatique*, April 2005

— (2006) in interview with the author, 14 July

Harding, Luke (2005) CIA's secret jails open up new transatlantic rift, *Guardian*, 5 December. Available online at: http://www.guardian.co.uk/usa/story/0,12271,1657839,00.html, accessed 6 June 2006

Hersh, Seymour (2004) The Gray Zone: How a secret Pentagon program came to Abu Ghraib, *New Yorker*, 24 May

— (2005) *Chain of Command*, London: Penguin

Hirsh, Michael, Hosenball, Mark and Barry, John (2005) Aboard Air CIA, *Newsweek*, 28 February

Huq, Aziz (2006) Extraordinary Rendition and the Wages of Hypocrisy, *World Policy Journal*, Spring 2006. Available online at: www.worldpolicy.org/journal/, accessed 6 June 2006

Ignatieff, Michael (2005) *The Lesser Evil. Political Ethics in an Age of Terror*, Edinburgh: Edinburgh University Press

Independent (2005) Britain and Europe must stand by their principles, 2 December p. 42

Jehl, Douglas and Johnston, David (2005) Rule Changes Lets CIA Freely Send Suspects Abroad to Jails, *New York Times*, 6 March 2005

Kellner, Douglas (2003) *Media Spectacle*, London: Routledge

Knightley, Phillip (1997) *A Hack's Progress*, London: Jonathan Cape

Laurin, Fredrik (2005) The Broken Promise, *Kalla Fakta* (Cold Facts), TV 4 Sweden, 17 and 24 May. Transcript available online at: http://www.hrw.org/english/docs/2004/05/17/sweden8620.htm, accessed on 6 June 2006

Leigh, David (2006) in email to author, 24 July 2006

Liberty (2005) UK Involvement in Extraordinary Rendition: Liberty and Justice. Supplementary Submission to the Joint Committee on Human Rights. Available online at http://www.liberty-human-rights.org.uk, accessed on 6 June 2006

Lull, James and Hinerman, Stephen (eds) (1997) *Media Scandals: Morality and Desire in the Popular Market Place*, Cambridge: Polity Press

Marty, Dick (rapporteur) (2006) Parliamentary Assembly Committee on Legal Affairs and Human Rights: Alleged secret detentions and unlawful inter-state transfers involving Council of Europe member states. Draft report: Part 11 (Explanatory Memorandum) 7 June. Available online at: http://assembly.coe.int, accessed on 6 December 2006

Mayer, Jane (2005) Outsourcing Torture. The secret history of America's 'extraordinary rendition' program, *New Yorker*, 14 February

McChesney, Robert (2003) The Problem of Journalism: a political economic contribution to an explanation of the crisis in contemporary US journalism, *Journalism Studies*, Vol. 4, No. 3 pp 299-329

McCoy, Alfred (2005) Cruel Science: CIA Torture and US Foreign Policy, *New England Journal of Public Policy*, Vol.19, No. 2 pp 209-262

— (2006a) *A Question of Torture: CIA Interrogation from the Cold War to the War on Terror*, New York: Henry Holt

— (2006b) Professor McCoy Exposes the History of CIA Interrogation, From the Cold War to the War on Terror, interview with Amy Goodman, Democracy, 18 February 2006. Available online at: http://www.zmag.org/content/print_article.cfm?itemID=9749&sectionID=1, accessed 24 July 2006

Observer (2005) Torture must stop: US 'rendition' shames its allies, 4 December p. 28

Parry, John T. (2005) The Shape of Modern Torture: Extraordinary Rendition and Ghost Detainees, *Melbourne Journal of International Law*, Vol. 6 pp 516-533

Peters, Edward (1996) *Torture* (2nd edition), Philadelphia: University of Pennsylvania Press

Pilger, John (ed.) (2004) *Tell Me No Lies; Investigative Journalism and its Triumphs*, London: Jonathan Cape

Porter, Henry (2005) Into harm's way: By 'rendering' suspects to torturers America sinks to the moral level of Saddam, *Observer*, 11 December p. 29

Priest, Dana and Gellman, Barton (2002) US Decries Abuse but Defends Interrogation; 'Stress and Duress' Tactics Used on Terrorism Suspects Held in Secret Overseas Facilities, *Washington Post*, 26 December.

Priest, Dana (2004) Jet is an Open Secret in Terror War, *Washington Post*, 27 December

— (2005a) Help From France Key In Covert Operations: Paris's 'Alliance Base' Targets Terrorists, *Washington Post*, 3 July

— (2005b) CIA Holds Terror Suspects in Secret Prisons: Debate is Growing Within Agency About Legality and Morality of Overseas System Set Up After 9/11, *Washington Post*, 2 November

Rennie, David (2006) Terror suspects 'vanish in spider's web', *Daily Telegraph*, 8 June p. 16

Risen, James (2006) *State of War. The Secret History of the CIA and the Bush Administration*, London: Free Press

Rose, David (2004) *Guantanamo: America's War on Human Rights*, London: Faber and Faber

Russell, Alec (2005) Secret CIA flights helped us save lives, insists Rice, *Daily Telegraph*, 6 December

Russell, Alec and Connolly, Kate (2005) CIA 'emptied secret jails' before Rice Europe trip, *Daily Telegraph*, 7 December

Sands, Philippe (2006) *Lawless World*, London: Penguin.

Schudson, Michael (1992) Watergate: a study in mythology, *Columbia Journalism Review*, May/June pp 28-33

Shane, Scott, Grey, Stephen and Williams, Margot (2005) CIA Expanding Terror Battle Under Guise of Charter Flights, *New York Times*, 31 May 2005

Snepp, Frank (2001) *Decent Interval: An Insider's Account of Saigon's Indecent End Told by the CIA's Chief Strategy Analyst in Vietnam*, Lawrence: University Press of Kansas, first edition 1977

Sunday Times (2005) A noble vision lost, editorial, 11 December p. 16

Suskind, Ron (2006) *The One Percent Doctrine: Deep Inside America's Pursuit of Its Enemies Since 9/11*, London: Simon and Schuster

Thompson, John (1997) Scandal and Social Theory, in Lull, James and Hinerman, Stephen (eds) *Media Scandals: Morality and Desire in the Popular Market Place*, Cambridge: Polity Press pp 34-64

— (2000) *Political Scandal: Power and Visibility in the Media Age*, Cambridge: Polity Press

Tomlinson, John (1997) 'And Besides, the Wench is Dead': Media Scandals and the Globalization of Communication, in Lull, James and Hinerman, Stephen (eds) *Media Scandals: Morality and Desire in the Popular Market Place*, Cambridge: Polity Press pp 65-84

Tremlett, Giles (2005) Spanish police expose more CIA links to secret flights of detainees: 42 operatives, the *Guardian*, 15 November

Tulloch, John (2005) Normalising the unthinkable: The British press, torture, and the human rights of terrorist suspects, *Ethical Space*, Vol. 2, No. 4 pp 25-32

Van Natta Jr, Don and Mekhennet, Souad (2005) German's Claim of Kidnapping Brings Investigation of US Links, *The New York Times*, 9 January 2005

Volkmer, Ingrid (2002) Journalism and Political Crises in the Global Network Society, in Allan, Stuart and Zeliger, Barbie (eds) *Journalism After September 11*, London: Routledge pp. 235-246

Whitlock, Craig (2005) Europeans Probe Secret CIA Flights, *Washington Post*, 17 November 2005 p. A22

Woodward, Bob and Bernstein, Carl (1974) *All the President's Men*, London: Quarto

Woodward, Bob (1987) *Veil: The Secret Wars of the CIA, 1981-1987*, London: Simon and Schuster

Chapter Three

Reporting Africa's Unknown Wars

Lara Pawson

I started working as the BBC's Angola correspondent in late November 1998. Within hours of my arriving in the capital, Luanda, the producer of Radio 4's Today programme requested a despatch on the kidnapping of two British diamond-mining workers by rebel soldiers in north-east Angola. Allaying my concerns about my unfamiliarity with the country, the unusually sympathetic producer explained he would email me some wire copy on which to base the piece, and then later talk through any necessary corrections. My predecessor was incredulous. Not once during her year in Angola had she filed a single report for Radio 4's 'flagship news show' despite repeated efforts to awaken their interest in Angola.

I soon realized that my brief foray with Today was nothing more than a case of beginner's luck. Two weeks after this event, Angolan government troops bombed the headquarters of the rebel group UNITA (*União Nacional pela Independência Total de Angola*). In retaliation, the rebels shelled the town of Kuito, in central Angola. Before the year was over hundreds of people had been killed in fighting and tens of thousands displaced. After four years of uneasy peace the United Nations' peacekeeping mission – which had cost the international community US$1.5 billion – had failed. The Angolan war had restarted. Yet this news story was of no interest to the Today producers, despite their appetite for the despatch on two missing British men a fortnight earlier.

I remained the BBC's correspondent for Angola until the end of December 2000. During that time, the situation worsened considerably, particularly in Malanje where the relentless shelling by rebels killed hundreds. Humanitarian agencies pulled out, fearing for the safety of their staff. Children had grown frighteningly accustomed to the shelling. The hospital had no fresh blood supplies. Many people were left to die. Food aid was siphoned off for the Angolan military or sold at the local market. Elsewhere in the country there were repeated sightings of mass graves and allegations that the Angolan army were using napalm. Humanitarian agencies reported that hundreds of thousands of people were dying from hunger. This stage of the conflict – known as Angola's fourth war – has since been described as more brutal than any phase in the country's conflict history since 1975.[1] Yet throughout this time I was never contacted by Today again. In fact, apart from a couple of interviews with Five Live, not one of the BBC news programmes broadcast in the UK – otherwise known as 'domestics'[2] – requested a report, even though they are marketed as programmes that cover the whole world.

This reflects a situation where most African wars are all but ignored by British mainstream media. Similar and more recent examples to Angola – whose war ended in April 2002 – can be found with Ivory Coast, the Democratic Republic of the Congo

(DRC), Burundi, Algeria, Somalia, Chad, north-east Sudan and Cabinda.[3] When conflicts are reported, the attention comes in brief bursts, produced by non-specialist reporters, and focuses primarily on the humanitarian aspects of the war, thus confirming the partial and paternalistic view that most Africans are helpless victims and their leaders unusually cruel and greedy.

In this chapter, I take a critical look at the way the British media represents African wars. I first provide examples of how the mainstream media attempts to report on certain conflicts, and highlight how some of the world's largest wars have received relatively scarce coverage. I examine the practice of modern-day newsgathering, which seems to encourage superficial rather than specialist reporting. I also question the notion of the qualitatively different African war and attempt to debunk the view that Africa's wars are more confusing than other conflicts. I show why Africa deserves more consistent and in-depth media coverage, highlighting in particular the entrenched relationship Britain has with certain African states (and their conflicts). Finally I argue that the wars themselves are often the only subject that the media is interested in, and thus the African continent is continually being misrepresented. If we really want to understand – and possibly prevent – these conflicts, we need to know about these countries before the violence erupts.

How the British media represents African wars

Within the 'domestic' media, the level of ignorance about Africa can have amusing manifestations, especially when editors resort to drastic measures to try to make a story relevant to the home audience. One journalist, interviewed for BBC Five Live about the abduction of British aid workers in Liberia during the civil war, recalled the presenter's concluding question: 'What impact do you think this will have on South Africa's 2010 World Cup bid?' The same journalist was interviewed by Radio Scotland on the same subject. This time the presenter asked him whether people going on holiday to Kenya should be worried about the events in Liberia, to which he responded: 'Only in the way that someone planning a holiday in Spain worries about the fighting in Yugoslavia.' He was never asked back on the show.[4] In case you are wondering, the distance between Liberia and Kenya is 5,354 kilometers, compared to the 1,863 kilometers separating Spain from the former Yugoslavia (Bosnia-Herzegovina, to be precise).

Another means to engage British audiences with African wars is via the tabloid-type story. Chris Simpson, the BBC's Angola reporter during the early 1990s, was once called by Five Live, who were interested in interviewing him about a runaway tiger that had killed a cameraman during an attempt to transport it from a crumbling private zoo in Luanda to South Africa. Simpson agreed to the interview on the proviso that they used the tiger story to segue into more serious questions about the Angolan war. Five Live agreed, but you have to wonder why it took a wild cat to raise interest in a country where hundreds were dying every day. After all, the British media did not need a tiger-ravaged cameraman to inspire them to cover the Bosnia war, in which 100,000 people were killed between 1992 to 1995.[5] The statistics of the Angolan war during the early 1990s show that, in terms of the number of deaths, it was clearly just as significant as Bosnia's. For the record, between October 1992 and October 1994, it is estimated that 3 per cent of the Angolan population – about 300,000 people – died as a direct result of the conflict.

Between May and October 1993, the United Nations reported that up to 1,000 people were dying every day in Angola, more than in any other conflict in the world.[6]

Am I suggesting that the number of deaths should be used to gauge a war's importance and therefore the amount of coverage it gets? Well, yes, I am, with the obvious proviso that it is not always possible to access reliable statistics quickly in the thick of war; but, if they are available, at least the statistics of casualties are a significant factor which could be taken into consideration when deciding how many lines or minutes a particular conflict is given, where it will appear in the running order and how often it will be covered.

On 24 July 2006, the Today programme reported that 30 people had been killed when a suicide bomb exploded in Baghdad. The presenter, Ed Stourton, told listeners about what he called 'an extraordinary statistic': that approximately a hundred people are dying each day in Iraq. Later this figure was repeated by the correspondent in Baghdad, Jane Peel, who reported that during the previous two months, 6,000 people had died a violent death in Iraq. At another point in the programme, presenter Justin Webb interviewed Martin Bell, ambassador for the UN children's body UNICEF, about a report he had authored on child soldiers in the DRC.[7] Bell explained that the highest concentration of child soldiers in the world is found in the Congo. He spoke of a 'child of 17' who had begun carrying a rifle when he was 13, and who had 'found it extraordinarily difficult to get out of this anarchy'. Ironically, given how little Today reports from (or on) the DRC, Webb responded: 'And extraordinarily difficult if the world takes no notice of what is happening.' To which Bell commented: 'That's the extraordinary thing about it. It's the only war I've ever known that the worse it gets, the less people seem to care. It's the great forgotten war of Africa. In eight years, four million people have died and they go on dying at a thousand a day.'

In fact, the UN's published statistics are worse. The UNICEF website states that every day 1,200 people are 'killed in the conflict-hit Democratic Republic of Congo (DRC) because of violence, disease and malnutrition'.[8] The same report states that more children under the age of five years die each year in the DRC than in China, which has a population 23 times the size of the Congo's. The International Rescue Committee calculates that the number of deaths in the DRC makes it the 'deadliest war since WWII'.[9] Even acknowledging that Iraq's population of 26 million is only half the size of the DRC's 53 million, it is nevertheless still the case that the DRC conflict is much larger, not only literally but also relatively. You would never think so if you relied solely on the British domestic media for your information about the world.

The practice of reporting African wars

In this section I look briefly at the cavalier practices of newsgathering, a world in which a reporter is required neither to speak the language of the people about whom he/she writes, nor necessarily to have visited the country. Indeed, often the most successful reporters are those who have traveled the most, as opposed to those who know the most about a place. Coupled with this is a cultural bias that tends to give English-speaking countries and former British colonies priority in the minds of British news managers, regardless of the story.

Issues of language

When the BBC first offered me the job as correspondent in Angola I told them I did not speak any Portuguese. The editor assured me this did not matter: he said that because I spoke French I would pick up Portuguese relatively quickly. This turned out to be untrue. I spent the first three months bribing my landlady's teenage son to translate the national radio news bulletins each day. I was lucky to be supported by a couple of Angolan journalists who answered my endless questions. Gradually, my Portuguese did improve but it took an enormous amount of effort, and a series of lessons which I, not the BBC, paid for. Of course you can use an interpreter, but few freelance correspondents can afford to pay one properly on a regular basis. Moreover, particularly in a country at war, interpreters are taking extreme risks to translate for a journalist. You have no guarantee that the interpreter will actually ask the minister of defense, for example, the frank question you posed. It might simply be too dangerous for the local interpreter to be so candid.

The UK broadcast media's rather lax approach to the importance of language also means that it is much harder to persuade an editor to broadcast a non-English speaker. Even at the BBC World Service – even within the Africa service – editors prefer to hear English speakers in reports and interviews. Some believe that a package or interview sounds too messy or cluttered if the original voice must be voiced-over in English; others think that the audience find it too hard listening to voice-overs and switch off. There are obvious limitations to this sort of policy, which fails to account for the millions of people who do not speak English in Africa, let alone the rest of the world. In Angola, English- speakers are largely members of the political and financial elite, and even these groups are not keen to speak a foreign language on air in case they make a mistake.

Related to this, it is worth noting that UK news managers favor English-speaking countries. In Africa, this means that former British colonies receive far more attention than the rest of the continent. Zimbabwe is a case in point. Even the BBC's African service programmes habitually favor Africa's so-called Anglophone to Francophone and Lusophone states. A similar pattern is seen in France and Portugal. The French media are more interested in Ivory Coast and DRC than Kenya and Nigeria; and the Portuguese media rarely cover any African countries other than Angola and Mozambique, with occasional reports from the three remaining Portuguese-speaking countries, Guinea Bissau, Cape Verde and São Tomé and Príncipe.

Unknown specialist or familiar generalist?

At the start of my career, a former BBC foreign correspondent welcomed me aboard, saying: 'We all cut our teeth in Africa: it's a good place to learn the job.' I was struck by this sentence, which I interpreted to mean that Africa is the foreign correspondents' kindergarten, where mistakes can be made and no one will mind too much. Perhaps there is so much ignorance about this huge continent, no-one would spot the errors anyway – particularly when there is a war taking place.

A few years later, I was warned not to stay too long in Angola. 'Whatever you do,' said another foreign correspondent, 'don't get trapped in Africa.' Perhaps this is why some regional correspondents on contract to Africa readily interrupt their work covering an entire continent for more prestigious assignments elsewhere. For example, between January to October 2005, the then Africa correspondent for the *Guardian,* Rory Carroll, was seconded from Johannesburg to Iraq.[10] He was kidnapped in Baghdad in October 2005. Ten months later, in August 2006, he ended his four-year stint as the paper's man in Africa.[11] Similarly, Hilary Andersson was the BBC Africa correspondent from 2001 until the end of 2005, although she also reported in Iraq and Afghanistan during her Africa tenure.[12]

Specialization and commitment to a region, or worse a single country, is not the best way to climb the foreign correspondents' ladder.[13] News managers tend to promote the idea that the more countries and more wars you've 'covered' the better the journalist you are, and if you want to go places you need to do a stint in the Middle East. It is alarming to think that a single journalist is considered so talented that he/she can not only cover an entire continent of more than 50 countries, but can also cross continents to file trustworthy reports from another region altogether.

One of the arguments put forward in favor of the generalist journalist who travels the world reporting on disaster after disaster, popping up one day in Kandahar, the next in Monrovia, is familiarity. Apparently audiences get to trust certain correspondents no matter where they appear. The BBC's John Simpson, Fergal Keane and, until recently, Ben Brown, are all reporters whose capacity to cover a major news story anywhere in the world seems to know no bounds.

On 13 September 2006, in the *Guardian,* Marcel Berlins asked: 'Is it better for viewers and listeners to be provided with information, opinions and arguments on serious topics by the people who know most about the subject or hold a particular office, even if they lack full fluency; or to use secondary speakers who may know a lot less but are more articulate?' Berlins had in mind a discussion he had heard on Today the previous Saturday, between John Humphrys and the Director for the Darfur Centre for Human Rights whose English, Berlins wrote, 'while obviously quite sound, was accented in a way that required concentration to fully penetrate – effort that is perhaps not compatible with breakfast listening, even on Radio 4'. Reluctantly, Berlins concludes his piece stating: 'Understanding is more important than rank.'

Indeed, there is no point broadcasting an interview if the target audience cannot understand it. But the choice is rarely so stark. The BBC's Sudanese journalist, Alfred Taban, won the UK Parliamentary Press Gallery's Speaker Abbot Award for his work in exposing the scale of the killing in Sudan's Darfur region. He speaks clear, fluent English, but I don't recall ever hearing him on a domestic radio or television programme talking about Sudan.

I am not suggesting that you must be a Somali to do good reports on Somalia – or a Briton to report well on Britain – but you do need to have spent time living among the people, learning to speak their language(s), to understand their ways of life, their attitudes to power, democracy and so on. There are already plenty of African reporters and specialist foreign reporters working for the BBC World Service in Africa, but they are low down the domestics' pecking order and are rarely heard talking about the country in which they live. Instead, British audiences are treated to regional reporters and drop-in star correspondents who fly into a place for a few days and know little of its peculiarities or history.

The culture of desk-bound newsgathering

Journalists are not paid to reflect or think or even, it seems, to investigate. Sometimes, we might as well not be there at all. With regards to my first report from Angola, the one about the two British men, the producer reassured me that my relative ignorance about the country did not matter because he would send me the wires. It struck me as highly questionable journalistic practice that London could simply email me some agency 'copy' which I could then crib, juggle and spew out as my own BBC report. How would I know whether the agency copy was correct? The same happened when I was in Ivory Coast, reporting on the West African region. I filed stories on Niger, Senegal, Mauritania and Liberia without setting foot in those places – all thanks to the wires.

During my first year as the BBC correspondent in Angola, I was also the Reuters correspondent. I learned that sometimes you could only sell a story to a BBC producer if they had already seen it on the wires. By contract, I was supposed to file to the BBC first and then to Reuters. If the BBC turned me down, I could file straight to Reuters. It was amazing the number of times the BBC would call me *after* seeing my report on Reuters and ask me to file exactly the same story I had offered hours earlier and they had rejected. Simply because the producers had seen the piece on the wires, they believed it (mattered). This proved a useful way for me to increase my meager freelance income – I could simply play the BBC off my agency work – but it never ceased to depress me. Copycat journalism can lead to inaccuracies becoming fact because no one has stopped to check the details for themselves. Yet this bad habit is inevitable as journalists come under pressure to file for more programmes to tighter deadlines.

The qualitatively different African war?

The challenge journalists face in trying to explain conflicts in a limited amount of time and space is immense. There is a tendency, seen for example in the mainstream coverage of the so-called war on terror, to reduce wars to the good versus evil narrative. The reality is usually far fuzzier. In the case of African conflicts, however, foreign journalists often appear to avoid the 'good versus evil' structure. Unfamiliar with the wars themselves, there is a tendency to present them as an anarchical mess, unique to Africa, where people are just fighting for the sake of it in a pitiful display of madness.[14] Bernard-Henri Lévy, a well-traveled journalist and philosopher, falls straight into this trap. He concludes that the wars in Burundi, Sudan and (formerly) Angola are what he calls 'the forgotten wars of the twenty-first century':[15]

> ...for the first time in the modern era, and because the great narratives that provided meaning have fallen silent, great masses of men are caught in wars without aim, without clear ideological stakes, without memory, as the wars last for decades, perhaps without outcome – and where it is sometimes difficult indeed to tell, between protagonists who are drunk with equal parts of power, money and blood, where lies the true, the good, the least evil, the desirable.[16]

Lévy contrasts these 'hidden' wars with: '...serious wars, which have a meaning. There still exist in the Near East, for instance, wars where everyone can see that the fate of the world is at stake.'[17] In dividing wars into two groups – those he sees as fuzzy, confusing, nonsensical ones versus the weighty, grown-up, meaningful ones – Lévy reveals his own ignorance. Why, for example, does he assume that 'everyone' views wars in the Near East in the same way? I doubt that the female peasant in eastern Congo thinks that the conflicts of the Great Lakes region in Central Africa are any less meaningful than the war between Israel and Palestine. From where she stands, the fate of her world is at stake in South Kivu, not the Near East.

Lévy's claim that it is harder to distinguish the good and evil protagonists in African wars (such as that in Sudan) than in other wars (such as Iraq's) highlights his myopic vision of African conflicts. While *he* may find it hard to distinguish the good from the bad in Darfur, it is unlikely that the Sudanese have the same problem. Perhaps they think all the sides are evil, perhaps not, but doubtless they will be able to make their own value judgments about the warring parties and their leaders. In my experience covering the Angolan and Ivory Coast wars, it is the London-based desk editors who struggle to understand how complex and fuzzy most wars are, not the locals.

Lévy goes to quite remarkable lengths to promote the European cliché of Africa. In Angola, he sees 'leprous slums...ten-year-old prostitutes...packs of children with nothing to do...women with gargoyle heads, men who no longer have any face at all'.[18] A little later he pronounces: 'It is definitely a war of the squalid, of the seamy, since I've seen only sleazy, squalid people since I've been here.'[19] So where was he looking? There are also children who go to school and women who could be on the catwalk. Did he not visit the young men who are given roses by the town's girls on the eve of a battle? Didn't he see any of them? Or did he feel they would not conform to the stereotype he had expected? When Lévy goes to the central highland city of Huambo, he finds 'everything in turmoil'.[20] Everything? Surely not.

When I visited Huambo (at around the same time he was there) there was a group of nuns who made and sold moisturizing cream, and another group of women selling pots of delicious homemade strawberry jam. These are important truths of the war, just as important as the amputees and shelled buildings. But all Lévy can see ahead of him is 'the same devastation, the same impression of a country in tatters – a dismembered, devitalized, lunar space, where everywhere you see traces of war but nowhere its logic, its meaning, or any sign of its end'.[21] Perhaps he did not know enough to spot the signs, to understand the meanings and logic and, indeed, the sign of its end: after all, the Angolan civil war ended a couple of years after his visit.

One of Lévy's final points about Angola is what he calls 'the paradox' of the conflict: 'They fight each other...wherever there's nothing but poverty, desert, villages plundered over and over...But wherever there are riches...a non-war is imposed, a gentleman's agreement...'[22] As I read this, I find myself pondering the so-called war on terror, replete with its own gentleman's agreements, and wonder why Lévy believes this to be so exclusively African.[23]

Lévy's account of the war he 'saw' in Angola was published, in a shorter version, in *Le Monde* in the early summer of 2001. His book – which includes the essay on Angola – was described by the *Jewish Chronicle* as an example of 'excellent journalism'. Yet it strikes me as a fine example of the sort of superficial response that so often emerges when foreign reporters drop in on a conflict. His analysis is trite and unhelpful. And yet Lévy was writing a whole book – his chapter on Angola is 18 pages long – whereas most reporters only have 500 words in a newspaper, or two minutes on the radio, or 50 seconds on the television. That is not enough time to explain the details of a civil war, and yet it is what the news corporations expect from a foreign correspondent. I recall a television presenter on a rolling news channel asking me, as if we were discussing the state of play on a Nintendo computer game, 'So who's gonna win the war Lara?' I had 40 seconds to answer. That ever-growing desire to keep the news short and simple makes life very difficult for any reporter trying to convey the complex narrative of a war.

Why should African wars be covered differently?

It is with mistaken arrogance that Lévy and too many other foreign journalists seek to point out the great gaps between 'them', the warring Africans, and 'us' who sit reading, listening or watching from the safety of our front rooms. Far more valuable and convincing journalism could be done informing audiences how we in Britain, and elsewhere in the West, are connected to these wars – not simply from a humanist and emotional perspective, but through real economic, political and military ties.

Geopolitical significance and economic interests

One of the reasons, you might argue, that Iraq receives more British media attention than the DRC is because of the relationship between Britain and Iraq. Put simply, there is one. What is more, it is a relationship that the British public could not fail to know about. We have been bombarded with information about our government's role in the Iraq conflict, as well as that of British troops, even British mercenaries and well-known British journalists. People in Britain know that Iraq has oil and assume that British companies are doing business there, even if they do not know the details.[24] Similar economic interests are apparent in African states but are less publicized and less visible. I believe that the fact that UK and US economic interests can actually contribute to, or escalate African wars, is why they are deserving of coverage.

For example, one of the reasons the conflict in the Congo escalated so quickly was because of the country's mineral wealth. Coltan, a vital ingredient for mobile telephones and Sony PlayStations, sparked a huge amount of commercial interest – and fighting.[25] So did gold. A UN panel of experts showed that up to eighteen British-based companies assisted in the plundering of Congo's minerals which fuelled the conflict in the east of the country.[26] However, despite the advice of the UN Security Council to follow up investigations into the likes of AngloAmerican and Barclays Bank, the British government has barely blinked, citing a lack of adequate evidence.[27] In 2005, the international organization Human Rights Watch (HRW) produced a report which alleged that AngloGold Ashanti, part of the mining giant AngloAmerican, developed links with mercenaries and warlords in order to gain access to gold-rich mining areas in eastern Congo.[28] These accusations have had little impact on AngloAmerican's chairman, Sir Mark Moody-Stuart, who played a leading role in UK Prime Minister Tony Blair's Commission for Africa.[29]

Britain also has big business links to Angola. The south-west African country produces almost 1.5 million barrels of oil a day (b/d), a figure that is expected to rise to 2 million b/d by 2008. BP, one of the UK's largest companies, and among the world's biggest oil and petrochemical groups, has substantial interests in Angola's expanding oil industry.[30] By its own admission, the company says: 'Angola is an important new profit centre for BP's exploration and production portfolio.'[31] Although this quotation is relatively recent, BP's involvement in Angola began almost four decades before the civil war ended in 2002. The company says it plans to have invested up to US$8 billion in Angola by 2010. Other British businesses operating in Angola include British Airways, De La Rue, Compass Group, KPMG, British American Tobacco and Crown Agents,[32] as well as smaller firms such as Hull Blyth[33] shipping agents, the oil and gas servicing company Terra Energy Services,[34] and diamond mining group Petra Diamonds.[35] According to the aid group Oxfam, British arms brokers were actively selling arms to Angola during the war.[36]

The US buys about 15 per cent of its oil from West African countries, a figure set to rise to 25 per cent by 2015. Currently, about 8 per cent of US oil imports come from Angola. The Cabinda Gulf Oil Company (Cabgoc), then a subsidiary of the US-based Gulf Oil, began oil explorations in Cabinda in 1954 and was pumping by 1969. Even when Angola gained independence in 1975, and the socialist-style *Movimento Popular de Libertação de Angola* (MPLA) took power, Cabgoc carried on operating. Production was not even affected by the US government's support for the UNITA rebels: Cuban troops actually protected the US company's Cabinda operations from potential rebel attacks, one of the lesser known ironies of the Cold War. Today, Cabgoc (now a subsidiary of ChevronTexaco) is still in Cabinda where offshore oil installations pump out half a million barrels of oil each day.

The fact that Cabinda alone – a small enclave of Angola – is of clear economic significance to the West has made very little difference to the mainstream media's interest in the place. In August 2006, a peace memorandum was signed between the Angolan government and Cabindan rebels, effectively ending three decades of conflict. The deal was struck just months before an Australian company was due to begin onshore oil drilling on the enclave.[37] This is big business, very big business, and yet it passed virtually unnoticed. If the Angolan war between UNITA and the MPLA was a forgotten war,[38] the Cabindan conflict was never even known, regardless of the titles of some academic papers on the subject.[39]

The impact of Africa's wars on Britain

The role of British (and Western) businesses in Africa is not the only reason we deserve to be kept informed. The conflicts on the continent also affect the British public at home. Refugees escaping war come to live in the UK. At the time of writing, the UK's Communities and Local Government Secretary, Ruth Kelly, has caused some controversy with her speech encouraging a national debate about multi-culturalism, immigration and asylum.[40] Kelly believes that in Britain, 'global tensions are being reflected on the streets of local communities' and that 'Muslims feel the reverberations from the Middle East'. She notes that some white British people are nervous about the presence of different ethnic groups coming from areas as diverse as Somalia, Afghanistan, Zimbabwe and South Africa. No doubt, this is true. And no doubt, their fears are fuelled – or, certainly not quelled – by the media's (re)presentations of these countries as dangerous, anarchical places. Certainly, there are elements of the British media that offer a full diet of Somali madness, a country shown to be dangerous and where beheadings are not uncommon. Meanwhile, there are thousands of Somalis living in the UK and each year, more try to enter the country.[41]

If there are Britons who are nervous about different ethnic groups, then surely the media have a duty to educate and inform them about the world in which we all live. I wonder how many members of the public are aware, for example, of the role the West has played in conflicts in the Horn of Africa, provoking many Somalis to flee their own country. In June 2006, the Somali capital, Mogadishu, came under the control of one central authority, the Islamic Courts Union (ICU), for the first time in 15 years.[42] The US Central Intelligence Agency (CIA) was no doubt appalled: they had been backing an opposing group of secular warlords known as the Alliance for the Restoration of Peace and Counter-Terrorism (ARPCT).[43] The US government's support for this group breaks international law: there is a UN arms embargo on Somalia.

For its part, Washington is nervous about the Horn of Africa, fearing that Somalia could be a home for international terrorists. The US has long suspected that Al Qaeda elements are operating out of Mogadishu, ever since the US embassy bombings in Kenya and Tanzania in 1998. It was because of these attacks that US President Bill Clinton ordered cruise missile strikes on Afghanistan, and also Sudan, where a pharmaceutical factory (not a chemical weapons plant, as alleged by Washington at the time) was destroyed. Four years later, an Israeli airliner and a hotel in Mombasa, Kenya, were attacked. In December 2002, the US established an anti-terrorism task force in Djibouti, including 1,600 American troops. More recently, in January 2007, the US carried out air strikes in southern Somalia reportedly targeting suspected Al Qaeda elements; this followed the US-backed Ethiopian invasion to overthrow the ICU in December 2006. Despite the clear relationship between the West and the Horn of Africa, Somalia receives little detailed coverage in the mainstream news other than the odd brief flurry of clichéd reporting when something big 'kicks off'. It would be helpful if the politics of the region were reported more frequently and more accurately within the British media, given the growing Somali population in the UK.

Conclusion: investing in war (and peace) reporting

Wars do not erupt out of thin air – they have roots, causes, histories and catalysts. In this chapter I have attempted to show why Africa's wars should be given more serious and considered coverage by the mainstream British media. The accepted hierarchy for news stories – which so often leaves Africa out, apart from the odd exaggerated burst of interest – is flawed. I believe this is partly due to a stereotypical view of the continent as a place where life is 'nasty, brutish and short', and partly due to ignorance. Greater investment in and use of specialist reporters living and working in currently ignored countries (as opposed to 'name journalists' who pop in) would help cultivate a more sophisticated understanding of the African continent. We also need to hear from local journalists, such as the BBC's Sudanese reporter Alfred Taban mentioned earlier, whose expert knowledge will help to challenge the narrow British perspective.

The focus should not only be on war, however. If we are to understand the continent and the conflicts that take place there, we need to start investing in the reporting of peacetime. This is not to suggest that journalists should refrain from writing about the horror of war when it is taking place – I am firmly against any attempts to sanitize or censor the truth of war – but it is a plea to end the portrayal of Africans as either crazed warmongers or helpless victims. The quest for variety and detail about how people live their lives from day to day – which could include small business ventures, acute political stories, local attempts to fight multinational and government corruption, as well as culture, to name a few – would reveal a plethora of material able to keep any single journalist in one country very busy. It would also pave the way for a more sophisticated understanding of the continent.

Notes

[1] For example, Prendergast, John, *Angola's Deadly War: Dealing With Savimbi's Hell on Earth* (Washington: United States Institute of Peace, 1999)

[2] For the purposes of this article, UK broadcast programmes include: for radio, Today, the World at One (WATO), PM, the World Tonight and Five Live; for television, BBC News at 1 pm and 6 pm. local time ('the One' and 'the Six'), the Ten O'Clock News ('the Ten') and the running news channel, News 24

[3] Cabinda, a province of Angola, is also an enclave sandwiched between the two Congos. A low-level conflict – distinct from the nation-wide war between UNITA and the MPLA – continued until 2003 to 2004 when the Angolan army conducted extensive military operations in the area. A peace deal was signed in August 2006. However, military activity and violence has continued. For further information, see Porto, João Gomes, *Cabinda: Notes on a Soon-to-be-Forgotten War* (Institute of Security Studies, Occasional Paper 77, August 2003). Available online at: http://www.iss.co.za/pubs/papers/77/Paper77.html accessed on 15 August 2006. For more recent information, see Cabinda Dreaming: The fight for Cabindan independence is being put to bed by the Luanda regime, *Africa Confidential*, 25 August 2006, Vol. 47, No. 17

[4] Antony Goldman. Email to author, 23 August 2006

[5] The number of deaths in the Bosnia war has caused much controversy. Initial estimates put the total number of dead at more than a quarter of a million people. However, that figure dropped by over a half when new research emerged from the Research and Documentation Centre in Sarajevo in 2005. See for example, Sarajevo Researcher Says 99,000 Killed in Bosnian War, by Croatian news agency HINA (17 December 2005). Available online at: http://www.csees.net/?page=news&news_id=48664&country_id=2, accessed on 25 August 2006

[6] Human Rights Watch Arms Project and Human Rights Watch/Africa, *Angola: Arms Trade and Violations of the Laws of War Since the 1992 Elections* (New York: Human Rights Watch, 1994)

[7] Martin Bell is a former BBC correspondent and a former British Member of Parliament.

[8] Child Alert: Democratic Republic of Congo, Martin Bell Reports on Children Caught in War (July 2006). Available online at: http://www.unicef.org/childalert/drc/content/Child_Alert_DRC_en.pdf, accessed on 14 October 2006

[9] The IRC is a humanitarian organization with headquarters in New York. *The Congo Crisis at a Glance: The Forgotten Emergency* is available online at: http://www.theirc.org/what/page.jsp?itemID=27814363, accessed on 14 October 2006

[10] In his absence, Andrew Meldrum in Pretoria, South Africa, and Jeevan Vasagar in Nairobi, Kenya, 'covered Africa'. Email from Rory Carroll to the author, 22 August 2006

[11] How I never quite fell for South Africa, *Guardian Unlimited*. Available online at http://www.guardian.co.uk/southafrica/story/0,,1844847,00.html, accessed on 15 August 2006

[12] For further details on Andersson's career, and in particular trips to the Middle East while working as the Africa correspondent, see: http://www.bbc.co.uk/pressoffice/biographies/biogs/news/hilaryandersson.shtml, accessed on 15 August 2006

[13] Mark Tully, the former BBC correspondent to India, is the most famous example of a journalist whose specialist knowledge was seen as almost an embarrassment by the corporation and eventually was squeezed out for younger, more television-minded staff

[14] A prime example is John Lloyd's Cry, the benighted continent: The west – ideally the UN – must intervene in Africa, even if it smacks of neo-imperialism, *FT magazine*, 5/6 August 2006 p. 10

[15] Lévy, Bernard-Henri, *War, Evil and the End of History*, London, Gerald Duckworth and Co. Ltd, 2004 p. 4

[16] ibid

[17] ibid p. 3

[18] ibid p. 10

[19] ibid p. 16

[20] ibid p. 13

[21] ibid p. 18

[22] ibid p. 25

[23] Dark heart of the American Dream, *Observer*, 16 June 2002, Vulliamy, Ed. Available online at http://observer.guardian.co.uk/magazine/story/0,,738196,00.html, accessed on 1 September 2006

[24] The value of UK investments in Iraq has not been made public. However, estimates vary between about £400 million and £1billion. See Corporate Watch. Available online at http://www.corporatewatch.org.uk/?lid=2646 accessed on 26 August 2006. Patrick Cockburn, who writes about Iraq for the *Independent*, told the author that it is currently almost impossible to know the value of British investment in Iraq. However, he did state that the majority of British interests were tied up in legal and less legal security companies. 12 December 2006 talk, Meltdown in Iraq: is it time for an exit? at the Institute of Contemporary Arts, London

[25] For example, http://news.bbc.co.uk/1/hi/world/africa/1468772.stm, accessed 25 August 2006

[26] For more information on the role that foreign companies have played in the DRC, see the Final Report of the Panel of Experts on the Illegal Exploitation of Natural Resources and Other Forms of Wealth of the Democratic Republic of Congo (October 2002). Available online at: http://www.globalpolicy.org/security/issues/congo/2002/1015letter.pdf, accessed 25 August 2006. Other useful sources of information include the international lobbying organizations Human Rights Watch and Global Witness

[27] Van Woudenberg, Anneke. Britain Must Confront Shameful Trade that Ruins Congolese Lives, the *Independent*, 31 October 2003. Available online at: http://hrw.org/english/docs/2003/10/31/uk12948.htm, accessed 25 August 2006. Mea culpa: How will the Blair Commission change British policy?, *Africa Confidential*, London: 18 March 2005, Vol. 46, No. 6

[28] *The Curse of Gold*, New York: June 2005. Available online at: http://hrw.org/reports/2005/drc0505/, accessed on 26 August 2006

[29] See Moral Choice, *Africa Confidential*, Vol. 46, No. 6, 18 March 2005
It is also worth noting that in April 2006, AngloAmerican reduced its shares in AngloGold Ashanti Limited to 41.8 per cent.

[30] For further details on BP's operations in Angola, see:
http://www.bp.com/sectiongenericarticle.do?categoryId=427&contentId=2000571, accessed on 26 August 2006

[31] BP in Angola. Available online at:
http://www.bp.com/sectiongenericarticle.do?categoryId=427&contentId=2000571, accessed 25 August 2006

[32] See the UK foreign office country profiles. Available online at:

http://www.fco.gov.uk/servlet/Front%3Fpagename%3DOpenMarket/Xcelerate/ShowPage&c%3DPage&cid%3D1007029394365&a%3DKCountryProfile&aid%3D101950110924, accessed 30 December 2006

[33] Available online at www.hull-blyth.com/angola, accessed 8 January 2007

[34] Available online at http://www.tesltd.com/index.htm, accessed 9 January 2007

[35] Available online at http://petradiamonds.com/content/, accessed 9 January 2007

[36] The Spoils of Peace: How can tighter arms export controls benefit both the poor and British industry, Oxfam 2002. Available online at:
http://www.oxfam.org.uk/what_we_do/issues/conflict_disasters/bp13_peace.htm, accessed 8 January 2007

[37] See Cabinda Dreaming: The fight for Cabindan independence is being put to bed by the Luanda regime, *Africa Confidential*, 25 August 2006 Vol. 47, No. 17

[38] Matloff, Judith, *Fragments of a Forgotten War*, Penguin 1997

[39] For example Porto, João Gomes, Cabinda: Notes on a Soon-to-be-Forgotten War op cit

[40] Community and local government secretary Ruth Kelly's speech on integration and cohesion, Guardian Online, 24 August 2006. Available at:
http://www.guardian.co.uk/race/story/0,,1857367,00.html, accessed on 28 August 2006

[41] For example, *The Somali Community in the UK: What we know and how we know it*, by the Information Centre about Asylum and Refugees in the UK, London: July 2004

[42] Islamist takeover, *Africa Confidential*, Vol. 47, No. 13, 23 June 2006

[43] ibid

Chapter Four

Unreported Mass Killings of Civilians

Jeremy Tunstall

For at least 200 years, journalism has given special attention to multiple violent deaths. Wars and civil wars, earthquakes and other disasters, and serial murder cases are still regarded as exceptionally high in news value, in ability to sell newspapers, and in capacity to grip radio and television audiences. But many mass killings of civilian victims have been largely ignored by the news media of their day. Here I briefly discuss eight episodes which received little, if any, immediate news attention, but which together involved the deaths of between 55 million and 80 million civilians.

One common circumstance is that the mass killings occur in remote and far away places where no Anglo-American correspondents or even local journalists are stationed. Often there is a deliberate cover-up by a government that wishes to keep secret the horrible deeds committed by its soldiers, prison guards or death squads. Strict censorship may prevent journalists from visiting the relevant location and may also make sending the story impossible; when large numbers of people are being killed, inquisitive strangers may be in deadly danger. Even if we exclude wartime military deaths and casualties, many of these events happen in the shadow of war – civilians are deliberately bombed or executed, or civilians may fail to survive the chaos of military defeat (Tunstall 2007: 57-69).

Another news reporting difficulty is that often the worst of the mass killing event happens in the first days or weeks. In its all-out attack, an army may kill every enemy soldier and civilian in sight; in an 'anti-guerrilla' campaign numerous villages may be attacked at dawn on the same day. Even if journalists are able to get to the scene of the massacre, genocide, or ethnic cleansing, it may be difficult to decide how many killings occurred. After mass killings, bodies may be burned, buried or eaten by animals; dead bodies are often thrown into rivers and washed downstream to resting points far from the original place of death.

Only three or four of these eight cases fall within the United Nations Genocide Convention's definition. The convention refers to acts committed with intent 'to destroy in whole or in part, a national, ethnical, racial or religious group' (Charney 1999; Gellately and Kiernan 2003; Power 2002). The following list contains examples which could be classified as genocides, massacres, mass killings, or perhaps ethnic cleansing. One particular mass killing may include elements of several of the above categories. Some mass killing episodes may begin with deliberate genocide or mass killing of certain sub-groups (such as men) while other sub-groups (such as women) may be punished by rape, beatings, starvation and expulsion from their homes.

Another relevant problem – which may be significant both for contemporary and for retrospective reporting – is the difficulty of establishing the 'who', 'when' and 'where' of a mass killing. The precise date and location are often problematic. Nor is the identity of the mass killers always self-evident; the army may claim that two factions, or ethnic groups, attacked each other in tribal warfare. Here are eight very varied examples of mass killings, each of which was either unreported, or very inadequately reported, at the time.

Eight examples of mass killings

The Congo, around 1900

Several million people died in the Belgian Congo from sleeping sickness but also from executions and a particularly brutal form of forced labour, amounting to semi-slavery. The Belgian colony had no civil administration but was administered by commercial interests being effectively the personal possession of King Leopold, who was a public relations pioneer. Leopold perfected the practice of (very carefully) guided tours for selected journalists (Ascherson 1999).

In Stalin's Soviet Union

Stalin's purges and the German invasion killed millions of civilians. Around 1932, an estimated 6 million people were starved to death, or executed, mostly in Ukraine, the North Caucasus and Kazakhstan. In Stalin's great terror (1937-38) some 650,000 (including many senior communists) were killed. During 1941-45 some 16 million civilian Soviet citizens were killed or starved to death in the fighting between the Soviet Union and Germany. Especially during Stalin's remaining years (1945-53), more millions died in the Gulag of labour camps.

A few of these cases were deliberately publicized in 'show trials' – especially of Stalin's political enemies and rivals during 1937-38. But the vast majority received no coverage in the fiercely censored Soviet media; during 1930-53 very few foreign reporters were based in the Soviet Union and they were largely confined to Moscow. Soviet public relations officers were adept at selecting sympathetic foreign journalists and intellectuals, who – after a brief visit – typically wrote positive stories about Stalin and the Soviet Union (Muggeridge 1940: 202-211; McCollam 2003: 43-48).

The Holocaust

About 6 million Jews – and 5 million Poles, Roma, Communists and other 'undesirables'– were killed in the Holocaust. Although the concentration camps began in 1933, the majority of killings occurred in 1942 and 1943; all of the extermination camps (as opposed to labour camps) were in Poland and 3 million died in Auschwitz-Birkenau (Gallately 2001). Roosevelt, Churchill and Stalin knew long before 1945 that what the Germans (and allies) were doing to the Jews (and others) went far beyond a somewhat larger version of the old pogrom.

In December 1942, the US and UK governments and nine others issued a statement confirming the existence of a German campaign to exterminate all Jews. What was happening to Europe's Jews in 1939-45 was not ignored by the US and UK media, but it was played down. Laurel Leff, in *Buried By The Times*, explores in detail how and why *The New York Times* deliberately played down the Jewish extermination story. The family publisher, Arthur Hays Sulzberger, preferred to see the Nazis' mass killings as targeted at several groups, including the Jews. Sulzberger, nevertheless, made special personal efforts to help his own Jewish relatives in Europe. Cyrus Sulzberger, the publisher's nephew, was a talented and flamboyant *Times* correspondent in Europe, but he was not especially interested in Jewish issues.

During the European war *The New York Times* carried 1,186 stories which dealt in whole or in part with Jews in Europe; but most of these were short pieces 'buried' deep inside the paper. Only 26 such stories reached the front page in 1939-45. Although *The Times* had a well-resourced Berlin bureau during 1939-41, no single journalist in New York (or in London) was subsequently designated as a specialist on Hitler and the Jews. The Jewish extermination story was often covered by *The Times* with AP and UP stories – an indication of lower importance on an elite newspaper.

The New York Times was also relatively reluctant to use stories from the Polish government in exile (in London); *The Times* did not subscribe to the specialist Jewish Telegraphic Agency (to which the *New York Post* and *Herald Tribune* subscribed). On 22 April 1943 listeners in Stockholm and London heard a radio transmission from inside the Warsaw ghetto, which said that 35,000 Jews were about to be killed by the German army. Although the Warsaw ghetto uprising had all the classic ingredients of a huge, and tragic, news story (Gilbert 1986: 557-567), *The New York Times* gave it the usual low key, brief, and undramatic coverage (Leff 2003: 330-358).

The British and American targeted bombing of civilians in Germany and Japan

This took place especially during 1942-45 and probably killed between 3 and 4 million civilians. The two atomic bomb raids on Japan in August 1945 killed about 200,000 people (with more dying later). The news media certainly reported hundreds of air raids each involving several hundred aircraft dropping thousands of tons of bombs. The aircrew members themselves were well aware that increasingly the prime objective was to burn down entire cities (Hastings 2004: 343-388; Knell 2003; Buruma 2004: 8-12), while the precise and accurate destruction of a major war factory was relatively rare. Any British or American journalist who looked around London could see that bombing was a somewhat inexact science. There was some criticism of 'Bomber Harris' who was Britain's bombing supremo; most of this criticism, however, occurred after the war was over. The city-bombing policy had been co-ordinated and agreed by Britain, the United States and Canada in late 1941. In retrospect American and British journalists could claim that several war-time conditions – censorship and self-censorship, patriotic support for our brave bomber crews, shortage of paper for lengthy background stories – would have made it difficult to get anti-bombing stories published.

Mao's Great Leap Forward campaign, China (1958-60)

Probably between 15 and 30 million people died of starvation and related illness during this 'campaign'. Although this was not a deliberately planned disaster, it does seem to qualify as a mass killing because Mao persisted with the policy well after its consequences were fully apparent. There was no coverage at all in the Chinese media, and almost none in any foreign media.

Guatemala during 1970s and 1980s

In Guatemala, some 200,000 civilians were killed by the army in several phases between the late 1970s and late 1980s. The great majority were Maya (the traditional inhabitants), so this qualifies as genocide targeted at a specific ethnic group. Many of the killings occurred in remote villages in mountainous areas, some of which were near the Mexican border; and many Mayans crossed the international border to evade the army. There was very little accurate coverage of these events in Guatemalan media; coverage did occur in foreign publications but it tended to focus on specific individual cases, such as a murdered nun who happened to be a US citizen (Grandin 2000; 2004).

Rwandan genocide 1994

A significant part of the entire population of this small African country were murdered, mainly with clubs and machetes, over a few weeks in 1994. Estimates of the total deaths vary between 400,000 and almost one million (Pottier 2002).

Congo massacres 2000

In 2000, the Congo experienced violence which probably produced more than 3 million deaths. This conflict had elements of an invasion (supported by other African governments) leading to civil war; much of the conflict seems to have involved local armed bands fighting each other to control local territories. This was a classic example of a conflict too obscure, too complex and too dangerous to allow reliable reporting. Much of the reporting was done from, and related to, the extreme west and extreme east of the Congo, with little about the 900,000 square miles in between (Lemarchand 2003: 26-29)

Later reporting of mass killings

Although these – and other – mass killings have been under-reported at the time, there are several cases of mass killings receiving more attention some years, or even decades, later. The Holocaust – after being heavily reported in 1945 in all the media (including cinema newsreels) – for some years attracted relatively little media attention. It was not until 1961 (and the televised trial of Adolf Eichmann in Jerusalem) that the 'Holocaust' became the accepted phrase and the media (and scholarly) coverage greatly increased (Novick 1999; Shandler 1999).

In other cases a major change of political regime led to a process of literarily digging up the bodies contained in secret burial grounds. This kind of development is described by Victoria Sanford (2003), writing about the 'buried secrets' of Guatemala. Sanford and her colleagues have used the new science of forensic archaeology to dig up these 'clandestine cemeteries', resulting from some 600 massacres conducted by the army in rural Guatemala. This process of digging up the dead reveals a complex pattern; the army killed some villagers (suspected of being guerrilla fighters) and also ethnically cleansed (or destroyed) the village – thus forcing villagers to depart higher up into the mountains or across the border into Mexico. Some of these villagers were then killed as they fled.

Further revelations may surface several decades after the violent events. In some cases old soldiers publish their memoirs and confess the torture and killings of their youth. Some trials are held of prominent people. Other prominent people establish some kind of 'truth and reconciliation' procedure. In Spain the bodies of political opponents killed by General Franco in the late 1930s were being dug up by villagers in the early 2000s. For example, clandestine cemeteries were being dug up, in 2002-3, near Segovia, about 50 miles north of Madrid. In three villages some 240 Republican sympathizers were killed (and buried) in December 1936, by Franco's soldiers, assisted by Franco-supporting villagers. The location of the unmarked graves was well known to the victims' relatives (Tremlett 2003; Feros 2004).

DNA and forensic archaeology techniques will continue to look back at past horrors; and we will have further opportunities to consider mass killings, which make the news today, but were not reported when they happened some decades ago.

References

Ascherson, Neal (199) *The King Incorporated: Leopold the Second and the Congo*, London: Granta Books

Buruma, Ian (2004) The Destruction of Germany, *New York Review of Books*, 21 October

Charny, Israel W. (ed.) (1999) *Encyclopedia of Genocide*, 2 volume, Santa Barbara, California: ABC-Clio

Feros, Antonio (2004) Civil War still haunts Spanish politics, *New York Times*, 20 March p. A15 p. 17

Gellately, Robert (2001) *Backing Hitler: Consent and Coercion in Nazi Germany*, Oxford: Oxford University Press

Gellately, Robert and Kiernan, Ben (eds) (2003) *The Spectre of Genocide: Mass murder in historical perspective*, Cambridge: Cambridge University Press

Grandin, Greg (2000) *The Blood of Guatemala: A history of race and nation*, Durham, North Carolina: Duke University Press

— (2004) *The Last Colonial Massacre: Latin America in the Cold War*, Chicago: University of Chicago Press

Hastings, Max (2004) *Armageddon: The Battle for Germany, 1944-45*, London: Macmillan

Knell, Hermann (2003) *To Destroy A City: Strategic bombing and its consequences in World War II*, Cambridge, Massachusetts: De Capo/Perseus

McCollam, Douglas (2003) Should this Pulitzer be pulled? Seventy years after a Government-engineered famine killed millions in Ukraine, a New York Times correspondent who failed to sound the alarm is under attack, *Columbia Journalism Review*, November/December

Muggeridge, Malcolm (1940/1989) *The Thirties: 1930-1940 in Great Britain*, London: Weidenfeld and Nicolson
Novick, Peter (1999) *The Holocaust in American Life*, New York: Houghton Mifflin
Palmowski, Jan (1997) *Dictionary of Twentieth Century History*, Oxford: Oxford University Press
Power, Samantha (2002) *'Problem From Hell': America and the Age of Genocide*, New York: Basic Books
Sanford, Victoria (2003) *Buried Secrets: Truth and Human Rights in Guatemala*, New York: Palgrave Macmillan
Shandler, Jeffrey (1999) *While America Watches: Televising the Holocaust*, New York: Oxford University Press
Tremlett, Giles (2003) Spanish civil war comes back to life. Old divisions resurface across the country as descendants dig up mass graves, the *Guardian*, 8 March
Tunstall, Jeremy (2007) *The Media Were American: US Mass Media in Decline*, New York and Oxford: Oxford University Press

PART II:

COMMUNICATING WAR THROUGH MEDIA INSTITUTIONS AND PRACTICES

CHAPTER FIVE

INFORMATION WAR: ENCOUNTERING A CHAOTIC INFORMATION ENVIRONMENT[1]

HOWARD TUMBER AND FRANK WEBSTER

> Today we're engaged in the first war in history – unconventional and irregular as it may be – in an era of: emails, blogs, cell phones, blackberrys, instant messaging, digital cameras, a global Internet with no inhibitions, hand-held video cameras, talk radio, 24-hour news broadcasts, satellite television. There's never been a war fought in this environment before.
>
> Donald Rumsfeld, US Secretary of Defense: Speech to Council on Foreign Relations, 17 February 2006

A turbulent world

The last two decades amount to the most sustained period of transformation in recorded history. Western capitalism's triumph over communism has unleashed market forces around the world, extensively and intensively spreading private enterprise, the profit motive, and the principle that market arrangements will determine who gets what, what gets made available and on what terms. Capitalism is inherently transformative: it never stands still, the search for value and return on investment encouraging continuous innovation and abandonment of arrangements that fail to deliver an adequate return.

In addition, the remarkable development of computer and communications technologies – and technology *tout court* – has facilitated the development of globalization on capitalist terms as well as contributing directly to the pace of change itself. We may now conceive, for the first time in human history, of a world society in which global action can take place in real time irrespective of distance, organized systemically on market principles (Castells 1996-8). The global search for most lucrative return, the capability of organization across thousands of miles, the movement of enormous sums at the touch of keyboards: these are all indicative of the scale of change as well as of its driving force.

One casualty of these trends has been the nation state, a body that provided much of the ordering of affairs in the past. It has not disappeared; nor will it do so in the foreseeable future. But the state has undoubtedly diminished in its capacity to organize economic, social and even political affairs as territory has declined in significance.

Consequences of this are evident just about everywhere, but amongst the most noticeable is that we now live with the expectation of uncertainty in each of our lives.

Many of us in the West have choices – in behavior, morality, relationships, movement – beyond the comprehension of our forebears. Despite this, perhaps even because of it, we are stricken by consciousness of the frailty and tenuousness of all that we do. Security of work cannot be assured because of the uncertainties of markets and the movement of locations of production. Coal mining was once amongst the most common occupations in Britain; in less than a generation it has become as scarce as weaving.

We no longer expect to live as our forebears did. There is no mould into which people may fit. In many respects this is liberating, leaving people free to choose how they may live and capable of resisting submission to fate. However, this uncertainty is also disconcerting: how can people be confident of paying the rent if the job may suddenly disappear? How do people choose when there are so many options as regards lifestyle, morality or even religious affiliation on offer (Bauman 1997)?

Fundamentalism on the rise

The turbulence that accompanies accelerating change affects all of us, but its effects are highly variable. In a world of over six billion people, many of those positioned in the metropolitan centers and equipped with capital and advanced level education are likely to find the upheavals exhilarating. Those on the periphery, lacking skills or resources, may have reason to resent the blandishments of consumer goods that they cannot afford, still more if they are accompanied by assaults on familiar mores and religious practices. It is here that fundamentalism, an assertion of certainty in an uncertain world, may thrive. This is not exclusive to the poorer parts of the world, but it is where conditions are especially propitious for its spread among the disadvantaged and disconcerted. Fundamentalism may be found everywhere, for example in Born Again Christian organizations inside the United States where literal interpretations of the Bible provide rules for living, or in Deep Ecology movements in Western Europe where subordination to Nature is the imperative of life. But it is also evident in peripheral regions where it can provide comfort for the insecure and destabilized.

Many fundamentalist organizations bring an ascetic withdrawal from the world so that undiminished attention can be devoted to a pure doctrine. They present little or no threat to social order and will make some pragmatic arrangement with the worldly life. However, in some forms, fundamentalism can lead to militant resistance, even military action in the name of absolute beliefs. One expression of this comes in the form of ethnic nationalism, the assertion of 'my country right or wrong', with evocations of long-held myths ('our people have always been here, living like this'). Ethnic nationalism has long played a part in the establishment of nations (Mann 2005). When leaders appeal to an organic vision of a nation as 'one folk', as they continue to do today in parts of the world, it may be accompanied with ethnic cleansing whereby minorities are stigmatized, forced into exile and frequently killed. The former Yugoslavia saw this expressed ferociously with a loss of more than 250,000 lives during the 1990s.

Fundamentalism is always territorially situated, and often makes claims for a place for its own folk. However, in recent decades fundamentalism with universal aspirations has emerged. It is a version that refuses the Western secularized ways of life, railing against the 'Great Satan' of America especially, and insisting on the rectitude of its version of the Koran. Terrorists of the loose-knit and for some inspirational network of

Al Qaeda – which does *not* reject Western technologies such as the satellite phone and semtex, though it uncompromisingly opposes secular capitalism – are the leading edge of such 'enemies without states' (Giddens 1994). It would be a mistake to imagine these are entirely placeless fundamentalists. Hence counter-measures need to take into account the origins of these people and their grievances. But there is no gainsaying that, with such 'enemies without states', there is little to negotiate since their hostility is implacable and murderous in intent.

Concern about war

Symptomatic of anxiety about the state of the world is the heightened concern about the likelihood and extent of war. The largest ever mobilizations against war took place across Europe on the eve of the American and British invasion of Iraq in 2003 when more than one million took to the streets of London, and even larger numbers demonstrated in Rome, Madrid and Paris. Opinion polls suggest that large numbers of Western populations are fearful about the likely outbreak of armed conflict and voice the opinion that the world is becoming a more dangerous place. This may not be surprising given continuing wars in Iraq and Afghanistan, not to mention such terrorist attacks of 9/11 in New York, March 2004 in Madrid, and July 2005 in London. In truth, war and casualties of war have been in steady decline for decades. The end of the Soviet system was one very important factor, removing the threat of nuclear annihilation from a battle between the superpowers, but also taking away the nasty proxy wars that were found in locations such as Korea, El Salvador, Guatemala and Vietnam.

Integrally related, globalization has contributed to the reduction of inter-state wars, which accounted for death and destruction of a vastly greater scale than anything seen in recent times. John Mueller (2005) aptly describes what we have today as the 'remnants of war', leftover and dirty conflicts conducted by terrorists of one sort or another, local fiefdoms and ethnic groups. *The Human Security Report* of 2005, produced at the University of British Columbia with support from ministries in Canada, Switzerland, Sweden and the United Kingdom, is authoritative. It charts a 40 per cent decline in the number of armed conflicts since the early 1990s (p. 3), noting that 'most wars are fought in poor countries with armies that lack heavy conventional weapons' (p. 5). The report records that 'international terrorism is the only form of political violence that appears to be getting worse' (p. 2). This is reason for public concern, but it also needs to be put in perspective. However lamentable the innocent deaths that come from terrorist attacks, they are minor compared to the great inter-state wars of the recent past. Indeed, the chances of being killed in a road accident are more likely for a British citizen than from a terrorist attack and the odds of premature death from poor nutrition much more of a worry to a population that faces an epidemic of obesity.

Nonetheless, there appears to be an increased public perception of the threat of war. It is difficult to avoid the conclusion that this owes much to the increased awareness of wars (mainly through heightened media attention) around the world, particularly those involving Western forces, as well as to the dramatic and disconcerting character of terrorist attacks that come without warning and aim at maximizing civilian casualties.

Information War

It is in this context of turbulence that one may situate the spread of Information War. This is war capable of pursuance only by affluent and defense-oriented nations and especially by the United States or the NATO alliance that it dominates. It is war that does not require the mobilization of the wider population to fight. Since a professionalized military is equipped with virtuoso weaponry, especially missiles and aircraft, that provides vastly disproportionate advantage, there is little need for the wider populace to be engaged in the war effort. Information War is most unlikely to be conducted between nations that each possesses its resources due to the widespread acceptance of the global market system and the diminishing of the former territorial concerns that previously motivated war. Instead, Information War is conducted, for the most part, in areas where there is marked turmoil and in cases where ethnic cleansing results in large-scale murder, as in Kosovo in 1999. It has also been practiced in the Persian Gulf, where the United States has pursued a 'rogue nation' that it fears will combine with terrorist groups against its interest. Enormous asymmetry ensures that possessors of Information War weaponry will quickly vanquish an enemy so long as it can be identified and that post-war conditions do not demand lengthy occupation by forces vulnerable to guerrilla attack. Though Information War is monopolized by a limited number of countries, 'weapons of the weak' (Mann 2003) such as explosives and the Kalashnikov rifle have proliferated, not least courtesy of the collapse of the former USSR and the marketization of arms dealing (Castells 1998: ch.3), factors that have 'transformed the prospect of violence *anywhere* on the globe' (Hobsbawm 1994: 560).

Irrespective of the wisdom of the US invasion of Iraq in the name of its declared 'war on terror', it is clear that a key feature of Information War is the mobilization of the public as spectators rather than active participants. We emphasize the formidable task this is today (even inside that exceptional nation, the United States). Nowadays when – and even before – Information War breaks out there is an astonishing amount of coverage ensuring that the public is saturated in information about the conduct of assaults, the casualty rates, and various factions involved. So sustained and wide-ranging is this information flow that Oliver Poole (2003), an embedded journalist in Iraq, is correct to insist that people in Europe and even in the United States 'had a far better idea of what was going on in Iraq [in 2003] than the average soldier who was actually there' (ibid: 116). This massive amount of reportage and comment provides audiences with an intense means of engagement with war, yet it is engagement at a distance and it is an engagement experienced with much argument and disputation. Despite this, however, the public is vital to the military endeavor, not least because at some point or other appeals to the legitimacy of the war in terms of 'our way of life' are always made.

Globalization of consciousness

Information war needs to be located in what one might term a growing *globalization of consciousness*. It is much harder nowadays to be unaware of the abject circumstances of the world's poor because of social movements, adeptly using advanced technologies and communications skills, working to ensure that we are made aware of conditions however far removed from them in terms of physical distance and standards of living. The globalization of consciousness more generally signals at once the spread of technologies such as satellites and television that distribute round-the-clock news, entertainment, music and sports programming, but also the messages that migrants carry with them as they travel, as well as the symbolic import of clothes and cuisines.

The globalization of consciousness means that, however uneven and complex is the process, increasingly we have a world in which people have knowledge of others – of their lives, conditions and beliefs. This by no means leads to a uniformity of outlook, but it does mean that, more and more, round the world there are shared reference points, common issues of discussion and awareness of the meanings of symbols.

A growing awareness of human rights and democracy is intimately connected to this globalization of consciousness. This awareness has received impetus from the collapse of communism, as it does from the radical legacies of the anti-Stalinist Left, and from the progress made by democracies around the world in recent decades. It sometimes leads to calls for military action to restrain anti-human rights actions and undemocratic regimes. News media are key participants in this heightening of consciousness, as Seib concluded: 'The strongest and richest nations do not have the moral right to avert their gaze from injustices they could halt or at least limit', so much so that 'the journalist's most important role... [is] to be the witness who arouses conscience' (Seib 2002: 121).

Frontline correspondents

Frontline journalists are essential contributors to public understanding of the war (Tumber and Webster 2006). Though there are important differences between these correspondents, in more than fifty lengthy interviews we found them to be thoughtful, well educated and conscientious about their work and their role. They operate in conditions of danger and discomfort, where threats to their safety are commonplace and ugly experiences are routine. They risk being shot at and bombed, even of being kidnapped and held for ransom and possibly worse. They have to function in inhospitable locations where something as mundane as pot-holed roads and incompetent driving can present significant risks.

The dangers encountered by foreign correspondents are nothing like so grave as those of local journalists (Pedelty 1995), but they are considerable and suggest a degree of passion that motivates the frontline correspondent. John Carlin told us[2] that, early in his career during the 1980s, when he was reporting for *The Times* from Central America, the 'rules of the game' were that combatants 'did not kill journalists, especially [those] from prestigious newspapers'. In other locations conditions became much less hospitable for the foreign correspondent. Iraq by 2004 had become such a deadly location for reporters that Tim Lambon, of Channel 4 News, commented: 'The hostile environments courses prior to the [Iraq 2003] war were teaching if you get abducted, just act the grey man, don't resist, do whatever they tell you, follow through with it, negotiations will take place, you'll be released. Now they're saying if somebody tries to abduct you, you take whatever chance you can to get away.'

Frontline correspondents operate under dangerous and stressful conditions. Increasingly they are trained for this by organizations staffed with ex-services people who have knowledge of field conditions, first aid and hostile environments. Advisors with military experience that helps ensure the journalists' safety may even accompany them into the field. Journalists have developed ways of coping with the pressures ranging from compulsively writing ('therapy on the go', in the words of John Carlin), to talking incessantly with intimate friends, to treating themselves with good food and wine when back home. It was noticeable how few felt able to take advantage of the professional counseling services made available by their employers.

It is striking, too, that just about all these journalists refused the title 'war correspondent', finding it limiting, somehow presumptuous, and often an uncomfortable reminder of a macho type that is seen as no longer relevant to serious coverage of conflict. As Luke Harding, of the *Guardian*, put it: 'Ernest Hemingway is long gone,' or as Colin Baker, of ITN, explained: 'I'm just a correspondent who's been to war, [who does] not like being called a war correspondent.' Most of the journalists we interviewed shared this sentiment.

Journalists and technological change

These journalists inhabit the same globalizing and fast-changing world we outlined above. Working for well-resourced organizations, they benefit from technological innovations, notably the satellite video phone and laptop computer that enables them to send pictures and text from the remotest areas with ease and immediacy. These technologies have a downside in making the journalists always connected to their organizational headquarters and, therefore, liable to be bombarded with requests from the centre for 24/7 continuous reportage that prevents them getting out of the hotel and into investigative mode. As Ben Brown, of the BBC, commented, this rolling news 'is a complete monster, which requires endless feeding'. The permanent connection of field reporters to the news headquarters is leading, as Julian Manyon of ITN warned, to the situation where 'increasingly news is driven from the centre'.

In addition, the Internet provides correspondents with the rapid capability to research background materials as well see what rival journalists are reporting. It also enables the subjects of the reports to read what was said about them with disconcerting immediacy.

Information War correspondents operate in a milieu of vague borders and lines of combat, when they may be reporting from inside 'enemy' lines (as, for example, Baghdad) and where contesting sides are unclear. They spend relatively short periods of time inside the war zones, where they rely on local fixers to get access to informants and supplies, as well as to interpret and provide background information. These, the 'unsung heroes', as Sky News's Peter Sharp described them to us, are 'the people we always leave behind'. The days in which the war correspondent accompanied the nation's forces, dressed in the uniform of their side, are diminishing in conditions of Information War.

Many of the seven hundred or so embeds during the 2003 Iraq War donned military attire – not an issued uniform, rather dress and equipment they purchased beforehand on the advice of the army and sometimes customized in the field – though how much this was for their own protection when risks from 'friendly fire' were real and how much as sign of endorsement of the invasion is unclear. Today's correspondent is less persuaded by appeals to 'my country right or wrong', and – if so disposed – there are likely to be many other correspondents in the combat zones from a variety of nationalities, so any unthinking reflection is likely to be contested. To be sure, the military go to considerable lengths to constrain and channel what the reporters see and produce.

Embedding and the military

Embedding journalists alongside the US and British forces in Iraq in 2003 is the latest attempt by military forces to gain greater control over what is reported. This time round it seemed that embeds, once given over to a military unit, were able to do their job largely unencumbered. Oliver Poole (2003), embedded with the US 3rd Infantry Division, echoed several of our interviewees when he observed 'amazement at the amount of freedom I was given to wander around and ask whatever questions I liked to whoever I chose. There was no minder and no censor' (ibid: 12-13). Audrey Gillan, of the *Guardian*, confirmed this from her own experiences as an embed: 'I wasn't a propaganda tool in any way; they didn't tell me to write stuff and they didn't tell me any lies.' What we learned from our interviews with frontline correspondents is that there is considerable self-awareness about the limitations of the embedded journalists. Some frankly refused to countenance what they regarded as an inherently limiting role, but others made a judgment that set against *de facto* censorship the access that being an embed allowed.

Frontline correspondents contribute a vital role in conditions of Information War. The military forces endeavor to enlist them in the war effort, to limit them to filing stories of derring-do and of brave men and women doing a tough but worthwhile job away from home. Some embeds are prepared to play this part. However, for the most part the reporters have more laudable goals, not least to 'tell it like it is', to get the story and tell it straight. As Orla Guerin, of the BBC, said, resonating many of our respondents: 'You want to feel that you're getting at the truth'. Kim Willsher, of the *Mail on Sunday*, added: 'You want to bear witness to what has happened; you want people to know what is happening in those places.' Barbara Jones put it similarly: 'We're gathering information, not for the military or for the government, but for the truth.' This is an admirable, though not a novel, aspiration for frontline correspondents; for instance, Peter Arnett recalled that throughout a forty-year career that began in Vietnam 'I believed that ... truth was the greatest goal I could aspire to' (1994: 321). It is a quality that finds support amongst journalists in a theory of democracy, that the public have a right to know what is being done in their name. It is also, as we have observed, something which military forces also find hard to ignore, since it risks media coverage that queries the legitimacy of the military action itself.

Aspirations to report truthfully are couched in the language of objectivity. We – and the correspondents themselves – know that objectivity is a weasel word (Knightley 2000). Legendary correspondent James Cameron, for instance, around 30 years ago asserted that 'objectivity was of less importance then the truth' (1978: 72), a distinction that would cause considerable consternation among many reporters. In the abstract, 'telling the truth' may mean reporting in a disinterested, detached and comprehensive manner, but in the practice of journalism it is more a matter of striving to get things right by reliance on sources that can be cited and evidence that can be confirmed by an accredited authority. In this sense it becomes a 'strategic ritual' (Tuchman 1978) that is manifested in practices and procedures, the journalist reporting that 'x says this' and 'y says that'. Inside a military unit as an embed it is hard to imagine how the inescapable reliance on the limited sources available could even approximate to objectivity.

The limitations of embedding

Nonetheless, frontline correspondents are well aware of the limitations both of being an embed and of an excessive focus on the drama of war in action. As Dan Edge, a field producer, told us: 'All an embed can cover is the mechanics and modalities of how a modern war is fought…but that's a miniscule percentage of what war reporting needs to be about.' Edge is by no means alone in his assessment. Pictures taken from atop a fast-moving military vehicle, with terse voice-over from a reporter, all recorded in real time, are likely to be deemed newsworthy. David Zucchino, of the *LA Times*, who joined with US marines in Abrams tanks as they sped into the centre of Baghdad, was candid about the limits of this reportage:

> What we didn't have access to is the decision-making at the Pentagon and at the National Security Council and at the White House…and that's really, the most important story – how decisions are made and what the rationale is… And part of the problem is the secrecy of the administration and the sort of duplicitous nature of a lot of… what they were doing, a lot of the claims they were making.

The embed for *The Times*, Chris Ayres (2005: 258), more bluntly, concluded that, though he was about as close to a frontline as could be imagined today, 'my battlefield perspective…was about as useful as Baghdad Bob's.[3] My mum knew more about the war than I did'. Another journalist 'constantly had to resist the temptation to generalize about what was going on across Iraq as a whole from the evidence available from my own isolated viewpoint' (Poole 2003: 259). Others recognized that the limitations of being embedded with troops, and even being a unilateral, restricted them to a particular time and place. This meant they relied on the central news organization collating different reports and putting together the jigsaw to produce a complete picture. This led James Meek, of the *Guardian*, to complain that 'I felt I missed the war because I hadn't seen it on TV' (quoted in Greenslade 2003: 6). Indispensable though frontline correspondents are to public knowledge of war, their perspective, no matter how assiduously it cites available sources, is not in itself the whole truth.

A focus solely on action can, indeed, be a distortion. There are the added difficulties that in circumstances in which combatants are all conscious that the mediation of the conflict can be of major significance, all sources are unreliable. As Dan Edge put it, 'there are fewer and fewer corners of the world where one's sources and interviewees are not hypersensitive of the power or lack of power of the media. And that informs everything they say'. The journalist's job is made that much more difficult when he or she is reliant for information on those who have an agenda. Sources endeavor to persuade the journalist that their perspective is the correct one, conscious that media play a key role in contemporary conflict. At other times sources by-pass journalists, going directly to news media especially to propagate their view. Nothing more vividly illustrates this than the production of hostage videos through 2004 in Iraq that were put out on sympathetic web sites.

Frontline 'definers of reality'

It is the frontline correspondents who act as the major definers of reality as regards war for the huge audiences back home who receive their reports through television, radio and the newspapers. These correspondents co-operate and compete with their peers in unscripted but calibrated relationships, manifesting camaraderie while striving to get out their own reports ahead of those of the others. As Orla Guerin of the BBC put it, 'though competition exists…you watch out for people in other organizations (because) you do not want to see any journalist hurt'.

Despite the frontline correspondents' words being the usual starting point for news, the copy they file is by no means untouched before receipt by viewers, listeners and readers. Editors in news organizations can play a crucial role in framing and contextualizing what the frontline correspondent sends through. In both activities the views of other participants (for example, government officials, party spokespeople, military experts, political commentators), as well as other sources of information (such as other reports from the theatre of operation, statements from combatants) are important elements of any product that goes out on air or appears in the press. This manufactured process involving many more hands than those solely of the frontline reporter is familiar to media analysts.

Bloggers as witnesses

A developing phenomenon, likely to be of increased significance in future, is the emergence of bloggers, those who put accounts, evidence and/or comment directly on the Internet, bypassing established media (though some of the most assiduous bloggers are journalists themselves). One may distinguish at least three ways in which bloggers contribute to the mediation of war. First, *bloggers as witnesses* who report from particular locations, the most renowned of whom in 2003 was architect Salam Pax, the Baghdad Blogger, who kept an online diary (http://dear_raed.blogspot.com/ and http://justzipit.blogspot.com/) to tell of his experiences inside the city as it was bombarded. Such blogs, as with emails direct from scenes of conflict, can become newsworthy and even news making.

There are other blogs as witnesses, for instance milblogs (military weblogs) where participants circulate stories of their experiences in the field. Direct emails back and forth to friends and family can also, if more widely circulated, become significant contributors to news. Such sources of information can play an important role on occasions, notably at times and at locations of conflict when regular journalists are not present. Here lightweight video equipment, digital cameras and even mobile phone photography can make a contribution, as was evident in the hundreds of digital images taken by soldiers and guards at Abu Ghraib prison, Baghdad, that were leaked to the media in May 2004 and have subsequently caused incalculable damage to the American effort to persuade opinion that they invaded to liberate Iraq (Hersh 2005).

Bloggers as commentators

Second, *bloggers as commentators* who have grown rapidly as Internet connectivity reaches larger majorities of the population. These appear to be read more avidly by journalists than by the rest of society, and by virtue of this they may increase their importance in the news making process. This category is itself wide, ranging from commentators promoting items overlooked by mainstream media to those bloggers who can make news by correcting reported versions of events. A renowned example of the latter was the way in which bloggers, after discrediting his evidence, forced CBS anchor Dan Rather to apologize in 2004 for a report on George W. Bush's service in the Texas Air National Guard.

Bloggers as amplifiers and inflectors of news

The third category is *bloggers as amplifiers and inflectors* of news, notably by extending discussion and debate in the blogosphere. Both this and the second categories appear to have played a role in the 2004 American election in the denigration of Senator John Kerry over military medals awarded for his part in the Vietnam War, and in the rise and fall of Howard Dean as Democrat contender. Though extravagant claims have been made for these developments one does not need to embrace notions of 'citizen reporters' or the 'end of journalism' to agree that they contribute appreciably to an already complicated information environment.

There is another factor that further complicates the information environment of conflict in ways that are surely set to grow (McNair 2006). On the one hand, as we have demonstrated, established media and news reportage is subject to change making television, radio and the press more diverse and complex for audiences. On the other hand, as the blogging phenomenon suggests, there have emerged – often adeptly using new media – alternative contributors to the scene. A very active anti-war and peace movement, for example, takes up mainstream media stories, orients them in ways that suit its own perspectives, and even offers its own information networks. Stop the War Coalition (StWC), which was established late in 2001 to oppose the invasion of Afghanistan, was at the heart of the mobilization for the 15 February 2003 demonstration in London against the impending Iraq War. StWC has a website (www.stopwar.org.uk), updated as a matter of routine, usually on a daily basis, to highlight stories amassed from diverse sources (minority magazines, newspapers, campaigning groups and all electronic media), notably from the United States and Europe.

The website offers particular emphases and oppositional interpretations of what is taking place in and beyond war zones. Thus it might highlight atrocities committed by occupying troops, the testimony of dissident and discontented soldiers, or the appeals of grieving parents whose sons have been lost in service of the military. It will present photographs in combination with text that challenge and on occasions amplify accounts found in more mainstream outlets.

Moreover, StWC may even by-pass established media with its amalgamated and inflected information. For example, in 2006 it was circulating a regular electronic newsletter to more than 20,000 subscribers highlighting news and events of import to the anti-war movement. In this way, with great speed, cost effectiveness and efficiency,

StWC contributes to what is now a remarkably rich and differentiated information environment about war.

Conclusion: the emergence of the transnational public sphere

Information War, for those people inhabiting advanced parts of the globe, is chiefly about mediated experiences. *Shock and Awe* was the name given to the US-led campaign during the invasion of Iraq in 2003. For the invading forces this attack was assisted by massive technological advantage over the enemy, while for those on the receiving end it brought death and rapid defeat. But Information War also involves communication. When conflict breaks out, even before it starts, there is an enormous upsurge of information from, about and beyond the war zone. Frontline correspondents play a central, but not solo, role in the presentation of what is often spectacle – vivid pictures of explosions, aerial images, cities lit up at night by tracer fire – to audiences around the world whose actual experience of war is far removed from combat. Audiences are presented, through virtuoso technologies, with astonishing pictures and sounds from the theatre of war.

Propaganda and persuasion are very much in evidence at every stage of this process. The winning of hearts and minds is of vital importance to the fighters of Information War. However, whatever the level of planning that goes into these efforts to massage public opinion, the ambiguities and complexities surrounding the informational dimensions of conflict nowadays make endeavors to control it always tenuous. If it were not so, how might one begin to account for the effects of the images that appeared of Abu Ghraib prison in Baghdad in the spring of 2004, images that have undermined the case for the overthrow of Saddam Hussein, and have sullied the name of the United States?

The 'fog of war', the unpredictability of events and an associated lack of clarity as regards information, is always present in conditions of armed conflict. The confusion of battle makes it hard to ascertain precisely what is occurring. However, it is the wider information environment pertaining today that is more responsible than the battle for the chaos. First of all, frontline journalists are not easily controlled nor manipulated to act as conduits for combatants and their leaders. They have a strong disposition towards 'telling it like it is', they cling to notions of 'objectivity', they have access to versatile equipment that allows them to report quickly and immediately back to their news organizations, the boundaries between fighting forces are often confused, and, perhaps more important, journalists are such a diverse group that once-powerful appeals to support 'our boys' have weakened. Furthermore, while embeds are severely constrained by virtue of their locations, news organizations now receive an enormous volume and variety of information. What gets into a finished programme or news report may be quite at odds with any single journalist's report.

What is also emerging, assisted by the growth of new media though by no means restricted to technological developments, is what Craig Calhoun (2004) has described as a transnational public sphere. This is not an equal playing field for contesting forces. However, it is one that is considerably more diverse than that available during the era of Industrial War, when national media systems projected images and carried reports in support of the nation's fighting forces. It is an information domain where Al Jazeera (Miles 2004) *and* CNN *and* the BBC co-exist, where claims and counter-claims may be encountered from a variety of disputing quarters, where images are posted that may be profoundly anti-pathetic to all sides in the confrontation. It is a domain where the digital camera and the Internet web site can play a key role in defining reality. It is one where even the weaker forces – who are acutely conscious that the media are globalized phenomena – can stage dramatic events through careful use of video cameras and the Internet. Such ambiguity and complexity come with the territory of Information War. The virtuoso weapons of war ensure massive asymmetry between combatants, but the media features are also crucial in the waging and long-term success of Information War. And these are much harder to predict or contain.

Notes

[1] This chapter draws on our book, *Journalists under Fire: Information War and Journalistic Practices* London: Sage, 2006. Funding for the research in this book came from the Economic and Social Research Council's (ESRC) New Security Challenges Programme (RES -223-25-0033)

[2] All the quotes from journalists in this chapter are taken from *Journalists under Fire* (Tumber and Webster 2006)

[3] Baghdad Bob, also known as Comical Ali (Muhammad Said Al-Sahhaf), was the Iraqi Information Minister for Saddam Hussein during the 2003 US invasion of Iraq, disparagingly named because of the divorce from known reality of his assertions

References

Arnett, Peter (1994) *Live from the Battlefield*, London: Corgi
Ayres, Chris (2005) *War Reporting for Cowards: Between Iraq and a Hard Place*, London: Murray
Bauman, Zygmunt (1997) *Postmodernity and Its Discontents*, Cambridge: Polity
Calhoun, Craig (2004) Information Technology and the International Public Sphere, in Schuler, Douglas and Day, Peter (eds) *Shaping the Network Society*, Cambridge, MA: MIT Press pp 229-52
Cameron, James (1978) *Point of Departure*, London: Panther
Castells, Manuel (1996-98) *The Information Age,* Three Volumes, Oxford: Blackwell
Giddens, Anthony (1994) *Beyond Left and Right*, Cambridge: Polity
Greenslade, Roy (2003) Fighting Talk, *Guardian,* 30 June. Available online at http://media.guardian.co.uk/mediaguardian/story/0,7558,987506,00.html, accessed on 28 November 2006
Hersh, Seymour M. (2005) *Chain of Command*, London: Penguin
Hobsbawm, E.J. (1994) *Age of Extremes*, London: Michael Joseph
Knightley, Phillip (2003) *The First Casualty*, London: Prion Books
McNair, Brian (2006) *Cultural Chaos*, London: Routledge
Mann, Michael (2003) *Incoherent Empire*, London: Verso
— (2005) *The Dark Side of Democracy*, Cambridge: Cambridge University Press
Mueller, John (20040 *The Remnants of War*, Ithaca: Cornell University Press

Pedelty, Mark (1995) *War Stories: The Culture of Foreign Correspondents*, New York: Routledge
Pickerill, Jenny and Webster, Frank (2006) The Anti-War and Peace Movement in Britain and the Conditions of Information War, *International Relations*, Vol. 20, No. 4 pp 407-423
Poole, Oliver (2003) *Black Knights: On the Bloody Road to Baghdad*, London: HarperCollins
Seib, Phillip (2002) *The Global Journalist: News and Conscience in a World of Conflict*, New York: Rowman and Littlefield
The Human Security Report (2005) University of British Columbia: Human Security Centre. Available online at http://www.humansecurityreport.info/, accessed on 28 November 2006
Tuchman, Gaye (1972) Objectivity as Strategic Ritual: An Examination of Newsmen's Notions of Objectivity, *American Journal of Sociology*, Vol. 77 No. 4 pp 660-679
Tumber, Howard and Webster, Frank (2006) *Journalists under Fire: Information War and Journalistic Practices*, London: Sage
Zucchino, David (2005) *Thunder Run: The Armored Strike to Capture Baghdad*, New York: Grove Press

CHAPTER SIX

TRUTH IN A WAR ZONE:
THE ROLE OF WARBLOGS IN IRAQ

DONALD MATHESON AND STUART ALLAN

During the 2003 US-led invasion of Iraq, familiar modes of war reporting were actively re-inflected, sometimes in surprising ways. While much debate ensued over the relative merits of 'unilateral' or 'embedded' news coverage, other developments enabled by the proliferation of new media technologies – from digital cameras and computer notebooks to satellite telephones – received far less attention. Among these new approaches to reporting war was the 'warblog', a mode we argue deserves particular scrutiny.

This chapter proposes to examine the emergent forms and practices of blogging as an augmentation of – and at times challenge to – war reporting. As will soon become apparent, however, we have not attempted the difficult task of comprehensively surveying the multiplicity of warblogs concerned with the invasion and its aftermath. Rather, we have chosen to investigate a small number, grouping them into three broad categories: warblogs associated with major news organizations; warblogs produced by freelance or 'sojo' reporters, as well as 'personal' or 'amateur' journalists; and warblogs posted by Iraqi citizens. In the course of our analysis, we draw upon insights provided by bloggers themselves, both from interviews conducted by ourselves as well as from other sources.[1] We suggest that these writers valued the use of blogging as journalism – characterized as it is by informality, subjectivity and eyewitness experience – for the ways in which it cuts across the fundamentals of ostensibly impartial news reporting. In this chapter's evaluation of warblogging's relative strengths and limitations, then, care will be taken to discern the extent to which it represents a challenge to certain longstanding tenets of war reporting.

Blogs as news sources

The advent of weblogging is currently the subject of intense debate within certain journalistic circles. Many of its advocates place blogging in the vanguard of new forms of citizen journalism enabled by digital technologies, which it is hoped will reconnect the profession with its diverse publics. Others speak of blogging and related phenomena as 'we media' (Bowman and Willis 2003), in which professional journalists are becoming marginalized in the course of a digital revolution reminiscent of the arrival of the printing press in the fifteenth century. Its detractors beg to differ, of course, with some even disputing the claim that such forms of discourse have anything more than a tangential relation to journalism. Blogging, they argue, is more akin to a form of subjective commentary, one where short, sharp bursts of opinionated argument about mainstream news items or events typically take the place of dispassionate, balanced and – crucially – investigative news reporting. Evidence to support these and related positions is readily available, needless to say, depending on where one looks in the virtual universe of the 'blogosphere'.

Weblogs, or blogs for short, may be aptly described as diaries or journals written by individuals with net access who are in possession of the necessary software publishing tools (e.g. those provided by sites such as Blogger.com) to establish an online presence. Emerging in the mid-1990s, they are currently believed to be flourishing in the millions across the webscape. Many news bloggers – a small minority compared to the number of ordinary netizens involved overall – consider themselves to be 'personal' journalists, intent on transgressing the border between 'professional' and 'amateur' reporting. While it is difficult to generalize, most seem motivated to share their analysis, comments or background knowledge about news events which matter to them so as to counterbalance mainstream news media coverage (Matheson 2004). Some post little more than *ad hoc* musings, offering a passing insight in the form of an occasional sentence or two, sometimes with accompanying excerpts and/or hyperlinks to pertinent news or information sites elsewhere. Typically, the more influential blogs, though, are those associated with a particular issue or concern, and are thereby committed to providing a fresh, 'unfiltered' perspective which sets them apart from other, rival blogs.

News-oriented blogs vary in form and practice, but many are informed by a shared ethos, namely that newsgathering and commentary need to be democratized. By acting as 'unofficial' news sources on the web, these blogs link together information and opinion which supplements – or, in the eyes of some advocates, supplants – the coverage provided by 'official' news outlets. Here it needs to be noted, however, that very few blogs actually provide new information. Instead, most bloggers pull together their resources from a diverse array of other sites, thereby situating a given news event within a larger context, and illuminating multiple dimensions of its elements. The apparent facts or claims being collected are usually time-stamped and placed in reverse-chronological order as the blog is updated, thereby making it easier for readers to follow its ongoing narrative.

Customarily the sources of the blogger's information are acknowledged explicitly, with the accompanying hyperlink enabling the user to negotiate a network of cross-references from one blog to the next, or to other types of sites altogether. In principle, the facts or claims presented in any one blog can be subjected to the relentless double-checking of users, some of whom may be even better informed about the events in question than the initial blogger. Any attempt by a blogger to present a partisan assertion as an impartial statement of truth is likely to be promptly recognized as such by other users.

In the months following the September 2001 attacks on the US, blogs became a site of intense debate in that country over the so-called 'war on terror'. A rapidly growing number of blogs – called 'warblogs' – devoted particular attention to the perceived shortcomings of the mainstream news media with regard to their responsibility to inform the public about possible risks, threats and dangers (see also Zelizer and Allan 2002). Warbloggers were divided, as one might expect, between those who favored US and UK military intervention in the Middle East, and those who did not. In both cases, however, an emphasis was placed on documenting sufficient evidence to demonstrate the basis for their dissatisfaction with what they deemed to be the apparent biases of the mainstream news coverage of the ensuing conflict in Afghanistan. For pro-war bloggers, a 'liberal bias' was detectable in much mainstream journalism, leading them to call into question the patriotism of well-known reporters and news organizations. In sharp contrast, bloggers opposed to the war were equally convinced that mainstream journalism, with its over-reliance on official sources, was failing to provide fair and balanced coverage. Many were able to show, with little difficulty, how voices of dissent were being routinely marginalized, when they were even acknowledged at all.

The heated debate over war in these warblogs (Wall 2005) contributed to growing activism among bloggers, both in relation to government policy and the media. Debates over the impacts of some bloggers are charted elsewhere (see, for example, Scott 2004; Haas 2005; Allan 2006) but there can be no doubt of the growing prominence of this mode of public debate. By April 2006, the news agency Reuters was announcing a partnership with an international network of bloggers, GlobalVoices, providing its members with funding and including their commentary on its newswires. At the same time, warblogs can be argued to have articulated and fed a general lessening of journalism's legitimacy and authority as the sole 'arbiter of events in society' (Zelizer 1993: 80).

Such concern could only be heightened by journalism's inevitably controversial position during the Iraq conflict, where any image construed as unpatriotic in the US was heavily criticized and where key parameters such as the claimed presence of 'weapons of mass destruction' in the country or the claimed end of the war in May 2003 proved so difficult to substantiate. As is discussed below, it was for precisely these reasons that some commentators argue that personal, unedited and non-professional blogs 'finally found their moment' as bombs were dropped on the city of Baghdad (Levy 2003). In this moment, we argue, the parameters of journalism were stretched in significant ways. As Reuters (2006) announced, blogs 'help our readers appreciate different perspectives and to engage in a global conversation'.

In order to explore the inter-relation of this phenomenon with the practices of journalism, particularly those of war reporting, we examine three relatively distinct (yet necessarily interrelated) approaches to warblogging below. In essence, their distinctiveness is defined in relation to the institutional basis, or lack thereof, underpinning their status as war reporters. We turn first to warblogs associated with major news organizations, such as the BBC (www.news.bbc.co.uk/), CNN (www.cnn.com), MSNBC (www.msnbc.msn.com/), the Spokane *Spokesman-Review* (www.spokesmanreview.com/) and Guardian Unlimited (www.guardian.co.uk/). Next, attention focuses on warblogs produced by solo or freelance journalists, including Christopher Allbritton's 'Back to Iraq. 2.0' (www.back-to-iraq.com). Lastly, warblogs posted by Iraqi citizens, such as that belonging to 'Salam Pax' are examined, before the chapter ends with several preliminary – and we hope conceptually suggestive – conclusions.

Blogging from a war zone

A glance at some of the blogs kept by Western journalists reporting on the invasion of Iraq for newspapers and broadcasters suggests there was little consensus at the start of the war about the role of blogging. Their warblogs varied widely in style and in the kind of knowledge they produced. Some, such as *Guardian* reporter Audrey Gillan's 'war diary' written while 'embedded' with the British Household Cavalry in early 2003, read like the more personal kind of newspaper column. The blog was, in effect, further space constructed by the news organization for the reporter's experience of war. Others, such as M.L. Lyke's blog for the *Seattle Post Intelligencer*, written during the three weeks she spent onboard the aircraft carrier USS Abraham Lincoln, were first-person accounts giving, at times, more space to her own birthday celebrations than the events of the war. Others, such as the 'Dispatches' of the *Christian Science Monitor*'s online journalist Ben Arnoldy 'embedded' in northern Iraq, shifted between the two styles. Others still, such as the BBC producer Stuart Hughes's blog, were near private sites, designed initially just for family and friends but rapidly gaining readerships of, in his case, the thousands. Tolerated by his employer, it was an experimental moment. Yet clearly, reporters, editors and readers were drawn to the warblog form in some numbers to augment the news.

The evolving status of Hughes's blog is emblematic of the fluid state of the warblog. Hughes, who produced reports for the BBC from northern Iraq during the war's initial months, was surprised that his blog was taken by readers as journalism. He typically posted entries to his blog immediately after filing his news items to the Corporation. He told us:

> I didn't think I was doing anything particularly pioneering. To go one step further and explain how my weblog came to be set up, it was never intended to be anything approaching journalism. I…only set it up for my immediate family and friends because I knew it would be difficult to stay in touch with them when I was Iraq. So I thought I'd post a picture and a few words every now and then and at least they'd know I was OK…And then gradually word started to spread about it and there were a few newspaper articles and it became a warblog, which it was never intended to be. It was like a daily dispatch to family and…[I wrote] literally what came into my head: this is what I've been doing, this is whom I've spoken to. But, interestingly, that tone and that approach and that style were exactly what people latched onto and they seemed to trust what I was telling them. They had no reason to, I mean I could have been making all those quotes up, for all anybody knows (Hughes, interview).

Hughes's blog, titled 'Beyond Northern Iraq' (stuarthughes.blogspot.com), focused on daily minutiae and personal responses to life on the ground, rather than on the major events of the war. Describing his blog as his 'guilty secret', he regarded it as a kind of 'sketchbook' for subjects to investigate. Others observed similarly that the line between the public and the interpersonal blurred on these sites. BBC News Interactive assignment editor Cathy Grieve observed that the Corporation's 'Reporters' Log', the weblog authored by its correspondents in Iraq, was often used by colleagues in the UK to check they were still alive and well (Grieve, interview). Indeed, she also recalled that it was used on one occasion by British officers, who had temporarily lost their charge in the desert.[2] For many news organizations, this blurring was attractive in that it offered to take the reader further than the formal news text into the journalist's experience of the news, giving them 'a dynamic look at the story behind the story of covering the news in Iraq', in the sales pitch of the NBC's 'Blogging Baghdad' (baghdadblog.msnbc.com).

A key feature of the blog which strongly attracted news organizations was the prominence the form gives to the latest information, and the ease with which a page can be updated. The *Spokesman-Review*'s online editor Ken Sands talked of the print newspaper as 'hopelessly behind' his newspaper's weblog (Sands, interview). The newspaper's print version was updated once a day, while its weblog, sitting to the side of newsroom routines, was updated with wire stories, links to newspaper and broadcaster websites around the world and commentary as often as Sands found something worth posting. The flexibility of blog posting, often without the intervention of subeditors, offered a sense of immediacy, taking readers vicariously to the scene of the conflict.

This type of immediacy, as one might expect, posed problems for established news practices. Even when codes separating ostensibly 'objective' reporting from 'subjective' comment were applied to their news blogs, news organizations often found that certain long-standing tensions between reporters and their editors were exacerbated. A decision to post material as soon as it became available, regardless of how 'raw' (un-edited) it might be, frequently sparked disagreements. Bill Mitchell was one of many who argued that the combination in any one journalistic blogger of such diverse skills as reporting, writing, editing and news judgment put at risk the reputation of the news outlet publishing it (Mitchell 2003: 66). To counteract the absence of institutional safety mechanisms, he suggested only experienced journalists should write news blogs.

Such an attitude partly explains the response of CNN's executives to the warblogging of it correspondent Kevin Sites. Published on his own site (www.kevinsites.net), Sites's blog provided his personal commentary about the events he was witnessing from one day to the next, along with various photographs and audio reports that he prepared. Perhaps in light of the media attention Sites's blog received, however, CNN ask him to suspend it on Friday, 21 March 2003. A Network spokesperson stated at the time that covering war was 'a full-time job and we've asked Kevin to concentrate only on that for the time being' (cited in Kurtz 2003). Sites agreed to stop blogging, later explaining that 'CNN was signing my checks at the time and sent me to Iraq. Although I felt the blog was a separate and independent journalistic enterprise, they did not' (www.kevinsites.net). Reactions from other bloggers were swift. CNN's response, according to Steven Levy (2003) of *Newsweek*, 'was seen in the blogosphere as one more sign that the media dinosaurs are determined to stamp out this subversive new form of reporting'.

In contrast, MSNBC supported its correspondents' blogging and maintained three warblogs focused on war coverage at the height of the conflict. 'Weblogs are journalism,' argued Joan Connell, one of the site's executive producers. 'They can be used to great effect in reporting an unfolding story and keeping readers informed' (cited in Mernit 2003). Nevertheless, while she does not share CNN's stance that blogs lack a sufficiently 'structured approach to presenting the news', she does believe that there is a necessary role for an editor in the process. In her words: 'Unlike many weblogs, whose posts go from the mind of the writer straight into the blogosphere, MSNBC's Weblogs are edited. Our editors scrutinize our weblogs for accuracy, fairness and balance, just as they would any news story' (cited in Mernit 2003).

Other news organizations similarly welcomed staff warblogs, and a few took the experiment with blogging a little further. BBC News Interactive assignment editor Cathy Grieve said her colleagues were motivated to produce a joint weblog of BBC foreign correspondents' thoughts because they 'wanted to do something more immediate' than more packaged news (Grieve, interview). Immediacy, in this sense, meant finding ways to engage with audiences in a more direct, less formal manner. The language of warblogs was usually much more colloquial in vocabulary and emotive in judgment. As Grieve stated:

> I just think it had more chatty language and was easier for people to understand and also correspondents were able to say what they really meant because it was a bit more personal and was about their thoughts. They weren't delivering a scripted and proper English Radio 4 piece as opposed to somebody having a chat with you (Grieve, interview).

For these journalists, warblogs were better able to convince audiences of their realness than more packaged reporting. A study by the Project for Excellence in Journalism of US television news reports in the conflict's first week found a similar attempt to use new communications technologies to produce more immediate accounts. The study found 80 percent of television reports included only reporters' voices, and 60 per cent of the reports were live and unedited. To Seib (2004: 55) the reports were like 'the reality itself – confusing, incomplete, sometimes numbing, sometimes intense, and not given to simple story lines'. Thus these warblogs exemplify a more general struggle within journalism to close the gap between the event and the telling of it, seeking to convince the news audience that they could experience the conflict through journalists' accounts. A claim to a particular kind of veracity is therefore also implicit in this quest for immediacy.

Independent voices

For some journalists, this claim to immediacy was interlinked with one to independence. These were the 'sojo' or solo journalists, a small but significant number of correspondents who were not backed by a major news organization, but who were able to write and edit their own copy for both online and print or broadcast media because of mobile technologies. Christopher Allbritton, Kevin Sites – when working freelance for NBC in 2003 and then Yahoo! as one of its news correspondents with a brief to tour the world's war zones within a year – and later in the conflict Steve Vincent (intheredzone.org), were among the more prominent. Equipped with a notebook computer and digital camera, or even a videophone and mini-satellite dish, these journalists had relative freedom of movement and claimed to be able, therefore, to pursue the stories which mattered most to them – and their readers. Herein lay the popularity of the warblogs amongst users, which in the opinion of journalist Bryony Gordon (2003) was hardly surprising: 'If a television reporter's movements aren't subject to Iraqi restrictions, then his [or her] report is likely to be monitored by the Allied Forces. Devoid of such regulations, the Internet is thriving.'

Moreover, for some journalist bloggers sites such as the *Spokesman-Review*'s and the BBC's were not 'real' blogging, precisely because they sought to curtail immediacy with editing. Real blogging, for them, as detailed below, involved the personal voice of the writer outside the confines of the news organization altogether. This sense of the incompatibility of conventional news routines and what blogging could offer can be summarized as a set of structural oppositions, which included tensions such as:

raw	polished
subjective	objective
first-hand	second-hand
unmediated	processed or packaged
independent	dependent
connective	distanced
behind the scenes	the official version
interactive	top-down

Such oppositions could be argued to be at work not only in blogging but also in a wider foreign correspondent tradition. The personal weblogs of a number of journalists in Iraq, therefore, made sense to them partly in terms of longstanding tensions around the role of the independent reporter, as well as a conviction that direct, eye-witness testimony was the most valuable mode of truth-telling. Equally important for warbloggers, however, was the personal control they experienced over their writing (the absence of an external editor being key), and the personal relationship they felt was constructed in the blog with their readers. This allowed them to construct a claim to connect readers to the 'real experience' of Iraq. Such oppositions appeared to inform, in turn, an implicit appeal to a sense of authenticity and trustworthiness in the blog itself.

Freelancer Christopher Allbritton (formerly a reporter with the AP wire service and *New York Daily News*) had announced his intention to be the web's first independent war correspondent in the months leading up to the invasion. His blog called upon readers to contribute to the financial support necessary to fund his travel and expenses in Iraqi Kurdistan. 'It's a marketplace of ideas,' he maintained, 'and those who are awarded credibility by their readers will prosper' (cited in Warner 2003). Support was such that his expenses were met by some 320 donors, allowing him to file daily stories from the country using a borrowed notebook computer and a rented satellite phone. As his blog's daily readership grew to upwards of 25,000, he became accustomed to receiving emails which posed questions and suggested story leads, while others provided useful links to online materials. 'My reporting created a connection between the readers and me,' Allbritton (2003) later observed, 'and they trusted me to bring them an unfettered view of what I was seeing and hearing.' This involvement on the part of his readers in shaping his reporting worked to improve its quality, in his view, each one of them effectively serving as an editor. 'One of the great things about the blogosphere,' he maintained, 'is that there's built-in fact-checking.' Given that so many people will 'swarm' over posts, 'generally the truth of the matter will come out' (cited in Glaser 2003).

By gaining this independence from the institution, however, journalist-webloggers such as Allbritton gave up the privileged access to power and authority which journalists attached to news organizations possess. He also forfeited the benefits associated with the assumed trustworthiness which newspaper mastheads and broadcast credits proclaim. 'This was journalism without a net,' he remarked, 'on the net' (Allbritton 2003: 83). Or rather, Allbritton used the blog to bring together an audience and to establish afresh his role as a journalist in speaking to that audience. Blogger and academic commentator Jay Rosen (2003) described the site as journalism that cut out 'the media', providing direct contact between writer and readers. 'Here you have a journalist collecting his own mini-public, a few thousand people on the web,' he observed, 'who then send him to report on events of interest to the entire world, via a medium that reaches the entire world.'

Of particular value here was what Allbritton called 'the personal connection that can be established through the interactivity of the medium' (Allbritton, 2003: 84). He wrote after he returned from Iraq: 'Throughout it all, I maintained a personal tone in my writing as I tried to let people know what it felt like to be working and surviving during such an extraordinary event' (ibid.). He quoted one of his readers who liked:

> ...the independence it gave you the reporter. No agendas except your own, which is perfectly acceptable to me. No one is totally objective, but you gave more personal perspectives of 'behind the scenes' of what it takes to do what you do, which was terribly fascinating to me (ibid).

Thus a claim to credible reporting emerged, not from the expert authority of the professional news organization, but from the personal attributes and relationship with readers of the reporter. As the quotation above suggests, independence, a consciously subjective telling which makes no claim to objectivity and access for the reader 'behind the scenes' are interdependent aspects of this claim. Allbritton's posts appealed as 'real' accounts precisely because they crossed the line between the public persona of the reporter and the individual filling that role, allowing readers to go more deeply behind-the-scenes to the life of the correspondent than blogs on news organization sites.

A considerable amount of 'sojo' journalism, as one would expect, found its way on to the news sites associated with major news organizations. In the case of the *Spokesman-Review*'s 'War in Iraq' weblog, for example, priority was given to filtering third-party material, some of it provided by 'sojos', but even more provided by 'personal' or 'amateur' journalist bloggers. Its editor, Sands, as noted above, valued the site for its immediacy, but he also argued – as Reuters also did three years later when announcing its partnership with GlobalVoices – that the blog's links to news material from around the world gave it a broader view of events than the news agencies and syndicated news services his print colleagues used. He thus gave users 'really interesting and important stories that simply were not picked up by the usual wire services'. He told us:

> We had amateurs around the world acting as editors, as aggregators actually, scanning the media and providing links to sources as varied as the BBC, *Jerusalem Post*, Al Jazeera, *Washington Post* and *The Spokesman-Review* (Sands, interview).

Sands also encouraged users to send in suggestions, thereby inviting an enhanced sense of interactivity between reporter and reader. It was precisely this interactivity which anchored, in turn, the authority of the warblog (see also Matheson 2005).

Across the blogosphere, a wide array of individuals – some self-described as 'personal' or 'amateur' journalists – did their best to contribute to news, comment or analyses about the invasion. Amongst the most popular, as judged by web user statistics, was the blog of 'L.T. Smash' (www.lt-smash.us), who claimed to be a reserve officer in the US Navy who had been recalled and deployed in the Gulf. His site, with its tagline 'Live from the sandbox', promised 'unfiltered' news – and received some 6,000 'hits' a day at the height of the conflict (doubts were initially raised about its authenticity, given that the pseudonym 'L.T. Smash' is also the name of a character on television's *The*

Simpsons). On one occasion, he even provided a self-interview of sorts, which included this Question and Answer exchange:

> Q. Can't you get in trouble for this sort of thing? Isn't this a violation of Military Regulations?
>
> A: I'm in the military – I can get in trouble for just about anything. But generally speaking, this form of communication is bound by the same rules as e-mail…I am voluntarily observing my own, stricter guidelines in regards to operational security.
>
> (Smash, cited in Kurtz 2003).

A vast number of similar blogs were posted by soldiers witnessing events firsthand, providing observations, impressions and opinions which, taken together, covered every facet of the pro- and anti-war continuum. Moreover, weblogs were posted by members of military families back home, almost always offering support for the troops, but some expressing reservations (at times passionately so) about the legitimacy of the war itself. Blogs also appeared from those on the ground in Iraq, but outside of the military. Wade Hudson, an anti-poverty worker from the US, posted his Baghdad Journal (www.inlet.org/wade/). Jo Wilding, a human rights campaigner living in Baghdad, posted her diaries on the Guardian Unlimited and the Voices in the Wilderness sites (www.vitw.org).

Iraqi bloggers

Iraqi bloggers, however, did more than any other group of citizen bloggers to extend public debate beyond journalism's previous parameters. These blogs provided viewpoints on the war rooted in the subjective experience of those at the receiving end of so-called 'precision bombing,' amongst other types of 'sanitized' wafare. Precisely what counts as truth in a war zone, of course, is very much in the eye of the beholder. Above dispute, in the view of many commentators, was that some of the best eyewitness reporting being conducted was that attributed to the warblog of 'Salam Pax' (a playful pseudonym derived from the Arabic and Latin words for peace), a 29-year-old architect living in middle-class suburban Baghdad. Begun in September 2002, the blog's original motivation was Salam's desire to keep in touch with his friend Raed, who had moved to study in Jordan. It was to his astonishment, then, that he discovered that the international blogging community had attracted such intense attention to his site. As word about 'Where is Raed?' spread via other blogs, email, online discussion groups, and mainstream news media accounts, it began to regularly top the lists of popular blogs as the conflict unfolded.

Enraged by both Saddam Hussein's Ba'athist dictatorship and George W. Bush's motivations for the invasion, Salam documented life on the ground in Baghdad before and after the bombs began to drop. This was 'embedded' reporting of a very different order, effectively demonstrating the potential of blogging as an alternative means of war reporting. His warblog entry for 23 March, 8:30 pm, was typically vivid:

> Today's (and last night's) shock attacks didn't come from airplanes but rather from the airwaves. The images Al Jazeera are broadcasting are beyond any description…This war is starting to show its ugly face to the world…People (and I bet 'allied forces') were

expecting things to be much easier. There are no waving masses of people welcoming the Americans, nor are they surrendering by the thousands. People are doing what all of us are doing – sitting in their homes hoping that a bomb doesn't fall on them and keeping their doors shut
(Salam Pax, dear_raed.blogspot.com)

Salam's posts offered readers a stronger sense of immediacy, an emotional feel for life on the ground, than more traditional news sites. For John Allemang (2003), writing in *The Globe and Mail*, 'what makes his diary so affecting is the way it achieves an easy intimacy that eludes the one-size-fits-all coverage of Baghdad's besieged residents.' As Salam himself would later reflect: 'I was telling everybody who was reading the web log where the bombs fell, what happened […] what the streets looked like.' While acknowledging that the risks involved meant that he considered his actions to be somewhat 'foolish' in retrospect, nevertheless he added: 'It felt for me important. It is just somebody should be telling this because journalists weren't' (cited in Church 2003).

This approach to warblogging, then, possesses the capacity to bring to bear alternative perspectives, contexts and ideological diversity to war reporting, providing users with the means to connect with distant voices otherwise being marginalized, if not silenced altogether, from across the globe. In the words of US journalist Paul Andrews (2003), 'media coverage of the war that most Americans saw was so jingoistic and administration-friendly as to proscribe any sense of impartiality or balance', hence the importance of the insights provided by the likes of Salam Pax. This 'pseudonymous blogger's reports from Iraq', Andrews believed, 'took on more credibility than established media institutions'. This point is echoed by Toby Dodge (2003) who argued that Salam managed to post far more perceptive dispatches than those written by 'the crowds of well-resourced international journalists sitting in the air-conditioned comfort of five star hotels'. Communicating to the world using a personal computer with unreliable internet access, he reported 'the traumas and more importantly the opinions of Iraqis as they faced the uncertainty of violent regime change'.

In the aftermath of the invasion, the number of warblogs appearing in occupied Iraq has multiplied at a remarkable rate. Such blogs provide web users from around the globe with viewpoints about what life is like for ordinary Iraqis, viewpoints otherwise routinely ignored, or trivialized, in their country's mainstream news media. The blog 'Baghdadee' (baghdadee.ipbhost.com/) has as its tagline 'An opportunity to hear from witnesses inside Iraq'. 'A Family in Baghdad' posts the online 'diaries' of mother Faiza and sons Raed, Khaled and Majid. This excerpt, written by Faiza, is indicative of its content:

Wednesday, 21 May 2003

Electricity is on at the hours: 6-8 p.m., 2-4 a.m., the Americans are spreading news about achievements they have accomplished…but on actual grounds we see nothing…we don't know whether they are truthful or not…The schools are open, they are teaching whatever, the importance being for the children to finish their school year. Some schools were destroyed during the war, so they merged the students with others from another school, and made the school day in two shifts, morning and afternoon…(afamilyinbaghdad.blogspot.com)

'Baghdad Burning', under the name 'Riverbend' (a 'Girl Blog from Iraq'), posted this entry on 7 August 2004:

300+ dead in a matter of days in Najaf and Al Sadir City. Of course, they are all being called 'insurgents'. The woman on tv wrapped in the abaya, lying sprawled in the middle of the street must have been one of them too. Several explosions rocked Baghdad today – some government employees were told not to go to work tomorrow.

So is this a part of the reconstruction effort promised to the Shi'a in the south of the country? Najaf is considered the holiest city in Iraq. It is visited by Shi'a from all over the world, and yet, during the last two days, it has seen a rain of bombs and shells from none other than the 'saviours' of the oppressed Shi'a – the Americans. So is this the 'Sunni Triangle' too? It's déjà vu – corpses in the streets, people mourning their dead and dying and buildings up in flames. The images flash by on the television screen and it's Falluja all over again. Twenty years from now who will be blamed for the mass graves being dug today? (riverbendblog.blogspot.com)

Words from blogs such as these ones speak for themselves, their importance for users looking beyond the narrow ideological parameters of much Western news coverage all too apparent. Indeed, Riverbend was nominated for a number of literary awards in 2005 and 2006 after her blog was published in book form.[3] From our position as Western media academics, what strikes us as strongly, however, is the authority sometimes accorded to such voices by major Western media organizations. From Salam's editing of a section of the *Guardian* to the *Daily Telegraph*'s interviewing of a Kuwaiti blogger for first-hand testimony of life on the edge of the war-zone to Reuters' inclusion of blogger commentary in its news services, the space given to the usually silenced voices of civilians is significant. News organizations had no shortage of articulate, English-speaking correspondents only a mouse click away who understood the country they were talking about, and they appeared to be willing to give them the status of authorized sources.

Conclusion

In light of this chapter's discussion, there can be little doubt that no definitive statement can be made about the larger implications blogs pose for journalism, in general, or war reporting, in particular. The blogs under scrutiny here represent a tiny fraction of those posted across the blogosphere, hence the need to avoid extrapolating from them to characterize broader trends or patterns. We would be cautious in describing the phenomenon as either a Napster-like threat to the news industry (Regan 2003: 69) or 'the first real democratization of the web' (*Guardian* 2003). The understanding of the blog as a news source and as a mode of communicating the experience of war explored above suggests to us, however, that the ideas and ideals of war reporting, which are so important to journalism's understanding of itself more widely, do not emerge unscathed from journalism's encounter with the online diary.

The dominant model of the foreign war correspondent, developed during the relatively information-scarce nineteenth-century, relied upon the correspondent having a monopoly of information and the status of an expert by dint of being present on foreign soil and having general journalistic skills. Such a model becomes less tenable when news editors and readers have instant access to multiple voices, both journalist and lay, experiencing the news event in question from an array of perspectives in multiple locations. In particular, the authority of the reporter as a witness to and interpreter of events carries less weight when he or she is only one among many witnesses being heard. Editors and news consumers are often, in fact, in a better position to judge the overall picture than the journalist (Pollard 2001).

The often subjective and impressionistic weblog fits into this context. While bearing in mind the relatively small audiences involved – from a few thousand for the *Spokesman-Review* weblog (Sands, interview) to tens of thousands for the most famous – such sites are likely to have a disproportionate effect upon the editors, producers, columnists and reporters who make up media elites. While a number of webloggers noted that the information about the war which they communicated was not necessarily suppressed or unavailable elsewhere (Hughes, interview; Allbritton, 2003), they emphasized the different nature of the knowledge they communicated. The *Christian Science Monitor* columnist Tom Regan (2003) notes unsympathetically that 'bloggers promise a more immediate experience of the news, one in which accuracy isn't regarded as being the most important element' (2003: 69). As we have seen, the emphasis upon the weblogger's subjectivity rearticulates the foreign correspondent tradition, working to establish a sense of connection and, therefore, an interpersonal trust. The BBC's Stuart Hughes describes his weblog posts as 'unchecked stories' whose accuracy he did not vouch for, but whose truth as his experience he did attest to. He observes: 'What I noticed when I was in Iraq particularly is that that kind of unmediated unfiltered flow of news was something that people really latched onto' (Hughes, interview).

It goes without saying, of course, that few readers of warblogs would have interpreted the reports posted as being unbiased or objective. Instead, the reports, at their best, were socially situated takes from the blogger's perspective, at once provisional, contingent and, at times, deeply emotive. For many users, the honesty of a report that acknowledges its political stance or commitment is to be valued over and above one which makes an appeal to a principle of detachment. Wall (2005) places this inversion of journalism's conventional wisdom within a wider cultural context of 'a growing tendency for audiences to blend with producers' and a rejection of institutional authority. Our discussion above leads us to slightly different conclusions, theorized less in terms of the activeness of the audience than in terms of a weakening of epistemological verities. Accordingly, we are inclined to theorize the rise of the weblog during the war as a partial revaluing of the subject of social knowledge, alongside the ostensibly objective record.

The phenomenon, thus, belongs to a steady trend in Western culture towards a weakening of the boundary between such opposed categories as public and private, shared and personal, real and imaginary, to which the increasing media saturation of culture has contributed. To draw on Manuel Castells' (1996) terms, we live within a culture of 'real virtuality', 'a system in which reality itself (people's material/symbolic experience) is entirely captured, fully immersed in a virtual image setting, in the world of make-believe, in which appearances are not just on the screen through which experience is communicated, but they become the experience' (1996: 373; see also Allan and Matheson 2004). The blog's emphasis upon daily experience fits, therefore, into a cultural mode where the media embrace ever-widening facets of lived experience, and where, as a result, there is a general reorientation of life around media representations of the social.

Indeed, as we have suggested throughout, blogs are not separable from the mediasphere to which they respond. The experiential journalism of Allbritton, for example, becomes a spectacle, an adventure of bribing his way across the Turkish-Iraqi border and hitch-hiking across Iraq with a borrowed laptop, an adventure taken further in Sites's Yahoo!-funded tour around the world's wars in a year. The form, therefore, finds part of its logic in the wider mediasphere. And, although many of the webloggers discussed here resist being turned into spectacles and seek to remain pseudonymous – Salam Pax, for example, for quite practical reasons of personal safety (BBC 2003) – the warblog phenomenon has become a spectacle of radical democratization of the web and of reality evading the propaganda. As Howard Rheingold (2003) notes, the key factor in the impact of new media on journalism and politics is not about the technology but 'a species of literacy – widespread knowledge of how to use these tools to produce news stories that are attention-getting, non-trivial, and credible'. The multiple uses of warblogs during the invasion and occupation of Iraq, we would suggest, provides a case study of such a literacy emerging.

Notes

[1] Four interviews were conducted in September and October, 2003: the US soldier, moja_vera and Ken Sands, online editor of the US *Spokesman-Review*, were interviewed by email; Cathy Grieve, assignments editor at BBC News Interactive, was interviewed by telephone; and Stuart Hughes, BBC news producer, was interviewed in person

[2] Grieve reports that some 70 per cent of the material on the 'Reporters' Log' was gathered when correspondents phoned in to file stories for the news network generally: 'When people were filing we'd have a quick chat and get something more impressionistic, or sometimes use material already filed for other BBC programmes or websites' (Grieve, interview)

[3] *Baghdad Burning* (Riverbend 2005) won third prize in the 2005 Lettre Ulysses literary reportage award, was long-listed for the 2006 Samuel Johnson non-fiction award and shortlisted for the 2006 Index on Censorship award

References

Allan, Stuart (2006) *Online news*, Maidenhead: Open University Press
Allan, Stuart and Matheson, Donald (2004) Online journalism in the information age, *Knowledge, Work and Society,* Vol. 2, No. 3 pp 75-95
Allbritton, Christopher. (2003) Blogging from Iraq, *Nieman Reports, Fall 2003* pp 82-84
Allemang, John (2003) Where everybody is a war reporter, the *Globe and Mail*, 29 March
Andrews, Paul (2003) Is blogging journalism?, *Nieman Reports, Fall 2003* pp 63-64
Bowman, Shayne and Willis, Chris (2003) We media: How audiences are shaping the future of news and information. Available online at:
http://www.hypergene.net/wemedia, accessed 13 October 2004
BBC (2003) Ask the 'Baghdad blogger', Have your say forum, BBCi, 22 September. Available online at:
http://news.bbc.co.uk/1/hi/talking_point/3116344.stm, accessed 20 October 2003
Castells, Manuel (1996) *The rise of the network society*, Oxford: Blackwell

Church, R. (2003) Interview with Salam Pax, CNN International, 3 October Transcript Number: 100302cb.k18.
Dodge, Toby (2003) An Iraqi in cyberspace, *The Times Literary Supplement*, 24 October
Glaser, Mark (2003) Reading between the lines in Iraqi blogs and newspapers, *Online Journalism Review*, 7 November. Available online at: www.ojr.org/ojr/glaser/1068169487.php, accessed 20 October 2003
Gordon, Bryony (2003) The internet Is having a field day: War 'blogs' are everywhere, the *Daily Telegraph*, 2 April. Available online at: http://www.telegraph.co.uk/connected/main.jhtml?xml=%2Fconnected%2F2003%2F04%2F03%2Fecnblog.xml, accessed 9 September 2003
Guardian (2003) If it's ever going to be Greg's year, this is it, GuardianUnlimited, 7 August. Available online at: http://media.guardian.co.uk/top100_2003/story/0,13483,992726,00.html, accessed 2 November 2003
Haas, Tanni (2005) From 'public journalism' to the 'public's journalism'? Rhetoric and reality in the discourse on weblogs, *Journalism Studies*, Vol. 6, No. 3 pp 387-96
Kurtz, Howard (2003) 'Webloggers' signing on as war correspondents, the *Washington Post*, 23 March
Levy, Steven (2003) Blogger's delight, *Newsweek Web Exclusive*, 28 March. Available online at www.msnbc.com, accessed 20 October 2003
Matheson, Donald (2004) Weblogs and the epistemology of the news: Some trends in online journalism, *New Media and Society*, Vol. 6, No. 4 pp 493-518
Matheson, Donald (2005) Negotiating claims to journalism: Webloggers and news genres, *Convergence*, Vol. 10, No. 4 pp 33-54
Mernit, Susan (2003) Kevin Sites and the blogging controversy, *Online Journalism Review*. Available online at: http://www.ojr.org/ojr/workplace/1049381758.php, accessed April 2003
Mitchell, Bill (2003) Weblogs: A road back to basics, *Nieman Reports, Fall 2003* pp 65-8
Pollard, Nick (2001) The challenges of satellite news, Reporters and Reported lecture series, Autumn. Available online at: http://www.cf.ac.uk/jomec/reporters2001/pollard.html, accessed 2 November 2003
Regan, Tom (2003) Weblogs threaten and inform traditional journalism, *Nieman Reports, Fall 2003* pp 68-70
Reuters (2006) Reuters forms alliance with Global Voices Online, Reuters Press Office, 13 April. Available online at: http://about.reuters.com/pressoffice/pressreleases/index.asp?pressid=2671, accessed 26 November 2006
Rheingold, Howard (2003) Moblogs seen as a crystal ball for a new era in online journalism, *Online Journalism Review*, 7 July. Available online at: http://www.ojr.org/ojr/technology/1057780670.php, accessed 11 July 2003
Riverbend (2005) *Baghdad burning: Girl blog from Iraq*, New York: Feminist Press

Rosen, Jay (2003) Terms of authority, *Columbia Journalism Review*. Available online at http://.cjr.org/issues/2003/5/alt-rosen.asp, accessed 6 October 2003

Scott, Esther (2004) 'Big media' meets the 'bloggers': Coverage of Trent Lott's remarks at Strom Thurmond's birthday party, case study, Joan Shorenstein Center on the Press, Politics and Public Policy, John F. Kennedy School of Government, Harvard University. Available online at: http://www.ksg.harvard.edu/presspol/Research_Publications/case_studies.shtml, accessed 15 September 2005

Seib, Philip (2004) Beyond the front lines: How the news media cover a world shaped by war, London: Palgrave

Wall, Melissa (2005) Blogs of war: Weblogs as news, *Journalism*, Vol. 6, No. 2 pp 153-172

Warner, Bernhard (2003) War bloggers Get reality check, MSNBC News, 9 April. Available online at www.msnbc.msn.com/id/3078669, accessed 6 October 2003

Zelizer, Barbie (1993) Journalists as interpretive communities, *Critical Studies in Mass Communication*, Vol. 10, No. 2 pp 219-37

Zelizer, Barbie and Allan, Stuart (eds) (2002) *Journalism after September 11*, London and New York: Routledge

Chapter Seven

Positioning the News Audience as Idiot

Oliver Boyd-Barrett

From mindful to mindless

In the film *Syriana*, a CIA agent sells a Stinger missile to a Middle Eastern terror group. The missile explodes as the terrorists stash it in a car. The same agent is implicated in an assassination plot against the crown prince of an unnamed Middle Eastern emirate. Defining a policy of autonomy and growth for his country, the prince engages anti-American jihadist movements. In regulating access to the kingdom's oil reserves, he favors the Chinese over the Americans. His ailing father, however, elevates his pro-American younger brother as heir. Just when the rejected brother initiates a *coup d'état*, he and his family are executed by a CIA remote-controlled bomb. The plot unfolds in the context of an alliance between the CIA, powerful and corrupt Washington politicians, and big US oil interests, reacting against China's increasing demand for oil. The conspirators seek rights, at any cost, to new sources of oil in the Middle East and Central Asia.

Syriana shares with genres of political, spy and detective thrillers a fascination with the Machiavellian dark side of formal political processes, international relations and criminal investigations, and exploits the audience's strong suspicion that 'real life is like that'. *Syriana* was, indeed, based on a non-fictional work by an ex-CIA agent (Baer 2004), reminiscent of other films inspired by the fictional works of ex-intelligence officers such as John le Carré (e.g. *The Spy Who Came in From the Cold*), Len Deighton (*The Ipcress File*), and Ian Fleming, creator of James Bond (as in *Casino Royale*).

My theme is the contrast between authorial presumptions of audience 'knowingness' in the context of fiction, and the positioning of audiences as 'innocents and idiots' in the day-to-day news coverage of mainstream media. I draw for inspiration from textual theories developed by Stuart Hall (1973) and Laura Mulvey (1975). While recognizing that texts and especially visual texts can be 'polysemic' (open to as many different interpretations as there are readers), as Roland Barthes (1974) argued, Hall and others recognize that texts and their meanings may be 'fixed' or 'inscribed' in ways that limit the likelihood of polysemic readings in favor of prevailing or 'preferred readings' that, within the context of culturally defined 'interpretive communities' (Radway 1984), may be predicted with some confidence.

In the context of mainstream Hollywood, Mulvey considered that texts 'position' audiences such that all audience members, regardless of gender, were encouraged to derive pleasure from the texts by adoption of the preferred 'male gaze'. David Morley (1980) tested Hall's theories to demonstrate that preferred readings are not always shared by audiences but are sometimes subverted, or ignored.

I shall argue that in matters of war and terrorism mainstream news media inscribe their reports in ways that are designed to privilege certain readings over others; they address the audience either as though it had no easy recourse through memory or alternative texts to readings that would subvert these privileged readings or, as though the audience was simply too distracted, careless or stupid to identify and care about gross inconsistencies between texts to which it was routinely exposed. Such positioning might suggest that audiences, regardless of gender, are encouraged to adopt a position – a 'feminine gaze' – that corresponds to the idealized role of the feminine in patriarchal society, whose features include passivity, trust and nurturing support for male authority. In short, the media address the audience as though it was either innocent or stupid. Oppositional readings, surely common, have limited social impact unless they give rise to oppositional textual productions that reach mass audiences.

In this paper I deal principally with US mainstream media coverage of events in which the US is a principal player. This is not because US mainstream media are unique, nor that the US itself is uniquely mendacious. The USA is currently the world's strongest power and the narratives that US media tell about their government's policies and its consequences bestow on these media a special and global significance. Audience positioning as innocents or idiots is an ever-present, though not necessarily all-pervasive feature, of US mainstream media "*as-though*" conflict reporting. It is exhibited for example, when:

- news reports employ the term 'terrorism' *as though* the violent acts that the term denotes could only ever be committed by countries or groups to which the U.S. is opposed, and never by the U.S. itself;
- the presence of U.S. troops in Iraq is framed *as though* motivated by selfless humanitarian intervention; and
- *as though* there was no important connection between war goals and the profits of war for the military-industrial complex;
- 'terrorist' groups are profiled *as though* completely 'other' to the USA and its allies, despite a dark history of covert penetration and redirection of such groups by security forces.

Journalism rules suppress the most important

That the media engage in such behavior reflects their relationship to principal news sources – by far the majority of these 'official' – and therefore, it is naively supposed, authoritative and credible. The 'feminine gaze' is refracted from the source-media to the media-reader relationship. In this relationship, behavior can be interpreted only within the frame of the explanations that dominant players publicly provide. Motives for action other than those that are 'officially' declared cannot be imputed. Hence, journalistic rules of evidence in the Anglo-American news tradition systematically suppress that which is often most important.

Precisely because motives in politics are sometimes unvoiced (and often complex, arising from unrevealed, maybe unspoken pacts between different interests, each party publicly saying one thing and secretly entertaining another), they can be accessed only indirectly through triangulation of evidence over long periods, claims of 'whistleblowers', informed assessment of undeclared 'interests,' and estimations of 'who gains' from different outcomes. Scholars categorize such reasoning as theory development, both deductive theorizing from existing evidence, and inductive theorizing through generation of new evidence. Journalists reject theorizing as a legitimate activity, depriving themselves of intellectual tools that might better direct them to appropriate sources, questions and methods. They too often depend on the superficial and convenient – what people in authority say are the reasons why authority does what it does.

Elsewhere (Boyd-Barrett 2004a) I have argued that it is precisely when the investigative resources of mainstream media are most needed, as at the start of war, that media are most vulnerable to manipulation and intimidation by powerful political and military sources, and most distracted by the operational demands of preparing to cover the *action*. Although such conclusions were buttressed by mainstream media apologies following the US invasion of Iraq in 2003 for their failure to interrogate administration claims that Saddam Hussein had weapons of mass destruction (Boyd-Barrett 2004b), their day-to-day coverage continued to frame the horrific consequences of occupation as merely a sad case of sectarian conflict – nothing to do with culpability for waging war on false pretext, nor with oil, nor with clearly articulated and accessible neo-conservative ambitions to reshape the Middle East.

Should we agree with Curtis (2005) that the principal frame that media apply to conflict is a presumption that Western governments act solely from good intentions, however incompetent and ineffective their actions? Could this be why media consistently privilege 'official' sources, failing not only to get beneath surface 'appearances' but misrepresenting even the appearances (see Boyd-Barrett 2004b; Mueller 2004)? I shall explore the implications with reference to the manufacture of pretexts for war, covert and 'false flag' operations, and the 'war on terror'.

Creating pretexts for war

Controversy over whether or not the immediate pretexts that elites give for war are genuine is the *norm* in international conflict. Not infrequently, an apparent 'victim' has engineered the aggression of another, to justify a war to its own people and evade legal consequences. In the short history of the US, the list of 'bogus pretext' and 'false flag' shenanigans is long, as it is for many powers throughout history. But mainstream media refrain from timely investigation and critique, ignore or marginalize opposing evidence, and, if truth finally emerges, routinely 'forget' to apply the lessons to future entanglements. Despite common knowledge of major controversies over egregious instances of false pretext warfare, mainstream media continued to give their administration all benefit of doubt, both in the lead up to the invasion of Afghanistan in 2001, and to the occupation of Iraq in 2003. That they should have so ignored the lessons of personally-lived history, which for most senior executives in US news media includes the Gulf of Tonkin pretext for US war in Vietnam, smacks of media-administration complicity at the highest levels. Let us recall a few examples of false pretexts:

a) The US went to war with Spain in 1898 alleging that the Spanish sank the *US Maine*. Yet the ship was sunk either by accident or was an American black operation (Gordon 2003); either way, it provided sufficient pretext for what eventuated as US domination of Cuba, colonization of the Philippines, and the Wilsonian project of opening the world to US business.
b) Stinnett (2001) is one of many authors (including Charles Beard's *FDR and the Coming of the War in 1941*, cited in Cockburn 2001; also Toland 1986) to question the official narrative of Pearl Harbor in 1941. In his book, *Day of Deceit*, Stinnett highlights, among other arguments, the role of Roosevelt's chief adviser, Commander Arthur McCollum of Naval Intelligence, who urged on Roosevelt a policy of provocation that included US denial of fuel to the Japanese, and concentration of the Pacific fleet in Pearl Harbor. This was against the advice of fleet commander James Richardson, who was removed after he explicitly warned that concentration would present an irresistible target. The stage was then set for a dramatic pretext to allow Roosevelt to drag a reluctant nation into war, a nation that had been assured there would be no war *unless America was first attacked*. The result of World War Two was US world hegemony. (For a hostile review by a USAF officer of Stinnett's book, see Geer 2006.)
c) The US war in Vietnam was justified by the Gulf of Tonkin incidents, known to be greatly inflated or even bogus by President Johnson within days of their occurrence if not at the time (Beschloss 2001). The *Maddox* was likely inside or had just emerged from South Vietnamese coastal waters, as part of or coincidental with a US strategy of provocation against otherwise clandestine Vietcong forces (Prados 2003). The 'incidents' entailing attacks on the *Maddox* and sister ship by small Vietcong vessels, may never actually have happened – even the ship's commander was confused – and, anyway, had minimal impact (Hanyok n.d.). The US should not have been in Vietnam. Had it supported international agreements for national elections, the country would have unified under the control of a potentially pro-American nationalist, Ho Chi Minh.
d) US pretexts for invading Panama in 1989, killing more than 3,000 Panamanian citizens, included President Noriega's drug dealings, undemocratic leadership, and protection of US lives. Panama had never been meaningfully 'democratic'. The US had previously paid Noriega substantial sums as a CIA asset precisely *because* of his drug connections. Threats to US lives resulted from provocations by US special operations forces. Instead, the US sought to crush the Panamanian military to ensure the country's malleability with the canal due to return to Panama in 2000 (Kasper 1992).

Covert operations and the United States' global reach

The documentation of US covert, special or 'black' operations, involving espionage, military and para-military activity, violent and non-violent persuasion, through government agencies or private contractors, US or foreign security forces, state or oppositional movements, is copious – so well known that related historical and fictional narratives are prevalent in entertainment media, familiar to people from all walks of life who commonly assume such operations occur. Politicians occasionally invoke them when exasperated with democratic or overt processes.

News reporting typically acts *as though* such things were never part of the equation. Opportunities for funding black ops are immense. Secretary of State Donald Rumsfeld admitted in 2002 that an accumulated $2.3 trillion of defense expenditure could not be traced. Leading officials claimed that the 2006 budget for the Office of the Director of National Intelligence alone was $1 billion (Pincus 2006). The total national intelligence community comprises 100,000 persons worldwide (Shrader 2006) and costs $44 billion (Shane 2005). The 2007 defense budget requested by the President was $439 billion, not including expenses for wars in Iran and Afghanistan ($120 billion in 2006; accumulated total to end of 2005 – $320 billion) (Baldor 2006).

In *Killing Hope*, William Blum (2004) provides accounts of fifty or more instances of US covert penetration, destabilization and egregious interference in the affairs of otherwise sovereign nations since World War II, many of them democracies. Spectacular examples include the two following cases:

a) In Italy, Germany, Greece, and other European countries the CIA set up secret armies for counter-insurgency (anti-socialist) operations. These were closely tied to terrorists, as in the case of the Gladio secret army in Italy. The 1980 Bologna railway station bombing was designed to look like a leftist plot and intimidate voters into supporting the Christian Democrats. The kidnapping and murder in 1978 of Aldo Moro (initially attributed to the Red Brigades), leader of the Christian Democrats, appears to have been the work of Gladio *agents provocateurs* (see Blum 2004: 63-4; 106-8). Just before his abduction, Moro announced he would enter into a coalition government with the Italian Communist Party. In 1990, Prime Minister Andreotti announced there were still 600 people on the Gladio payroll in Italy. In Belgium in 1983, to convince the public that a security crisis existed, Gladio operatives, in conjunction with police, staged a series of random shootings in supermarkets. In 1984, a party of US marines parachuted into Belgium with a view to attacking a police station. Guns used in the operation were later planted in a house used by a communist splinter group (for a book length study of Gladio, see Gasner 2005).

b) In Iran, in 1953, the CIA worked with the British to unseat democratically-elected Mohammed Mossadegh – described by Blum as rich, reactionary, feudal-minded (Blum 2004: 64-72) – whose support for or from the communist Tudeh party was unstable. CIA agents penetrated the Tudeh for the purpose of staging demonstrations, presenting the Tudeh and, by implication, Mossadegh, as anti-religion. The mob that supposedly overthrew Mossadegh was significantly paid for by the CIA (Blum 2004: 66, quoting, among other sources, a 1979 book by the CIA instigator, Kermit Roosevelt). Contrary to US propaganda, the Soviet Union tried to restrain, not encourage, the Tudeh. Mossadegh's overthrow brought to power the repressive regime of Mohammad Reza Pahlavi, America's friend. Reaction to his regime fostered fundamentalist Islamic power under the leadership of Ayatollah Khomeini, whose supporters overthrew Pahlavi, the Shah, in 1979.

'False flag' warfare

Operation Northwoods

In a 'false flag' operation a combatant disguises his identity by waving the flag of some country other than his own. The purpose is to hide from view of the target and/or third parties the true identity of the assailant, and may be intended to deceive the target into exacting vengeance against the country whose flag is waved. The 'false flag' principle pertains to tricks that are played among parties to any dispute when tricksters disguise their identities while taking aggressive action against a target individual or organization. An additional twist occurs when assailants stage attacks – while waving the flag of an opponent – against their *own* people or assets, often with a view to initiating hostilities without seeming to be the aggressor, and/or to mobilizing popular support. A classic US example was Operation Northwoods in 1963. Proposed by the security establishment but rejected by President Kennedy, the real target would have been Cuba. To win the support of Americans for outright war against Cuba, the plan was to stage terrorist acts against US military and civilian targets, and attribute responsibility to Cuba (Bamford 2000: 82-91).

Media and 9/11 as 'false flag' warfare

Operation Northwoods is often quoted as precedent by writers of the 9/11 Truth Movement which is sceptical of the official version of 09/11 events. Recent research (Boyd-Barrett and Sun 2006) identified several book-length investigations into 9/11 that questioned the narrative of the official 9/11 Commission, arguing that the events were either foreseen and 'allowed' to happen by elements within government, or that such elements conspired to facilitate the events. On the basis of LexisNexis searches of US daily newspapers up to April 2006, they noted that none of the principal books examined had received sustained or widespread coverage in the newspaper press. Indeed, they were virtually ignored. On the few occasions they *did* attract coverage, attention was not typically negative, it was merely very slight (e.g. short reports in inside pages of provincial newspapers). Longer reports were more critical. The evidence provided weak support for our hypothesis that books espousing 'incompetency' theories (i.e. stressing inefficiency within, or over-zealous competition between, intelligence agencies) would receive more coverage and more positive coverage than theories that postulated a government of malign intent.

Following this research and in the lead-up to the five-year anniversary of 9/11 there were notable exceptions to this pattern of media avoidance. These included a CSPAN broadcast of the Scholars for 9/11 Truth conference (29 July 2006), followed by mainstream reports of 9/11 Commissioners Keane and Hamilton's book, *Without Precedent*, which revealed that some commissioners sought criminal investigations to punish misleading testimony from Pentagon and Defense witnesses. The Pentagon issued a rebuttal, and the same week saw the apparently unofficial release of NORAD tapes manifesting substantial confusion among respondents as a direct result of numerous simulated exercises operational on 9/11 itself, simulations that had often been referred to by alternative theorists but acknowledged only in passing by the official commission. Mainstream media failed to ask or research the obvious questions: why had the original report virtually ignored these simulations, how was it that the hijackings exactly coincided with the simulations, and through what processes had such massive system vulnerability been allowed?

My continuing investigations of media coverage of alternative 9/11 theories include critical mainstream press coverage during the summer of 2006 by *The New York Times*, *Washington Post* and *Time* magazine. Provisional conclusions are that such coverage, when it occurs, often attacks *ad hominem* the integrity and sanity of those who dare question official versions, and selectively quotes *other people's* investigations or assertions in preference to undertaking even modest levels of original investigation. No distinction is allowed between the asking of good, critical questions (which the mainstream seems rarely to do), and the adequacy of answers provided (which the mainstream happily attack).

By far the most substantial wrestling with alternative 9/11 theories, though barely mainstream, appeared in *Popular Mechanics*, later published in book form (Reagan et al 2006). Only one, alternative, broadcast program, *Democracy Now!* had the imagination to bring the authors of this book into direct debate with the makers of a popular, critical 9/11 documentary *Loose Change* (Avery and Rowe 2006). Mainstream media appear unreasonably trusting of official sources and institutions, possibly perceiving their foremost responsibility in such circumstances to be one of social control. More than is common in almost any other reporting, media frame such stories within a not-so-subtle tone of mocking disbelief and ridicule (hallmarks of propaganda).

Taliban as a creation of Pakistan's ISI, Saudi intelligence and CIA

What follows are examples of 'false flag' strategies that even now appear only in the margins of mainstream media, totally forgotten or repressed precisely when their lessons need most to be recalled and applied as guides to the questions that journalists should ask. I am particularly indebted to accounts provided by Ahmed's *War on Truth* (2005), as well as by Chossudovsky (2001) and Bovard (2003).

The Soviet-backed party, PDPA, spearheaded a 1978 *coup d'état* in Afghanistan overthrowing the government of Muhammad Daud. By 1979, perhaps earlier, the US began covert operations *before* the Soviet invasion of December 1979 – to *provoke*, not prevent, invasion (Brezinski 1997). The Soviets invaded to counter US destabilization. Working with Pakistani intelligence (ISI) the US encouraged local warlords to form mercenary rebel groups. In effect, these were used to preserve the Afghan feudal system. Central to the strategy was the attempt to manufacture an extremist religious ideology that fused Afghan feudal traditions with Islamic rhetoric. This included the production of school books that promoted the war-values of murder and fanaticism.

Osama Bin Laden was crucial to the conspiracy, with the approval of Saudi Arabia and the CIA. The US facilitated entry of Bin Laden mujahedin to the US for guerilla training by means of a special US visa program for unqualified applicants, organized from Saudi Arabia. (Ahmed 2005:. 3-30; 219). Another player was warlord Gulbuddin Hekmatyar to whom the CIA and Pentagon provided half a billion dollars in arms, planning, and training, channelled through ISI, possibly supplemented by drug money organized by ISI. Such funding helped construct an international Islamist financial empire in which Bin Laden played a key role, and which gave the CIA a route through which to recruit, finance and train terrorist groups that would help destabilize nationalist and communist movements threatening to US interests.

The structure was sustained after the 1989 Soviet retreat and a 1991 meeting between the CIA, Saudi intelligence and Osama Bin Laden (Ahmed 2005: 12). The Saudis wanted to preserve the alliance between Osama Bin Laden and Pakistan, with CIA support for this bulwark against Shi'ite Iran. Saudi intelligence wanted to limit Osama Bin Laden's contacts with the extremists he had helped create, and discipline him for opposing the presence of US soldiers on Saudi soil. But Osama, still with influence in Saudi royal circles, struck a deal with the head of Saudi intelligence that permitted him to exit Saudi Arabia with funding and followers intact plus Saudi financial support for operations outside Saudi Arabia.

State penetration and manipulation of terror groups

The history of terrorism provides frequent examples of terrorist groups that have been penetrated and used by security forces. Moreover, mainstream coverage of terrorism demonstrates its blindness to the symbiotic charade between terror groups and security forces, and gullibility in its handling of 'false flag' propaganda texts such as video and audio tapes allegedly compiled and released by terror groups, when the *timing* of their release (as possible propaganda at the service of the State) is as significant as their content, whose authenticity is often 'established' by reference to assurances from security forces.

Undercover security agents sometimes actively instigate terrorist actions that may not necessarily have happened otherwise, in order to furnish evidence that can later be used to convict, if only on the basis of *intent* to cause a terrorist attack. This appears to have been the case of the 'Liberty City' seven about which Van Auken (2006) concluded there was 'every indication that the purported terrorist threat was manufactured by the FBI, which used an undercover agent posing as a terrorist mastermind to entrap those targeted for arrest'. Agents may remain in terrorist organizations for many decades. Their presence may explain the frequency with which selective parties appear to receive advance warnings of terror attacks, as in the case of the 2005 London bombings (see below).

British security agents have routinely climbed to high-ranking positions within the IRA and its political arm, Sinn Fein, their cover blown only after decades, demonstrating that security services have remained undercover even during significant terrorist actions. Two cases in point include Dennis Donaldson, a leading figure of Sinn Fein, exposed in 2005, and Freddie Scappaticci, deputy head of the IRA's internal security, exposed in 2004 (James and Marsden 2006). Penetration may sometimes reach the point that the terrorist organizations become instruments of security forces, manipulated to serve covert foreign policy objectives or even personal, criminal gain.

Australian channel SBS's Dateline programme (Global Research 2005) about the 2002 Bali bombings, quoted the former President of Indonesia, Abdurrahman Wahid, as speculating that Indonesian police or army were the likely culprits behind the bombing. Another source, Umar Abduh, a convicted Islamic terrorist, told Dateline: 'There is a not a single Islamic group, either in the movement or the political groups that is not controlled by Intel.' Umar said he was incited to terrorism after infiltrators showed him a letter saying Muslim clerics were to be assassinated.

The mujahedeen who fought with Western, Pakistani and Saudi support to oust the Russians from Afghanistan in the 1980s, were later channeled north by Western security agencies to accomplish Western objectives in promoting the fragmentation of ex-Yugoslavia, and of the old Soviet empire in Chechnya and elsewhere (Ahmed 2005: 31-57).

The presence of security agents under cover in terrorist organizations does not necessarily serve only noble or official causes. Ahmed relates the history of Algerian radical Islamic group GIA, set up by the Algerian security forces after 1992 (when the victory at the polls of the official Islamic party, FIS, was suppressed) to discredit the Islamic movement by random but massive acts of savage terror. Sometimes these acts also served the interests of individual army officers or politicians (Ahmed 2005: 65-77).

Coverage of the London transport bombs, July 2005

The Blair government consistently rejected an inquiry into intelligence failures surrounding the London bombings of 7 July 2005 (which killed 52 people and injured 1,800). Failures included a downgrading by the Joint Terrorism Analysis Centre of the threat level facing the UK in June from 'severe general' to 'substantial', notwithstanding the meeting of the G8 nations in Scotland that month. A *Sunday Times* investigation tracked an April 2003 report of the Joint Intelligence Committee (JIC), signed off by the heads of MI5, M16 and GCHQ warning Prime Minister Tony Blair that Al Qaeda was planning a 'high priority' attack specifically aimed at the London Tube (Leppard 2006).

The Israeli embassy was informed of the bombings shortly beforehand – in time to dissuade Israeli finance minister Benjamin Netanyahu, then in London, from attending a hotel conference situated just above the subway station where one of the blasts occurred. Such a warning, if it did not come *before* the blasts as one report indicated, would at least have come after the first blast but before the London authorities had concluded that the blast was a terrorist attack. Other sources suggest that Mossad warned MI5 of the expected attacks weeks in advance. Amy Teibel, of Associated Press, even claimed it was British police who had alerted the Israeli Embassy in London minutes before the explosions (though this does not square with evidence that, at least officially, authorities did not realize the first explosion was a bomb). The *Observer* reported that Saudi Arabia had warned Britain less than four months previously that such an attack was pending, specifying the London Underground as target (Bright, Barnett and Alkhereiji 2005).

British security forces later admitted that three alleged bombers had been known to them for at least two years. Investigative journalist Susskind (2006) claims that the alleged leader had once been denied entry into the United States on security grounds. MI5 had kept the alleged leader, Mohammad Sidique Khan, under temporary surveillance 18 months before the bombings, in connection with an alleged plot to explode a truck bomb outside a London target, but had then assessed him as not an immediate threat, despite receiving an extensive CIA file on him. Bomber Shehzad Tanweer had been under surveillance for two years. A third suspect, Haroon Aswat, had been of interest to federal prosecutors in Seattle, in connection with a failed attempt to set up a terrorist training camp in Bly, Oregon, in 1999.

Yet the Justice Department had blocked efforts to bring criminal charges (Bernton and Heath 2005). Former US federal prosecutor John Loftus claimed that Aswat was a British-backed double agent. In September 2005, senior Labour member of Parliament and former Environment Minister Michael Meacher, writing in the *Guardian*, feared that an investigation would be thwarted by the intelligence services. Meacher recalled how Britain had aided Muslim terrorists in Bosnia, even using the al Muhajiroun group in London to recruit Islamist militants with British passports in preparation for fighting against the Serbs in Kosovo. Meacher has previously linked such considerations to possible CIA involvement in 9/11 (Marsden 2006).

Other anomalies include claims that IDs of bombers were found in separate piles of rubble at blast sites; and that the bomb on the tube train was thought by some witnesses to be *under* the carriage as opposed to *inside* (the official version) where passengers would surely have spotted something amiss. The Metropolitan Police failed to shut down cell phone networks that might have prevented the triggering by mobile signal of explosive devices, as was the case with the train bombings in Madrid in March 2004, thus possibly indicating foreknowledge that cell devices would not be used.

There were conflicting accounts as to whether or not military explosives had been used. The managing director of Visor Consultants, a crisis management company, informed BBC Radio Five Live on 7 July that Visor was running a simulation exercise 'for a company of over a thousand people' based on simultaneous bombs going off precisely at the railway stations where the actual blasts occurred (see Marsden 2005). Paul Watson and Alex Jones, of Prison Planet, speculate that such simulations 'act as a cover for the small compartmentalized terrorists to carry out their operation without the larger security forces becoming aware of what they're doing, and, more importantly, if they get caught during the attack or after with any incriminating evidence they can just claim that they were just taking part in the exercise'. That London's Commissioner for Public Transport, Bob Kiley, was an ex-CIA agent, once executive assistant to CIA director Richard Helms, is curious. Some months before the attack, as Isikoff and Hosenball (2004) reported in *Newsweek*, FBI agents ceased to travel on London's subway for fear of terror attacks.

Conclusion

Media audiences are generally no fools. They have been well educated by Hollywood, ironically, to entertain the idea that beneath the surface appearance of things there often lurk darker, complicated and unpalatable truths. Have audiences been socialized to anticipate such unpleasant twists *only* in the world of fiction?

Media researchers, like journalists, too often underestimate the extent to which news media are framed within an all-encompassing project of propaganda, quietly constructed and perfected over so many generations that only a relatively few and privileged people are entirely aware of its purpose and methods. Helping along the deception are the many ways that journalists tell themselves how journalism should be practiced, through 'objectivity as strategic ritual' (Tuchman 1978). Most reasonable people are content to go along with the idea of such a methodology because they consider it self-evidently superior to the crass products of the controlled press of authoritarian countries.

But the methodology has grave flaws. 'Facts' and 'evidence' are not reducible to what people say, however many people are interviewed, and still less are they reducible to what powerful people say. Powerful people are not authoritative, in the sense of credible, simply *because* they are powerful. Further, 'facts' are not enough in themselves. One first needs to consider what kinds of fact are going to be most interesting, important, and relevant. This process of 'consideration' is similar to, if a little less formal than, the scientific process of theory development. A journalism that is unaware of its own theorizing or disdains the importance of theory is easy prey to spin-masters.

References

Ahmed, Nafeez (2005) *The war on truth. 9/11, Disinformation and the Anatomy of terrorism*, Northampton, Massachusetts: Olive Branch Press

Associated Press (2005) Powell calls pre-Iraq U.N. speech a 'blot' on his record, *USA Today*, 8 September

Avery, Dylan and Row, Korey (2005) *Loose Change* (2nd edition), A Louder Than Words Production, New York: Oneonta

Baer, Michael (2002) *See no evil*, New York: Arrow

Baldor, Lolita (2006) Bush to request $439.3B Defense Budget for 2007, Associated Press, 2 February

Bamford, James (2002) *Body of secrets: Anatomy of the ultra-secret National Security Agency*, New York: Anchor

Barthes, Roland (1974) *S/Z: An Essay* (trans. Miller, Richard), New York: Hill and Wang

Bernton, Hal and Heath, David (2005) Effort here to charge London suspect was blocked, *Seattle Times*, 24 July

Beschloss, Peter (2001) *Reaching for Glory*, New York: Simon and Schuster

Blum, William (2000) *Killing hope: U.S. military and CIA interventions since World War II*, Monroe, ME: Common Courage Press

Bovard, James (2003) *Terrorism and tyranny*, New York: Palgrave Macmillian

Boyd-Barrett, Oliver (2003) Doubt foreclosed: US mainstream media and 11 September 2001, in Demers, David (ed.) *Terrorism, Globalization and Mass Communication*, Spokane: Marquette Books pp 3-34

— (2004a) Understanding: The Second Casualty, in Allan, Stuart and Zelizer, Barbie (eds) *Reporting War: Journalism in Wartime*, London: Routledge pp 25-42

— (2004b) Judith Miller, The New York Times, and the Propaganda Model, *Journalism Studies*, Vol. 5, No.4 pp 435-450

Boyd-Barrett, Oliver and Sun, Kang (2006) Media coverage of 9/11: The benign state. Paper presented at the annual conference of the International Communication Association, Dresden, June

Bright, Martin, Barnet, Anthony, and Alkhereiji, Mohammed (2005) Saudis warned UK of London attacks, the *Observer*, 7 August

British Broadcasting Corporation (2001) Bob Kiley: going underground. BBC, 13 January. Available online at http://news.bbc.co.uk/1/hi/uk/1113837.stm, accessed on 30 September 2006

Bryzinski, Zbigniew (1997) *The grand chessboard: American primacy and its geostrategic imperatives*, New York: Basic Books

Caghan, Stephen (2006) writer/director, *Syriana*, Section 8 Productions: Warner Home Video

Chossudovsky, Michel (2005) *America's war on 'terrorism'*, Ottawa: Global Research

Carré, John le (2001) *The spy who came in from the cold*, New York: Scribner (reprint edition)

Cockburn, Andrew (2001) Things you can't say in America. FDR knew about the attack on Pearl Harbor, Anti-war.com. June 8. Available online at http://www.antiwar.com/cockburn/c060801.html, accessed 30 September 2006

Curtis, Mark (2003) *Web of deceit: Britain's real role in the world*, London: Vintage
Deighton, Len (1995) *The Ipcress File*, London: HarperCollins
Fleming, Ian (2002) *Casino Royale*, New York: Penguin (reprint)
Gasner, Danielle (2005) *NATO's top secret stay-behind armies and terrorism in Western Europe*, London: Frank Cass
Geer, Judith (2001) Did FDR know? Salon.com, June 14. Available online at http://archive.salon.com/books/feature/2001/06/14/fdr/index.html, accessed 30 September 2006
Global Research (2005) Inside Indonesia's War on Terror. Former President of Indonesia Abdurrahman Wahid conforms involvement of Indonesian Military Intelligence, Center for Research on Globalization, 14 October. Available online at: http://www.globalresearch.ca/index.php?context=viewArticle&code=20051014&articleId=1085, accessed 30 September 2006
Gordon, William (2003) Remember the Maine, Star-Ledger, August 15. Available online at http://newsmine.org/archive/deceptions/war-pretext-lies/remember-the-maine-pretext-rush.txt, accessed on 16 August 2006
Hall, Stuart ([1973] 1980): Encoding/decoding, in Centre for Contemporary Cultural Studies (ed.) *Culture, Media, Language: Working Papers in Cultural Studies*, 1972-79, London: Hutchinson pp 128-38
Hanyok (n.d.) Skunks, bogies, silent hounds, and the flying fish: the Gulf of Tonkin Mystery, 2-4 August 1964. Available online at National Security Agency at www.nsa.gov/Vietnam/releases/relea00012.pdf, accessed 2 August 2006
Hersh, Seymour (2006) Watching Lebanon, *New Yorker*, 14 August
Isikoff, Michael and Hosenball, Mark (2004) The real target? *Newsweek*, November 22. Available online at: http://www.msnbc.msn.com/id/6514619/site/newsweek/, accessed on 16 August 2006
James, Steve and Marsden, Chris (2006) Northern Ireland: the Donaldson affair and the threat to democratic rights. World Socialist Web Site, January 19. Available online at http://www.wsws.org/articles/2005/dec2005/irel-d22.shtml, accessed 30 September 2006.
Kasper, David (1992). *The Panama Deception*. Directed by Barbara Trent
Kean, Thomas and Hamilton, Lee (2006) Without precedent: The inside story of the 9/11 Commission, New York: Knopf
Kellner, Douglas (1992). *The Persian Gulf TV war*, Boulder, San Francisco, Oxford: Westview Press
Labeviere, Richard (2000) *Dollars for terror: the United States and Islam*, New York: Algora Publishing
Lance, Peter (2003) *1000 years for revenge: International terrorism and the FBI – The untold story*, New York: Regan Books
Leppard, David (2006) Spies warned of tube attack, *The Sunday Times*, December 18
Marsden, Chris (2005). London bombings: Why does Blair oppose an inquiry into intelligence failures? World Socialist Web Site, 13 July. Available online at http://www.wsws.org/articles/2005/jul2005/lond-j13.shtml, accessed on 30 September 2006
— (2005) British MP Michael Meacher suggests Security Services are shielding July 7 bomb plotters, World Socialist Web Site, September 14. Available online at

http://www.wsws.org/articles/2005/sep2005/brit-s14.shtml, accessed on 30 September 2006

Morley, David (1980) *The Nationwide Audience*, London: British Film Institute

Mueller, Susan (2004) *Media Coverage of Weapons of Mass Destruction*, Baltimore: University of Maryland

Mulvey, Laura (1975). Visual Pleasure and Narrative Cinema. *Screen*, Vol. 16, No. 3 pp 6-18

Pallister, David (2005) UK-based dissident denies link to website that carried Al Qaeda claim, *Guardian*, 9 July

Pilger, John (2003) *The new rulers of the world*, London: Verso

Pincus, Walter (2006). Intelligence director's budget may near $1 billion, report finds, *Washington Post*, 20 April

Prados, John (2003) *The White House Tapes*, New York: The New Press

Radway, Janice (1997). Reading the Romance, in *Studies in Culture: An Introductory Reader*, Gray, Ann and McGuigan, Jim (eds) London: Arnold pp. 62-79

Reagan, Brad et al (eds) (2006) Debunking 9/11 myths: Why conspiracy theories can't stand up to the facts, Popular Mechanics

Roosevelt, Kermit (1979) *Countercoup: The struggle for control of Iran*, New York: McGraw Hill

Shane, Scott (2005) Official lets slip US spy budget, *New York Times*, 9 November

Shrader, Katherine (2006) Intel chief says personnel number 100,000, Associated Press, 20 April

Socialist Equality Party (Britain) (2006) One year on: Lessons of the London bombings, *World Socialist*, 6 July. Available online at http://www.wsws.org/articles/2006/jul2006/lond-j07.shtml, accessed on 30 September 2006

Stinnett, Robert (2001) *Day of deceit: The truth about FDR and Pearl Harbor*, New York: The Free Press

Suskind, Ron (2006) *The One Percent Doctrine*, New York: Simon and Schuster

Tiebel, Amy (2006) Netanyahu changed plans due to warning, Associated Press, 7 July

US Department of Defense (2002) Testimony before the House Appropriations Committee: Fiscal Year 2 Defense Budget Request. Available online at: http://www.dod.gov/speeches/2001/s20010716-secdef2.html, accessed on 30 September 2006

Toland, John (1982) *Infamy: Pearl Harbor and its aftermath*, Garden City: Doubleday and Co

Tuchman, Gaye (1978) *Making News: A Study in the Construction of Reality*, New York: The Free Press

Usborne, David (2003) WMD just a convenient excuse for war, admits Wolfowitz, Truthout.org. Available online at: http://www.commondreams.org/headlines03/0530-05.htm, accessed on 30 May 2006

Van Auken, Bill (2006) Miami 'terror' arrests – a government provocation, World Socialist Web Site, 24 June. Available online at: http://www.wsws.org/articles/2006/jun2006/miam-j24.shtml, accessed 30 September 2006

CHAPTER EIGHT

FIGHTING DISCOURSES: DISCOURSE THEORY, WAR
AND REPRESENTATIONS
OF THE 2003 IRAQI WAR[1]

NICO CARPENTIER

War, antagonism and hegemony

When a nation or a people go to war, powerful mechanisms come into play to turn an adversary into the enemy. Where the existence of an adversary is considered legitimate and the right to defend their – distinct – ideas is not questioned, an enemy is excluded from the political community and has to be destroyed (Mouffe 1997: 4). The transformation of an adversary into an enemy is supported by a set of discourses, articulating the identities of all parties involved. These discourses play a crucial role, as Keen has put it:

> In the beginning we create the enemy. Before the weapon comes the image. We think others to death and then invent the battle-axe or the ballistic missiles with which to actually kill them (Keen 1986: 10).

Moreover, little room is left for internal differences, which is evidenced by the words of the German Emperor Wilhelm, who during the First World War claimed that 'he would no longer hear of different political parties, only of Germans' (Torfing 1999: 126). The American President George Bush used an updated version during his address to the Joint Session of Congress and the American People on 20 September 2001, saying: 'Either you are with us, or you are with the terrorists.' The antagonistic discourses on the enemy tend to become very quickly hegemonic, excluding other discourses.

A brief overview of Laclau and Mouffe's discourse theory

Particularly relevant to any analysis of hegemonic discourse is the work of Ernesto Laclau and Chantal Mouffe who argue that all social phenomena and objects obtain their meaning(s) through discourse. This they define as 'a structure in which meaning is constantly negotiated and constructed' (Laclau 1988: 254). In what they call a 'radical materialist' position they argue that the discursive component of reality is a necessary condition for accessing reality. Moreover, they see 'the' social reality as contingent: in other words the present socio-political constellation is not defined as a necessity, but as the result of the complex interaction between subjects, subject positions and discourses.

Their major text, *Hegemony and socialist strategy* (1985), can be read on three interrelated levels. The first level – discourse theory in the strict sense – refers to their social ontology and to the position they negotiate between materialism and idealism, between structure and agency. A second – strongly related – level is what Anna Marie Smith (1999: 87) calls their political identity theory, which is tributary to conflict theory. Key concepts on this level are social antagonism and (of course) hegemony. Their post-Marxist approach becomes even more evident at the third level, where their plea for a radical democratic politics situates them in the field of democratic theory.

When focusing on the key notions of hegemony and antagonism, Smith (1999) rightfully relates Laclau and Mouffe's work to the notion of identity. Embedded in their social ontology, identity becomes fluid, flexible, over-determined, undecided and discursively articulated. Identity is seen as the way in which social agents can be identified and/or identify themselves within a discursive environment. This component of identity is termed a subject position, and defined as the positioning of subjects within a discursive structure: 'Whenever we use the category of "subject" in this text, we will do so in the sense of "subject positions" within a discursive structure. Subjects cannot, therefore, be the origin of social relations – not even in the limited sense of being endowed with powers that render an experience possible – as all "experience" depends on precise discursive conditions of possibility' (Laclau and Mouffe 1985: 115).

Traditionally antagonism is viewed as a collision of social agents that dispose of a fully developed identity. Laclau and Mouffe, however, revert to early semiology by claiming that 'all identity is relational and all relations have a necessary character' (ibid: 106). When this position is applied to antagonism, this implies that social agents can never attain a completely developed identity: 'the presence of the Other prevents me from being totally myself' (ibid: 125). Antagonisms have both negative and positive aspects, as they attempt to destabilize the 'other' identity but desperately need that very 'other' as a constitutive outside to stabilize the proper identity. When the question arises how these antagonisms are discursively constructed, Laclau and Mouffe refer to the logic of equivalence and the creation of chains of equivalence. In such chains different identities are equated to each other or made equivalent, and opposed to another – negative – identity. When existing chains of equivalence are broken down and the elements of these chains are articulated in another discursive order, Laclau and Mouffe use the concept of the logic of difference. This process results in the weakening of social antagonisms – relegating them to the 'outskirts' of society.

When discourses begin to obtain social dominance, Laclau and Mouffe refer to the concept of hegemony as developed by Gramsci. Originally, Gramsci defined this notion in function of the formation of consent, rather than as the (exclusive) domination of the other, without however excluding a certain form of pressure and repression (Gramsci 1999: 261). From Laclau and Mouffe's perspective, hegemony refers to the 'articulation of a plurality of identities into collective wills capable of constituting a certain social order' (Torfing 1999: 103). Hegemony is thus the ability to fix meaning, within a specific context of space and time, taking into account the constant struggle of different groups and social forces 'in order to control the direction, policies and future of the society' (Kellner 1992: 58).

Discourses on the enemy and the self

Following Galtung and his colleagues (Galtung and Vincent 1992; Galtung 1998; Galtung 2000; McGoldrick and Lynch 2000; Galtung, Jacobsen and Brand-Jacobsen 2001), it is contended that the discourses on the self and the enemy that transform an adversary into an enemy are based on a series of elementary dichotomies: good/evil, just/unjust, innocent/guilty, rational/irrational, civilized/barbaric, organized/chaotic, superior to technology/part of technology, human/animal-machine, united/fragmented, heroic/cowardice and determined/insecure. A second layer of dichotomies structures the meanings attributed to the violent practices of both warring parties, which include: necessary/unnecessary, last resort/provocative, limited effects/major effects, focused/indiscriminate, purposeful/senseless, unavoidable/avoidable, legitimate/illegitimate, legal/criminal, sophisticated/brutal and professional/undisciplined.

All these dichotomies can be defined as floating (or empty) signifiers (Laclau and Mouffe op cit: 112-113; Žižek 1989: 97), binary oppositions and/or central oppositions (Berger 1997). Floating signifiers have no fixed meaning, but they are (re)articulated before, during and after the conflict and attributed positions in different chains of equivalence. At the same time they play key roles as nodal points in hegemonic projects, which attempt to fix their meaning. Both sides claim to be rational and civilized, and to fight a good and just war, attributing responsibility for the conflict to the enemy. The violent practices of both sides are focused, well considered, purposeful, unavoidable and necessary. The construction of the enemy is accompanied by the construction of the identity of the self, clearly in an antagonistic relationship to the enemy's identity. In this process not only the radical otherness of the enemy is emphasized, but the enemy is also considered to be a threat to 'our own' identity.

Although the discourses that constitute the construction of the enemy are widespread, specific groups of actors tend to play a vital role in the hegemonization of these discourses. These groups can benefit from unequal power relations that increase the weight of their statements. A first group of actors is usually referred to as the state, unifying among others governments, parliaments, political parties, advisory bodies and not in the least the military. Not only does a state hold decision-making powers, has to assume responsibility for waging war and will be held accountable for the course of war, but as a political organ – representing and governing 'the people' – its statements (and actions) can play a vital role in establishing or supporting an hegemonic process. As war is considered a very specific condition – which threatens the existence of numerous human beings and possibly 'even' the survival of the state itself – not only the legitimization of war is considered appropriate. The support of the 'home front' (or national unity) and a military victory become prime political objectives, legitimizing policies of hegemonization.

From this point of view, propaganda could be seen as one of the available (and widely used) instruments for the purpose of hegemonization. Propaganda is supplemented by censorship, which can be considered a second instrument for hegemonization. The specific characteristic of propaganda is its emphasis on *a priori* planning by organized groups, which can range from a small number of special advisors to large bureaucratic organizations responsible for the propaganda and counter-propaganda efforts (Taylor 1995: 6; Jowett 1997: 75). This characteristic also marks the difference between propaganda and hegemony, as the latter is seen here as the rigid but ultimately unstable result of a societal process determining the horizon of our thought in a specific spatial and temporal setting. Although propaganda can be instrumental in establishing hegemony, the societal construction of the collective will to fight a war supersedes all propaganda efforts.

One of the major targets of the state's propaganda efforts are the mainstream media, which – as Kellner (1992: 57) remarks – should not be defined as hypodermic needles, but as 'a crucial site of hegemony'. A wide range of information management techniques have been developed in order to influence the (news) media's output. Nevertheless, the existence of these strategies does not imply that the mainstream media are defenseless victims. Here, the media's specificity should be taken into account, at both the organizational level and the level of media professional's identities. The majority of the Western media can still be considered relatively independent organizations, with specific objectives and specific values.

Even in the most liberal normative theories of the media, the mainstream (news) media claim to inform their audiences and to subject state practices to public scrutiny. Moreover, media professionals claim access to the description of factuality and the representation of truth or authenticity, which potentially counters (some of) the propaganda efforts of the states at war. This implies that substantiation for this claim to truth-speaking becomes unavoidable. Journalistic ethics and ritualistic procedures (Tuchman 1972) are required to guarantee the integrity, reliability and status of journalists as 'truth speakers' – by analogy with Foucault (1978) – or 'truth-reporters':

> The journalist's profession...might be described as that of 'authorized truthteller' or 'licensed relayer of facts'...Journalistic ethics can be seen as a device to facilitate the social construction of legitimacy, to mobilize the trust of the audience in what they are reading, hearing or seeing (McNair 1998: 65).

The 2003 Iraqi War – Persian Gulf War 2[2]

The 2003 Iraqi War attracts global media attention combined with the deployment of large-scale media management. The state apparatus have initiated their ideological positioning long before the actual war started, firstly by categorizing Iraq as one of the rogue states, part of the 'axis of evil' (Bush 2002) that forms a potential threat to world peace. Further building on the constructions of the enemy that were born out of the 1991 Gulf War and out of the cat-and-mouse game of disarmament that followed, Iraq is singled out of the relative safety of the group of rogue states. The events of the past decade are translated into an antagonistic positioning between the US (and its allies) representing the (military) struggle against terrorism on the one hand and Iraq, representing terrorism and the threat to world peace on the other.

The nodal points of this articulation of the enemy thus become again centered on the Iraqi leader, Saddam Hussein, who is defined through the state-as-person metaphor, as the main (individualized) threat to the (Western) world. His evilness is constructed (this time even more than in the previous 1991 Gulf War) on the basis of the (alleged) possession of WMD, and his will to effectively put them to use. Strategic support for this decision is found in Iraq's brutal (military) history, especially in the First Gulf War (when between 1980-1988 Iran and Iraq fought a very bloody war) and Iraq's use of chemical weapons in March 1988 against the Iranian troops that occupied the Kurdish city of Halabjah, which resulted in the death of more than 5,000 civilians. Also Iraq's violent oppression of the Shi'ites and Kurdish minorities adds weight to the 'evilness' of the regime. Based on this historical evidence and new (but faulty as it later turned out) evidence of Iraq's Nuclear, Biological and Chemical programs, Iraq and its military system are seen as a major threat to world security.

When the pre-conflict phase develops the ideological model evolves further. The processes of demonization are further strengthened by the discursive creation of a victim. More specifically, the Iraqi people are positioned as the victims of the brutal dictatorship of Saddam Hussein. The enemy chain of equivalence also includes the fragmented nature of the Iraqi society. At the civil level the fragmentation becomes intertwined with the process of victimization, as the Iraqi people (as a whole) are disarticulated from the regime, which is defined as a threat to its own people.

At the level of the military the fragmentation of Iraq is constructed by distinguishing between the elite Republican Guard and the regular army. The elite forces that support the regime are again dehumanized and considered part of the military technology. The regular army is seen as less supportive and remains (at least in the first phase) part of the 'people', ready to be freed from oppression. From a different perspective, all Iraqi resistance thus becomes intrinsically linked with the regime, excluding all other legitimizations for resistance.

On the other hand the so-called coalition positions itself as the heroic safeguards of world security. This positioning partially moves the process of victimization to the level of the potential. The American (and other Western) people are potential victims of the Iraq military force, directly through Iraq's potential possession and usage of WMD and indirectly through the supposed support for terrorist networks. The need to protect their populations legitimizes the use of violence, which is seen as the last resort, and thus unavoidable and necessary. At the same time the discourse on the self is oriented towards the perceived need to become the future liberators of the main victim of the pre-war situation, the Iraqi people. This articulation provides further support for the construction of a chain of equivalences that articulates the Western states as good, just and determined.

The virtualization of war

This process of 'heroization' is strengthened by the emphasis on the mastery of superior technology, which is rationally and carefully used, capable of 'surgical strikes' with only limited effects, rendering human suffering almost invisible. This virtualization of war excludes not only the destruction of enemy human bodies from the discourses of war, but also embeds the 'accidental' loss of civilian life in the rhetoric of necessity. It furthermore detaches the good operator of military technology (the coalition soldier) from the actual effects of that technology (death and destruction). These processes of exclusion and detachment serve but one purpose: to protect the goodness of the professional coalition soldier, who only kills out of bare necessity. Finally, their goodness is articulated by the homogenization of the self. In contrast to the divided enemy, the coalition, regime, military and civilian population (the 'home front') are united in their support for the just cause.

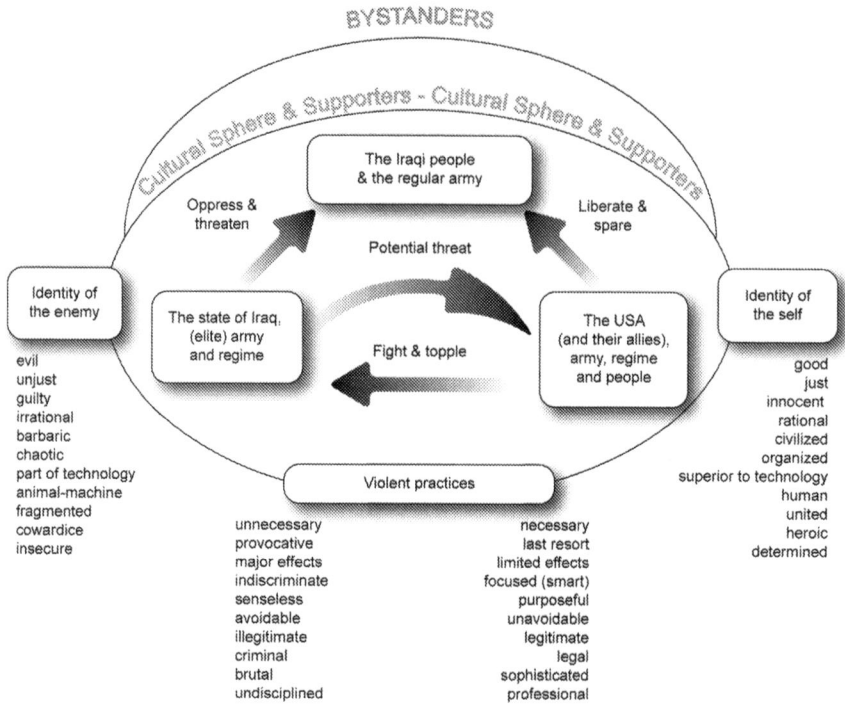

Figure 8-1: The Ideological Model of War

This ideological model of war (see Fig 8-1) is supported by a huge propaganda effort, organized to manage the media outputs. Key elements of the media management are the installation of the international press center at US Central Command in Qatar and the (re-)use of the embedding system. Although unembedded journalists ('unilaterals') are working at great risk in Iraq – for an overview, see Gopsill (2004) – the images produced by the embedded journalists, driving along with the advancing troops through southern Iraq, dominate a major part of the media coverage. *Chicago Tribune* television critic Steve Johnson calls this 'a heroic picture of a rush to Baghdad' (quoted in Seib 2004: 7). Embedded journalists produce this low-tech looking imagery of tanks and armed troop carriers speeding through the desert by using hi-tech videophones. Comments are often as heroic as the images, as, for instance, when CNN reporter Walter Rodgers (embedded with the US Army 3rd Infantry Division's 7th Cavalry Regiment) refers to 'a giant wave of steel' that was 'ever pushing towards the Iraqi capital of Baghdad' (Rodgers 2003).

The ideological model under pressure

The ideological model, as described above, cannot be considered as stable or fixed during (or before and after) the war. In the case of the Iraqi War a number of events put a major strain on the 'original' ideological model. After the initial rush through the desert, the resistance of Iraqi forces increased, slowing down the advance. Illustrative for the surprise this has caused is the repeated miscommunication on the 'falling' of Umm Qasr (and its harbor), showing how the interpretations based on the original ideological model are contradicted by new events (e.g. the continued resistance). Especially the resistance by (parts of) the regular army, that does not surrender *en masse*, requires a first rearticulation of the ideological model, separating the regular army from the Iraqi people again.

It is further complicated by the emergence of a new category of soldiers, the Fedayeen, and the first signs of civil resistance, said to originate from members of the Ba'ath party. Secondly the military and technological superiority of the coalition forces comes under pressure by a number of 'undesirable' events, such as the Iraqi civilian deaths, the relative large number of American and British soldiers who die in accidents and 'friendly fire' and the bizarre grenade attack by an American soldier on his 'own' staff officers at Camp Pennsylvania on 22 March 2003. But especially disturbing is the capture of a number of American and British soldiers by Iraqi forces. During the Nassiriya incident in April 2003, units of the 507th Maintenance Company (consisting out of diesel and heavy equipment mechanics, a computer technician, supply clerks and sergeants, and cooks) ended up in the eastern suburbs of Nassiriya and were attacked. Nine soldiers of the 507th lost their lives. Two other soldiers and at least two Marines were killed during the rescue. Fourteen other Marines were killed in other actions on that day in Nassiriya (Rosenberg 2003). Six of the soldiers were captured and appeared soon on different television channels.

The US choose to deal with this threat to the ideological model by reverting to propaganda of the act and 'airlifted' on 1 April one captured and injured soldier (Jessica Lynch) from the Nassiriya hospital. Afterwards, Lynch's capture was translated into a heroic event that – instead of threatening the ideological model – strengthened it. On 3 April 2003, Fox News Channel website summarized this heroic story as it appeared in the *Washington Post*, based on statements from 'unidentified US officials':

> The *Washington Post* reported Thursday that the 19-year-old Army supply clerk shot several Iraqi soldiers during the March 23 ambush that resulted in her capture. She kept firing even after she had several gunshot wounds, finally running out of ammunition, the newspaper said, citing unidentified US officials (Fox News Channel 2003).

From 4 April onwards the focus is placed on the battle for Baghdad, which poses no real threat to the ideological model. In this final phase all disruptive events, such as the high number of Iraqi people killed and the death of three journalists on 9 April can be countered and incorporated by the victorious end of the war that is in sight. In this short phase the war can legitimize itself, as one of its main aims, the 'liberation' of the Iraqi people is close to realization. When the statue of Saddam Hussein at the Firdos Square is toppled on 9 April the war (at least symbolically) ends and the 'postwar war' (Seib 2004: 1), which will not be extensively discussed in this chapter, commences.

When the WMD cannot be found, this fundamentally threatens the structural integrity of the ideological model, as the goodness of the Anglo-American self is now based on preventing the use of non-existing WMD. Different strategies to cope with this near-dislocation are used, in an effort to keep the model intact (at least during the war itself). Firstly, the blunt denial of the problem is often used, invoking arguments of time and space. The second strategy is based on the repeated communication of important discoveries related to WMD. On 27 March, the BBC, for instance, reports on the discovery of gas masks and protective suits in an Iraqi command post, which according to the UK defense secretary, is 'categorical proof' of the possession and readiness to use of chemical and biological weapons (BBC 2003). Meanwhile little evidence of WMD has been presented, leading to a number of political crises after the war. The above-described strategies have, nevertheless, been successful in keeping the possible existence of WMD unresolved until after the war.

Ideology and structural bias in the media

Although media professionals and organizations like to believe they are outside the operations of ideology – what Schlesinger (1987) has called the macro-myth of independence – the ideological model on the war is difficult to escape. As these discourses on the enemy and the self have been hegemonized and turned into common sense, they also become the interpretative frameworks of media professionals. Taking Westerståhl's (1983) approach to objectivity as a starting point, this ideological privileging of a specific interpretative framework strongly affects the construction of factuality and directly impacts on journalistic practices. In other words: what is to be defined as relevant and truthful, and what will become represented in the media is contingent upon the ideological model of war.

The problems in the representation of war are strengthened by the application of the specific procedures and rituals (Tuchman 1972) that media professionals use to guarantee or legitimize their truth-speaking (and objectivity). On a number of levels these procedures create so-called structural biases that feed into the operations of the ideological model of war. Journalistic daily practices and procedures are regulated through key concepts as balance, relevance and truthfulness, which have an important impact on the actual representations journalists produce. As these fluid concepts have to be transformed into social practice, their content is rendered highly particular and specific. In some cases, as discussed below, this specificity favors the discourses of war. The always-specific articulation of these key concepts through the media professionals' daily practices thus finds itself in a sometimes-strange alliance with this ideological model of war.

The specific articulations of relevance that are customary within the media system are strongly focused on elite sources. Bell (1991: 191) summarizes this as follows: 'News is what an authoritative source tells a journalist...The more elite the source, the more newsworthy the story.' During periods of war this often provides the political and military leadership often-unmediated access to the media, for instance through live and uninterrupted broadcasts of speeches-to-the-nation and press conferences. Koch (1991) claims that journalists tend to focus on journalistic events, and ignore the actual occurrences (termed 'boundary events') that precede them, shifting the question of factuality from the fact-of-the-event to the fact-of-the-statement. These preferences also allow the military and political representatives of states at war to communicate their ideological frameworks, and discourses of the enemy and the self, maximizing the impact of their specific vocabularies and media management.

The impact of this specific articulation of relevance is further strengthened by the role of another key signifier: balance. Balance is often transformed into journalistic practice by guaranteeing access to 'legitimate elites on all major sides of a dispute' (Entman 1989: 37). In the case of war this implies trying to complement the statements made by the political and military representatives of the self by the political and military representatives of the enemy, although problems with access to the latter category might skew the balance. Nevertheless, balance is often translated into a personalized balance, built on a comparison of (categories of) individuals. An argumentative balance, which creates a balance between arguments and/or discourses, is only seldom used. Moreover, this type of balance is highly problematic because of internal and external constraints. The result is that 'during warfare, objectivity in the sense of giving as much credibility to the enemy as to the spokespersons of one's own nation is close to impossible in the mainstream media' (Tumber and Palmer 2004: 165).

Contextualization by the military

The focus on members of the political and military establishment is further complemented by the contextualization by military experts, often-retired military or academics that comment upon the military strategies under development. The media attribute high relevance to the narration of war, supported by a continuous flow of images. Out of the complexity of military events they try to extrapolate a number of storylines allowing them to narrate the conflict on a daily base. This narration is not only supported by the comments of military experts, but also by elements of the geography of war (maps and satellite pictures) and images considered representative for the 'events of that day'. These images often testify of the media's fascination – or glorification as Galtung and Vincent (1992: 211-212) call it – with the technology of death and destruction, but media organizations tend to shy away from showing the effects of its use (human suffering). In other words, they dissociate themselves from the war's materiality (Carruthers 2000: 276).

In many cases this problem has lead to speculation and misinformation, fed by assumptions based on the ideological model. These instances were (as mentioned before) especially centered on the issue of the existence of WMD. Other examples were the counter-attack of a column of ghost tanks from Baghdad, and the mythical popular uprising in Basra.

Finally, direct and indirect political and economic pressures (including censorship) have had their impact on the media output as well, not just in limiting the media's access to Iraq (before, during and after the war), but also on the representations of war. An interesting example is the Pentagon's ban on making images of dead soldiers' 'homecomings' at Dover Air Force Base public, broken after legal action instantiated by a website called the Memory Hole[3].

Media resistance

Although the processes described above often characterize the mainstream media output, care should be taken not homogenize the diversity of media organizations and practices. In a number of cases have mainstream media managed to produce counter-hegemonic discourses. They have provided spaces for critical debate, in-depth analysis and humor. They have on a number of occasions shown the horror of war. They have also attempted to counter some of the basic premises of the ideological model[4], to give a face to the Iraqi victims, to pay attention to the strong European and the less strong US popular resistance against the war. Tumber and Palmer (2004: 164) summarize the situation in the UK as follows: 'Unlike the anti-Vietnam protests...the anti-war protest over Gulf War II, consisting of a politically and socially diverse coalition, was given space and prominence in the media.'

It should also be remarked that outside the mainstream media other public spheres are used to critique or complement the hegemonic ideological model. As was the case during previous wars, (part of) the Internet serves as a critical sphere, with websites like ZMag, Truthout and Oneworld, and with web logs like the Salim Pax blog. Also other spheres, like the streets, books, magazines, cartoons, and from a broader perspective, popular culture can contain discourses that attempt to disrupt the hegemonic discourses of war. An almost visionary example can be found in George Michael's pop song and video clip 'Shoot the dog', containing a (rather amusing) critique on the British relationship of dependence towards the US, depicting Tony Blair as Bush's puppy, thus attempting to disarticulate the homogeneous Anglo-American self.

Conclusion

The discursive-theoretical approach adopted here highlights both the stability and the contingency (or the fixity and non-fixity) of the representations of war. On the one hand the complex series of events that a war is composed of appears to be highly elusive and impossible to represent in its entirety. Moreover, these processes of mediation are highly politicized. Influencing them becomes an important objective of the hegemonic projects of the states at war. A variety of the discursive strategies that aim to stabilize and fix these meanings engulf the practices of war and propagate a dichotomized ideological model of war, built on the traditional good/evil, just/unjust, innocent/guilty, rational/irrational, civilized/barbaric, organized/chaotic, superior towards technology/part of technology, human/animal-machine, united/fragmented, heroic/cowardice and determined/insecure dichotomies.

Laclau and Mouffe's theoretical elaborations emphasize the operations of hegemony, and its impact on all societal levels. Hegemony (and the related notion of social antagonism) provides a crucial theoretical tool to improve the understanding of the inter-connectedness of discourses emanating from state and media, the powerlessness of media to escape the ideological model and the (direct or indirect) legitimization of war.

This model is built on its taken-for-grantedness and, indeed, becomes the social horizon for the majority of social actors, including journalists. Within the media system, the workings of this ideological model are merely increased by propaganda and censorship, and by structural, military, technological and political pressures, leading to media representations that can only be described as exclusionary towards a considerable number of other meanings, interpretations and discourses. The specific articulation of objectivity through journalistic practice leads to an over-representation of military and political representatives of the states at war, which is skewed towards the representatives of the US and UK, the contextualization of war by military experts, and an emphasis on the episodic narration of war. One of the main consequences of these specific articulations is the de-contextualization of the conflict in time and space, resulting in the under-representation of the complex causes of the conflict, of the motives and interests of all parties involved and of the future power structure. The human cost of the conflict and its long-term impact are also to often lost in the fever of triumph.

Notes

[1] Special thanks to Maite Ceusters for assisting in the research project on North Belgian media representations on war, and to Sofie Van Bauwel for her comments on an earlier version of this chapter. The responsibility for the final text remains with the author alone.

[2] The name of this conflict is in itself already problematic, as in most cases the count tends to exclude the 'first' Persian Gulf War, namely the Iran-Iraq war (1980-1988). The absence of clear Western involvement seemed to warrant its exclusion from the count. For this reason the more neutral '2003 Iraqi War' has been chosen. Media are of course confronted with similar problems, and some choose differently, as Bodi (2004: 244-245) remarks: 'Al Jazeera's tag for the conflict was "War on Iraq", in contrast to the BBC's neutral "War in Iraq" and Fox News' jingoistic "Operation Iraqi Freedom" which merely parroted the Pentagon's name for the conflict.'

[3] http://www.thememoryhole.org, edited and published by Russ Kick.

[4] A modest but interesting example is provided by the North Belgian newspaper *De Morgen* on April 4, 2003, when referring to the coalition as a 'mini-coalition'.

References

Aksoy, Asu and Robins, Kevin (1992) Exterminating angels: morality, violence, and technology in the Gulf War, in Mowlana, Hamid, Gerbner, George and Schiller, Herbert I. (eds) *Triumph of the image: the media's war in the Persian Gulf – A global perspective*, Boulder, San Francisco, Oxford: Westview Press pp 202-211

Baudrillard, Jean (1995) *The gulf war did not take place*, Bloomington: Indiana University Press

BBC (2003) 'Proof' of biological weapons found, BBC, 27 March. Available online at http://news.bbc.co.uk/1/hi/world/middle_east/2892077.stm, accessed on 22 April 2004

Bell, Allan (1991) *The language of news media*, Oxford: Blackwell

Berger, Arthur Asa (1997) *Narratives in popular culture, media and everyday life*, London: Sage

Blix, Hans (2004) Disarming Iraq. The search for weapons of mass destruction, London: Bloomsbury

Bodi, Faisal (2004) Al Jazeera's war, in Miller, David (ed.) *Tell me lies. Propaganda and distortion in the attack on Iraq*, London: Pluto Press pp 243-250

Bush, George (2001) Address to a Joint Session of Congress and the American People, 20 September. Available online at: http://www.whitehouse.gov/news/releases/2001/09/20010920-8.html, accessed on 22 April 2004

Bush, George (2002) President Delivers State of the Union Address, 29 January. Available online at: http://www.whitehouse.gov/news/releases/2002/01/20020129-11.html, accessed on 22 April 2004

Carpentier, Nico and Biltereyst, Daniel (2000) *Fighting discourses: the construction of the self and the enemy. Media covering war: Vietnam, Persian Gulf and Kosovo*. First University of Essex Graduate Conference in Political Theory: Contemporary Theory and Politics for the New Millennium, University of Essex (12-13 May 2000)

Carruthers, Susan L. (2000) *The media at war: Communication and conflict in the twentieth century*, London: Macmillan

Ellul, Jacques (1973) *Propaganda: the formation of men's attitudes*, New York: Vintage Books

Entman, Robert M. (1989) *Democracy without citizens. Media and the decay of American politics*, New York, Oxford: Oxford University Press

Foucault, Michel (1978) *History of Sexuality, Part 1: An introduction*, New York: Pantheon

Fox News Channel (2003) Report: Lynch Was Shot, Stabbed in Fierce Struggle With Iraqi Captors, Fox News Channel, 3 April 2003. Available online at: http://www.foxnews.com/story/0,2933,82923,00.html, accessed on 15 March 2004

Freedman, Des (2004) Misreporting war has a long history, in Miller, David (ed.) *Tell me lies. Propaganda and distortion in the attack on Iraq*, London: Pluto Press pp 63-69

Fuss, Diane (1989) *Essentially speaking: Feminism, nature, and difference*, London: Routledge

Galtung, Johan and Vincent, R. C. (1992) *Global glasnost: toward a new world information and communication order?* Cresskill, New Jersey: Hampton Press

Galtung, Johan (1998) *The Peace Journalism Option*, Taplow, Bucks: Conflict and Peace Forums

— (2000) Conflict Transformation by Peaceful Means: The TRANSCEND Method, Geneva: UNDP

Galtung, Johan, Brand-Jacobsen, Carl G. and Frithjof Brand-Jacobsen, Kai (2001) *Searching for Peace. The Road to TRANSCEND*, London: Pluto Press

Gerbner, George (1992) Persian Gulf War, the movie, in Mowlana, Hamid, Gerbner, George and Schiller, Herbert I. (eds) *Triumph of the image: the media's war in the Persian Gulf - A global perspective*, Boulder, San Francisco, Oxford: Westview Press pp 243-265

Goff, Peter (ed.) (1999) *The Kosovo news and propaganda war*, Wien: International press institute

Gopsill, Tim (2004) Target the media, in Miller, David (ed.) *Tell me lies: Propaganda and distortion in the attack on Iraq*, London: Pluto Press pp 251-261

Gramsci, Antonio (1999) *The Antonio Gramsci Reader: Selected writings 1916-1935*, London: Lawrence and Wishart

Hall, Stuart (1973) The determination of news photographs, in Cohen, Stanley and Young, Jock (eds) *The manufacture of news: social problems, deviance and the mass media*, London: Constable pp 226-243

Haraway, Donna (1991) A Cyborg Manifesto: Science, Technology, and Socialist-Feminism in the Late Twentieth Century, in Haraway, Donna (ed.) *Simians, Cyborgs and Women: The Reinvention of Nature*, New York: Routledge pp 149-181

Hoon, Geoff (2003) Government press briefing by the Defense Secretary, 14 April 2003, Available online at: http://www.number-10.gov.uk/output/page3496.asp, accessed on 22 April 2004

Hume, Mick (2000) Nazifying the Serbs, from Bosnia to Kosovo, in Hammond, Philip and Herman, Edward S. (eds) *Degraded capability: The media and the Kosovo crisis*, London: Pluto Press pp 70-78

Jowett, Garth S. (1997) Toward a propaganda analysis of the Gulf War, in Greenberg, Bradley and Gantz, Walter (eds) *Desert Storm and the mass media*, Cresskill, New Jersey, Hampton Press pp 74-85

Keen, Sam (1986) *Faces of the enemy*, New York: Harper and Row

Kellner, Douglas (1992) *The Persian Gulf TV war*, Boulder, San Francisco, Oxford: Westview Press

Koch, Tom (1991) *Journalism in the 21st Century: Online information, electronic databases and the news*, Twickenham: Adamantine Press

Laclau, Ernesto (1988) Metaphor and social antagonisms, in Nelson, Cary and Grossberg, Lawrence (eds) *Marxism and the interpretation of culture*, Urbana: University of Illinois pp 249-257

— (1990) New reflections on the revolution of our time, London: Verso

Laclau, Ernesto and Mouffe, Chantal (1985) *Hegemony and socialist strategy: Towards a radical democratic politics*, London: Verso

McGoldrick, Annabel and Lynch, Jake (2000) Peace journalism. How to do it? Available online at http://www.transcend.org/pjmanual.htm, accessed on 15 March 2004

McNair, Brian (1998) *The sociology of journalism*, London, New York, Sydney, Auckland: Arnold

Michael, George (2002) Statement on 'Shoot the dog'. Available online at: http://george.michael.szm.sk/Lyrics/lyrstdog.html, accessed on 15 March 2004

Mouffe, Chantal (1997) *The return of the political*, London: Verso

Pax, Salam (2004) *The Baghdad Blog*, London: Atlantic Books

Pilger, John (2000) Censorship by omission, in Hammond, Philip and Herman, Edward S. (eds) *Degraded capability: the media and the Kosovo crisis*, London: Pluto Press pp 132-140

Rodgers, Walter (2003) Imagine a giant wave of steel, CNN.com, 21 March. Available online at: http://www.cnn.com/2003/WORLD/meast/03/21/btsc.irq.rodgers/, accessed on 15 March

Rosenberg, Howard L. (2003) Bloody Sunday. The Real Story of What Happened to Jessica Lynch's Convoy, ABC News, 17 June. Available online at:

http://abcnews.go.com/sections/primetime/World/iraq_507convoy030617_pt1.html, accessed 22 April 2004

Schlesinger, Philip (1987) *Putting 'reality' together*, London and New York: Methuen

Seib, Phillip (2004) (ed.) Lessons from Iraq: The news media and the next war: The Lucius W. Nieman Symposium 2003, Milwaukee: Marquette University

Smith, Anne Marie (1999) *Laclau and Mouffe: The radical democratic imaginary*, London and New York: Routledge

Taithe, Bertrand and Thornton, Tim (1999) Propaganda: a misnomer of rhetoric and persuasion? in Taithe, Bertrand and Tim Thornton (eds) *Propaganda. Political rhetoric and identity 1300-2000*, Phoenix Mill: Sutton Publishing pp 1-24

Taylor, Philip M. (1995) *Munitions of the mind: a history of propaganda from the ancient world to the present era*, Manchester: Manchester University Press

Taylor, Philip M. (1998) *War and the media*, Manchester: Manchester University Press

Torfing, Jacob (1999) *New theories of discourse: Laclau, Mouffe and Žižek*, Oxford: Blackwell

Tuchman, Gaye (1972) Objectivity as a strategic ritual: an examination of newsmen's notions of objectivity, *American Journal of Sociology*, No.77 pp 660-679

Tumber, Howard and Palmer, Jerry (2004) *Media at war: The Iraq crisis*, London: Sage

Westerståhl, Jörgen (1983) Objective news reporting, *Communication Research*, No. 10 pp 403-424

Williams, Kevin (1987) Vietnam: the first living-room war, in Mercer, Derrick, Mungham, Geoff, Williams, Kevin (eds) *The Fog of War: The Media on the Battlefield*, London: Heinemann pp 213-260

Žižek, Slavoj (1989) *The sublime object of ideology*, London: Verso

Chapter Nine

Keeping the Peace:
Media Representations of the Anti-Gulf War Movement in the British Press

Chris Atton

Introduction: mediatizing protest

News media have tended to portray social movement activists as marginal to wider political processes, often trivializing their methods and constructing them as deviant. These representations present a reductive focus on participants as troublemakers, emphasizing violence, incoherence and criminality (for example, Ashley and Olson 1998; Gitlin 1980; Halloran et al. 1970; van Zoonen 1992). The mass support for anti-war protests in the UK (against the invasion of Iraq) in 2003 and 2006 brought together a 'rainbow coalition' of trades unionists, church members, NGOs, non-aligned activists and members of political parties that would lead us to expect a shift in normative depictions of protest away from the standard frames of deviance and conflict towards ones that emphasized consensus and normalization. Mobilizations such as Globalize Democracy, Jubilee 2000, Make Poverty History and various G8 summit protests have also exhibited this catholic mix. Has the news media been able to address this shift in protest activity? To what extent is it still bound by the enduring framing devices that marginalize protest except under conditions of 'professionalization' (for example, the PR successes of large, international NGOs such as Greenpeace and Friends of the Earth)?

The recent history of the peace movement has seen it move from a narrow, specialist interest social movement to one that is able to mobilize millions of citizens internationally, cutting across nation-states, class and political affiliation through a variety of strategies. How have the news media responded to this new complexity of protest within a peace movement that is diverse and networked, yet apparently internally coherent and focused on common aims? This chapter will explore these issues through a comparative examination of British national press coverage of the anti-war protests of February 2003 (before the invasion of Iraq) and March 2006 (on the third anniversary of the invasion).

Media representations of protest

There are few studies of the media coverage of anti-war protests. Two remain central to the field; both deal with protests and demonstrations against the Vietnam War. Halloran et al.'s analysis (1970) of the media coverage of the 1968 London demonstration set the agenda for numerous studies of protest and social movements. It found that media coverage emphasized 'forms of action to the neglect of underlying causes' (Murdock 1981: 210); that activism was equated with violence; and that the political content of the demonstration was ignored. The consistency of coverage across 'quality' and popular titles and across political allegiance was largely due to the ideological closure of the demonstration as an event that could be described as 'objective' and hard news, rather than as a complex of political actions requiring interpretation.

Gitlin's analysis (1980) of the media coverage of the anti-Vietnam activities of the Students for a Democratic Society (SDS) found a similar focus on the event at the expense of explanation. Applying Goffman's (1974) frame analysis method, he found that negative coverage of the movement was achieved through many devices, including trivialization, marginalization and disparagement (quantitatively by under-counting numbers on demonstrations and qualitatively by questioning the effectiveness of the SDS).

Both studies explored the impact of journalistic practices on the coverage. Gitlin paid close attention to the dominance of elite and official sources in news reports; the use of delegitimizing quotation marks when reporting SDS spokespeople and the emphasis on the rhetoric of violence. Halloran et al. focused on broader, ideological consensus of the political elite and the socialization of journalists to produce stories that fit with this consensus.

These two studies remain the classic models for analyses of the mediatization of demonstration and protest. Their conclusions continue to be replicated in many subsequent studies of media representations, for example, of the women's movement (Ashley and Olson 1998; van Zoonen 1992). Studies of the representation of ethnic minorities have found similar dominant themes of marginalization, trivialization and deviance, and the framing of action through discourses of violence, fanaticism and criminality (Cottle 2000; Fowler 1991; van Dijk 1991; Poole 2002; Richardson 2004). Of particular relevance to the present study are the studies of British newspaper coverage of Muslims since the terrorist attacks of 11 September; the dominant findings show significant negativity towards Muslims (Poole and Richardson 2006).

Whilst in general, studies are critical of the media's tendency to focus on internal dissent, more recent social movement studies have identified the emergence of global, coalition-based movements such as Globalize Democracy, Make Poverty History and Jubilee 2000 (Mayo 2005). These movements differ from the largely student-based movements of the 1960s in three important ways. First, coalition movements of the 1990s and 2000s draw on an extremely wide range of groups and organizations, including political parties, trades unions, faith groups and NGOs. Second, no longer is protest considered the province of the young radical: we see 'the emergence of a class of ordinary citizens who increasingly see the sites of their political action as ranging from local to global' (Bennett 2003: 27). Drawing on the work of Mittleman (2000), Bennett argues that the collective nature of such activism is less rooted in the membership of ascribed social groups than in 'individual choices of social network' (op cit: 31).

Finally, because many of the issues around which coalition movements organize do not proceed from ascribed social group membership, social justice issues like debt, poverty and the environment are able to attract commitment even from those who might not consider themselves as 'activists'. Social movement theory has addressed this through a critique of collective identity. Rather than seeking to explain new social movements by static notions of 'identity politics' and 'common traits', globalized protests may be better understood as the dynamic 'public experience of self' and as 'a shared struggle for personal experience' (McDonald 2002: 125).

There is evidence of a shift towards portrayals that approach this complexity, for example in liberal newspapers such as the *Guardian* (Atton 2002). Here, though, the representation is filtered through the reliance on the classic primary definers (representatives of elite groups), at times supplemented by 'expert' eyewitness testimony from journalists themselves. Similarly Bennett et al. (2004) found that media coverage of the World Economic Forum meetings and protests was dominated by elite sources. Rojecki's (2002) study of the protests in Seattle in 1999 against the World Trade Organization finds that mass media coverage of the demonstrations took into account the diversity amongst protesters. Gitlin's study, however, argued that coverage of divergent approaches within SDS activities was evidence of the mass media's emphasis on dissent (and, therefore, incoherence) within the movement. Rojecki shows that 'the range of views in the news and the commentaries was as wide as that expressed by the protesters themselves' (ibid: 166). For Rojecki, this shift is explained primarily by the erosion of state sovereignty in a globalized world, which results in conflict and dissent within political elites. It is important to note, however, that Rojecki's findings are not borne out by other studies of Seattle (Boykoff 2006; McFarlane and Hay 2003). Nevertheless, Rojecki's arguments and findings offer a potentially useful avenue through which to revisit the media framing of protests, taking into account political-economic factors as well as professional, media-economic considerations.

As elite dissensus develops, so journalistic practice is able to take critical advantage of it. In terms of Hallin's (1986) model of the three spheres of practice, this is to move the elite agenda from the sphere of consensus to that of legitimate controversy. As political reporting moves to controversy and interpretation in response to the fracturing of elite consensus, we might see a similar shift in the journalistic response to public protest.

Moreover, as protest activities become more populous with a heterogeneous membership, so the likelihood grows that protesters will be drawn from mass media audiences. Media depictions of protest are likely to move away from the standard frames of deviance and conflict (Hallin's sphere of deviance) to ones of 'legitimate controversy'. Editorial accounts would, thus, become sensitive to the convergence of elite dissensus and public consensus: the former enabling critical journalism based more on interpretation than on fact-gathering, the latter taking account of its audience's stance even where this might conflict with editorial stance. To study the mass media in this way is 'to look not for reality, but for purposes which underlie the strategies of creating one reality instead of another' (Molotch and Lester 1974: 111).

However, this is not say that the strategies of representing the 'non-activist' or the 'ordinary' protester are not themselves circumscribed by conventions of media representation. Langer (1998) has shown how the 'ordinary' is typically constructed as a type of celebrity. The 'celebrityhood' of ordinary people derives from their achievement of remarkable results in the face of adversity. According to Langer, they tend to be located within a story 'constellation' that emphasizes the overturning of expectations: how the 'unremarkable' may be capable of extraordinary achievements. The ordinary actors in such stories are considered as heroic in a sense, achieving remarkableness ('celebrityhood') through their own achievements and their mastery of their world.

Methodology

A study of media representations of contemporary protest needs to take into account the characteristics of coalition protest and to identify the extent to which media representation takes account of those characteristics. The inclusiveness of a coalition and the normalization of the politics of protest might be reflected in the forms of media representation. This could be prompted by editorial awareness of public opinion and specifically of a readership's attitudes. This is shown in Tumber and Palmer's (2004) study of newspaper coverage of the pre-invasion phase of Gulf War Two. Around the time of the February 2003 anti-war protests, even those newspapers whose editorial stance was pro-war recognized the strength of feeling against the war amongst their own readers. Whilst Tumber and Palmer's study was not concerned with coverage of the protests themselves, they suggest that this recognition may explain 'a substantial part of the negative coverage of US policy found in these [hitherto pro-war] titles' (ibid: 87).

On the other hand, Robinson et al.'s (2006) study of British media coverage of the war found that 'controversial issues such as… anti-war protest accounted for considerably less than 10 per cent of news stories' (ibid:. 24). The authors establish that anti-war protesters also had much less access to the media (both as direct and indirect sources) than other political actors, such as members of the government and the military. Robinson has also noted that media coverage of the anti-war movement was 'much more positive prior to the conflict' (cited in Bhattacharyya 2006). However, the 2006 study found that the marginalization of 'substantive' issues such as discussion of the rationale for war meant that this coverage focused on the events, rather than the reasons behind the protests.

The present study examines press coverage of two anti-Gulf War protests across British broadsheet and tabloid titles. The first protest took place on Saturday, 15 February 2003, before the invasion of Iraq, and has been assessed as an 'historic, unprecedented global peace protest' in more than 600 cities in over 60 countries (Simonson 2003: 13). The second occurred on Saturday, 18 March 2006, on the third anniversary of the invasion. These protests have been chosen because of the comparisons they offer in their relative political and military contexts. The 2003 protest falls within the 'pre-invasion' phase of the war, with that of 2006 firmly within the post-invasion phase. These contexts are significant in terms of elite consensus and dissensus, as well as in terms of public opinion. Both factors, as we have already seen, might well help to shape the media's framing of events.

To obtain a representative spread across political allegiance, sector and editorial position on the war the following titles were chosen:

Independent on Sunday (anti-war)
News of the World (pro-war)
Scotland on Sunday (pro-war)
Sunday Express (pro-war)
Sunday Herald (anti-war)
Sunday Mail (Glasgow edition) (anti-war)

Sunday Mirror (anti-war)
Sunday Telegraph (pro-war)
Sunday Times (pro-war).

Press coverage of each protest was restricted to the day immediately following it (the Sunday papers of, respectively, 16 February 2003 and 19 March 2006). To contextualize each paper's stance toward the protests a small number of sample articles were selected from a wider period (both before and after the two weekends). These additional articles are not used in the following analysis. The coverage of the 2003 and 2006 protests was analysed quantitatively and qualitatively. These methods bring together themes derived from the findings of previous studies of social movement protests and those particular to the newspaper coverage of the Iraq conflict undertaken by Tumber and Palmer (2004).

First, the analysis focused on contextualization. Tumber and Palmer, in their more general analysis of media coverage of the Iraq crisis, found that during the pre-invasion phase left-wing titles gave more space to reporting than did right-wing titles. Comparing sectors, they also found that tabloid coverage emphasized 'hard news values', focusing on 'the major facts of any sets of events', whereas the broadsheets presented 'the maximum possible background and analytic material' (ibid: 81). These findings suggest that, contrary to previous studies of protest coverage, we might find strong evidence of contextualization in the broadsheet sector.

Second, the analysis looked for evidence (or its absence) of the 'classic' themes of protest coverage:

- trivialization;
- marginalization;
- disparagement by numbers (under-counting);
- disparagement by questioning the effectiveness of the protest;
- delegitimization through use of quotation marks;
- focus on event rather than context;
- equation of protest with violence;
- sourcing practices that emphasize elite groups;
- negative lexical indicators ('riot,' 'disturbance');
- homogenization of protesters.

Sunday, 16 February 2003: contextualization and extent

By the time of the protests, the British press had been reporting and commenting extensively on the arguments, purposes and rationale for war against Iraq. On the day following the protests we still find this: none of the titles in the sample restricts itself only to coverage of the demonstrations. However, there is little detailed context in either the reports of the protests or the editorial and comment pieces. The anti-war papers contain the largest number of articles and the greatest range. The *Sunday Mirror* contains nine articles: five report on the protests in the UK and worldwide under the umbrella heading of 'The people's march' (around 6,000 words); others include a report on Prime

Minister Tony Blair's conference speech in Glasgow, a personal account of the London march and an editorial.

The pro-war titles offer the least coverage. The *News of the World* gives a little under 1,000 words to the demonstrations but, despite its stance, publishes an anti-war comment piece by Alex Salmond, the former leader of the Scottish National Party. Generally, coverage is leanest in the pro-war titles, but the *Independent on Sunday* (anti-war) devotes less than a 1,000 words to its coverage. Conversely, the pro-war *Scotland on Sunday* contains the largest number of articles (12), including an editorial and three opinion pieces. Despite the lack of context in the papers, arguments and rationale are explored in the reports themselves, almost entirely in the words of the protesters. We shall turn to these later, but first we shall examine more general representations of the protesters.

The Protesters: homogenization and diversity

All reports of the protests note the diversity amongst the participants to varying degrees. This is most apparent in reports of the marches in the UK and Ireland by staff writers. As the most populous, the marches in London, Glasgow, Belfast and Dublin are given the greatest attention. We can assume that reliance on agency reports for other countries largely prevented the observational detail necessary to makes claims about the composition of the demonstrations. In its coverage of the Belfast march, *The Sunday Times* displays only 'moderate' indicators of diversity, emphasizing the range of organizations involved: trades unions, churches and 'left wing organizations'. It notes 'a marked absence of mainstream political figures', a theme developed in its report on the Dublin march, the appeal of which 'went well beyond the left-wing activists who organized it'. In addition to 'politicians, celebrities and entertainers,' the paper finds a 'mix of generations': a mother with her son and grandchildren; a 24-year-old student; a father and daughter. In Rome, the protesters range 'from pensioners to dreadlocked teenagers'. The paper's pro-war stance is shared by *Scotland on Sunday*, but here, too, we see diversity acknowledged:

> Muslims and Christians, pot-smoking youths and smartly-dressed pensioners, punks, hardened activists and families from the suburbs ('Anti-war voices unite for protest' p. 5).

The paper finds this composition novel: 'an incongruous collection of doctors, students, teachers, manager, pensioners and parents with young children'. It is amongst the anti-war papers, perhaps predictably, where we find the greatest emphasis on diversity. In these cases it sits besides unity and solidarity: the cause is held in common, despite the variety of backgrounds, ages, professions and political allegiance. The *Independent on Sunday* describes the protest in Rome as 'a dazzlingly colorful tide of people… uniting monks and nuns, communists and anarchists and hundreds of thousands of ordinary Italians'.

The *Sunday Mirror* finds the London march populated by 'worried mums and dads of all ages, all races and religions'. Religious and ethnic diversity is noted throughout the papers, both pro- and anti-war. This is particularly notable in the coverage of the Belfast and Dublin marches, both of which are seen to cross the sectarian divide. All the papers find some space (if not a large amount) to point out representatives from Muslim and

Middle Eastern communities. The *Sunday Herald* calls the London demonstration 'the most ethically and socially diverse march Britain has ever seen'.

Amongst the anti-war papers (and, to a lesser degree, amongst the pro-war titles) there is an emphasis on first-time protesters. The *Sunday Mirror* devotes a report to these 'protest virgins' who were 'middle-class, middle-aged, politely-mannered and jolly angry'. A headline in the *Sunday Mail* runs: 'Auntie war protest: ordinary folk call for peace.' Despite acknowledging the various politicians and entertainers taking part or speaking at rallies, the protest is consistently presented as 'ordinary'. The pro-war *Sunday Telegraph* identifies the presence of 'many "hard-left" groups' but emphasizes the 'tens of thousands of "moderate" protesters' in London. The *Sunday Mirror* calls it 'the people's march' and the 'people's revolt'; the *Sunday Mail* writes of 'people power' and of the confluence of people who 'in their everyday lives... probably had little in common'. *Scotland on Sunday* reports that '[p]rotester after protester said they had never been on an anti-war rally before'.

Disparagement and demonization

These 'millions of ordinary citizens' (*Independent on Sunday*) are depicted as coming together in a show of solidarity that prompts rather obvious descriptors across all the papers, such as 'rainbow coalition'. The 'ordinary' and 'moderate' composition of the protests seems to prevent reports that present the protesters as deviant. The protests are uniformly presented as taking place in 'carnival atmosphere' (another popular phrase). There is a marked absence of coverage that focuses on violence, which is unusual for protest coverage. The papers unanimously agree that the UK protests passed off peacefully, with few arrests. *The Sunday Times* offers a typical account from Dublin: 'police... were hugely outnumbered but they need not have worried'.

Sources for these assessments comprise reporters' eyewitness accounts and police spokespeople. There is, therefore, little that is negative to report though, as Gitlin (1980) and Halloran et al. (1970) have shown, such an absence has not prevented media coverage of previous protests emphasizing violent incidents, however minor. The breaking of shop windows and the throwing of a petrol bomb by 'anarchists' at the demonstration in Rome is briefly mentioned by all papers in their round-ups of protests across the world, but nowhere is this headline news. By contrast, many of the papers highlight how the protests 'helped bridge bitter ethnic rivalries' (*Sunday Times*) and 'cross-community action' (*Independent on Sunday*) in Bosnia and Cyprus.

Even though the protests disrupted travel across the cities where protests took place, this is never emphasized negatively: 'the centre of the capital was paralyzed by noisy but peaceful people from many political backgrounds' (*Sunday Telegraph*). Only one paper (*The Sunday Times*) details security measures. In its brief coverage of a demonstration in South Africa, it itemizes the police's use of 'sharpshooters' and 'radiation detectors'. The only disruption that features consistently in the coverage of the UK protests is that suffered on the rail network. This is of particular interest to the papers in Scotland, where many protesters were unable to travel from Edinburgh to the Glasgow march.

Even in the anti-war titles the representations of the protests, the protesters and their aims are, at the very least, classically objective, in that they appear to present factual accounts of the events. The congruence between the anti-war and pro-war titles seems to confirm this. The sincerity of the protesters is never doubted, neither is the seriousness of the issue. There is no evidence of disparagement in any of the news coverage. Only in an editorial does the pro-war *News of the World* write of 'knee-jerk rent-a-mob agitators like Tony Benn and Ken Livingstone', whom the paper compares unfavorably to the 'many sincere protesters'.

Gitlin (1980) has shown how media reports might also disparage by under-counting the numbers of protesters in a demonstration. This tactic is entirely absent from the coverage of the 2003 protests, even in the pro-war titles. The papers are in agreement that many of the protests are the largest ever seen, particularly those in the UK. In all reports of the UK marches, estimates are presented both from the marches' organizers and from the police. As is typical in this method, police figures are significantly lower. The *Sunday Telegraph* headlines: 'One million march against war' in London, whilst quoting an official figure in its story of 750,000. It points out that police officers 'privately said that the total appeared certain to have reached at least one million'. In the anti-war papers the numbers for the protests in the UK and Ireland are presented emphatically: they are 'staggering... massive' (*Sunday Mirror*) and 'three times bigger than predicted' (*Sunday Mail*). The *Sunday Herald* calls the police estimate for the London march 'simply risible'. The *Sunday Mirror* headlines '5m in worldwide demo' and the *Independent on Sunday* cites organizers' claims of three million in Rome alone.

Sourcing practices

All papers employ elite sourcing practices in their coverage of the demonstrations in the UK and Ireland. In all cases (except for the use of police sources and the occasional transport spokesperson), sources are drawn from those participants in the demonstrations and speakers at the rallies. These include politicians, city officials (such as the Lord Provost of Glasgow and the Mayor of London), representatives of the Stop The War Coalition and the many entertainers and other celebrities who were present. In those papers with briefer coverage (mostly the pro-war titles), members of these categories are used either exclusively or most frequently. The *News of the World*, for example, only quotes rock musician Damon Albarn and a protest organizer from those present in London.

In its coverage of the Dublin march, *The Sunday Times* quotes singer Christy Moore and one of the protest's organizers. Some anti-war titles use a similar approach. The *Sunday Herald* devotes 2,250 words to the opinions and arguments of 25 'prominent Scots from all walks of life', including writers, lawyers, politicians and academics. The *Sunday Mirror*'s lengthy piece (almost 1,200 words) on r'n'b singer Ms Dynamite is largely an interview with her about her reasons for marching and performing in London. The piece continues with quotes from Tony Benn (veteran socialist), Mo Mowlam (then Labour MP, critical of the build-up to war), Michael Foot (former Labour leader), Charles Kennedy (Liberal Democrat leader), Bruce Kent (of the Campaign for Nuclear Disarmament) and Ken Livingstone (Mayor of London). In this case, however, the piece is only one of several on the paper's news pages. In the others there are numerous quotes from 'ordinary' protesters.

As we have seen, all the papers characterize the protests in terms of the significant presence of 'ordinary' and 'moderate' protesters. Most of the titles also note that many of these protesters are taking part in a demonstration for the first time. This is an important feature for all the papers and is displayed by the use of quotations from these participants. The content of these quotations is, arguably, less important than their presence. The opinions expressed add little to those of the primary sources, which, in turn, add little to the arguments rehearsed in the previous months. Motifs across all titles include: the experience of first-time protest; the motivation to join the protest; and the commitment to the protest for the sake of others, whether for the Iraqi people or for the speakers' own friends and family. They offer little deep insight but cumulatively 'humanize' what otherwise might have been a rather arid presentation of numbers, occupations, locations and family relationships.

This practice occurs most frequently in the anti-war papers. The *Sunday Mirror* clusters these sources together in its reports. Its reports from Dublin and Glasgow each feature four 'ordinary sources'. Personal details are provided; these indicate a wide range of occupations, ages and geographic locations. This method is consistent across the other anti-war papers. The placement of these sources alongside elite sources lends credibility to their 'ordinariness'. The language and arguments used by both are similar. There is a sense of unanimity, of a public protest that is representative of society at large. There is no evidence in any of the news reports of delegitimization, scepticism or marginalization. These practices appear only in the editorial, comment and opinion pages of the pro-war papers. Rather than finding protesters homogenized and stereotyped, we find their diversity acknowledged, their views recorded in some detail.

Sunday, 19 March 2006

Three years later, the extent of coverage is very different. The estimated numbers for the London march are substantially lower than those for 2003 (all papers cite the police estimate of 15,000 and the organizers' estimate of 80,000 to 100,000). There is no coverage of the three-year anniversary marches in three of the nine papers in the sample (*Sunday Express*, *Sunday Telegraph* and *The Sunday Times*). In its foreign news section, *The Sunday Times* notes American polls that show the unpopularity of President Bush over his conduct of the war. *Scotland on Sunday* and the *Sunday Mail* similarly embed news of the protests in their news stories about then-Defense Secretary John Reid's assessment of anti-war protesters as 'aiding terrorism' and 'disgraceful.' The *Independent on Sunday* notes the protests briefly in a special report on Iraq 'three years on', which examines the claims of success in Iraq made by Reid, Tony Blair and President Bush. A sidebar to this article quotes anti-war 'voices', amongst them a Stop The War Coalition organizer, a 'student marcher' and a labourer in Kirkuk.

Only three papers publish specific reports of the marches. The *Sunday Herald* presents some 500 words opposite its report on John Reid. This focuses on the London demonstration and briefly covers protests in other countries. Its sources are few: it quotes an organizer ('wonderful'); Tony Benn; and an 'ordinary' protester ('Naomi Sly, 20, who had traveled from Leicester for the protest'). The *Sunday Mirror*'s report of around 150 words mentions only the London rally (it too quotes Benn); the second half of the article is taken up with John Reid's comments and a final paragraph about the latest US military casualties in Iraq. Finally, the *News of the World* prints a 37-word report ('War march is global protest') with no quotes. The only sources are organizers and police (both estimating numbers for the London march). The size of the protests may have reduced their newsworthiness. The limited coverage (at least compared to the overall coverage in 2003) of the 2006 marches can also be explained by the presence of other articles in some papers. The *Sunday Herald* features an 'Iraq eyewitness' column and an examination of the deaths of British soldiers in Iraq by the paper's diplomatic editor. *Scotland on Sunday* devotes two pages (including a 'picture essay') to answer the question: 'Three years on and was it really worth it?'

Conclusion

We have seen that, in the press coverage of the 2003 protests, the mobilization of public opinion against the war was recognized by all papers, regardless of political allegiance, sector or editorial stance on the war. Coverage of the anti-war movement is far from the generally negative representations identified by previous social movement studies. The strength of public opinion – cutting across political, social and cultural lines – is expressed through emphases on 'ordinary' protesters. Readers might well see themselves – or those similar to them – represented in the reports. Therefore, for the pro-war titles, reports are held in tension to maintain an editorial stance towards the war without alienating readers. This confirms the findings of Tumber and Palmer (2004). The analysis also clearly shows the convergence between elite dissensus and public consensus. The coverage of the 2003 protests highlights the heterogeneous nature of the protesters, their 'ordinariness' – protest becomes normalized as a public practice, not merely the preserve of an expert culture of 'activists'. This is to shift significantly both protesters and their representation from the status of deviancy to one of legitimacy.

Nevertheless, there is a significant 'remarkableness' to this representation: protesters are portrayed as 'ordinary heroes'. They are transformed into celebrities of the everyday by a process similar to that described by Langer. Moreover, the transformation occurs within specific, transient events. There is more than a whiff of the spectacle about this. The absence of any substantive presentation of the issues underlying the protests suggests that, as Robinson et al. have shown, press coverage is driven by the remarkable nature of the events and not by the significance of their underlying rationale. This argument may also be applied to the coverage of the 2006 protests, if in an apparently contradictory way. The spectacular representation of an event depends to a large degree on its novelty. If the newsworthiness of the 2003 protests resided largely in the 'remarkable ordinariness' of the demonstrators, then their recurrence three years later would hardly be news. Neither were the numbers of protesters high enough to trigger the statistical hyberbole of 2003.

These factors not only marginalize the 2006 protests, they call into question the apparent shift in press coverage of the protests three years earlier. If this coverage was largely prompted by news values familiar to us from other forms of reporting (the spectacle, the heroic in the ordinary), then was it truly exceptional? Was it not instead simply perpetuating a common representation of ordinary people as heroes? It might well challenge dominant and chronic representations of protest, but does it signal any fundamental shift in those representations? The coverage of the 2006 protests suggests that it does not.

By the time of the 2006 protests, elite dissensus was perhaps more acute; insurgency within Iraq showed no signs of abating; the Hutton Inquiry (into the BBC's coverage of the run-up to the invasion) and the death of Dr David Kelly (Andrew Gilligan's source for his controversial Radio 4 report on the government's WMD claims) had reinvigorated the debate over the reasons for going to war; there were frequent calls for withdrawal and regular criticism of the actions of US forces (such as those at the Abu Ghraib prison in Baghdad). The post-invasion phase was characterized by the movement of opposition to the war into the mainstream. At this point the coverage of Iraq was itself 'normalized'. The papers carried daily reports, comment and opinion on all aspects of the crisis – military, economic, humanitarian, religious, social and cultural. The war was over, but the crisis was not. The press were examining the everyday lives of Iraqis, providing death tolls on a daily basis and continuously critiquing the strategies and tactics of the Allies and the Iraqis. Against this normalization of the Iraq crisis, it should come as no surprise that the protests of 2006 provide only a minor sidelight.

References

Ashley, Laura and Olson, Beth (1998) Constructing Reality: Print Media's Framing of the Women's Movement, 1966-1986, *Journalism and Mass Communication Quarterly*, Vol. 75, No. 2 pp 263-277

Atton, Chris (2002) News Cultures and New Social Movements: Radical Journalism and the Mainstream Media, *Journalism Studies*, Vol. 3, No. 4 pp 491-505

Bennett, W. Lance (2003) New Media Power: The Internet and Global Activism, in Couldry, Nick and Curran, James (eds) *Contesting Media Power: Alternative Media in a Networked World*, Lanham: Rowman and Littlefield pp 17-37

Bennett, W. Lance, Pickard, Victor W., Iozzi, David P., Schroeder, Carl L., Lagos, Taso, Caswell, C. Evans (2004) Managing the Public Sphere: Journalistic Construction of the Great Globalization Debate, *Journal of Communication*, Vol. 54, No. 3 pp 437-455

Bhattacharyya, Anindya (2006) Iraq and the information war, Socialist Worker online, 2 December. Available online at: www.socialistworker.co.uk/article.php?article_id=10230, accessed on 15 January 2007

Boykoff, Jules (2006) Framing Dissent: Mass-Media Coverage of the Global Justice Movement, *New Political Science*, Vol. 28, No. 2 pp 201-228

Cottle, Simon (2000) *Ethnic Minorities and the Media: Changing Cultural Boundaries*, Milton Keynes: Open University Press

Fowler, Roger (1991) *Language in the News: Discourse and Ideology in the Press*, London: Routledge

Gitlin, Todd (1980) *The Whole World is Watching: Mass Media in the Making and Unmaking of the New Left*, Los Angeles and London: University of California Press

Goffman, Erving (1974) *Frame Analysis: An Essay on the Organization of Experience*, New York: Harper and Row

Hallin, Daniel C. (1986) *The 'Uncensored' War: The Media and Vietnam*, New York: Oxford University Press

Halloran, James, Elliott, Philip and Murdock, Graham (1970) *Demonstrations and Communication: A Case Study*, London: Penguin

Langer, John (1998) *Tabloid Television: Popular Journalism and the 'Other News'*, London: Routledge

McDonald, Kevin (2002) From Solidarity to Fluidity: Social Movements beyond 'Collective Identity' – The Case of Globalization Conflicts, *Social Movement Studies*, Vol. 1, No. 2 pp 109-128

McFarlane, Thomas and Hay, Iain (2003) The Battle for Seattle: Protest and Popular Geopolitics in the *Australian* Newspaper, *Political Geography*, Vol. 22, No. 2 pp 211-232

Mayo, Marjorie (2005) 'The World Will Never Be the Same Again'? Reflecting on the Experiences of Jubilee 2000, Mobilizing Globally for the Remission of Unpayable Debts, *Social Movement Studies*, Vol. 4, No. 2 pp 139-154

Mittleman, James H. (2000) *The Globalization Syndrome: Transformation and Resistance*, Princeton: Princeton University Press

Molotch, Harvey and Lester, Marilyn (1974) News as Purposive Behaviour: On the Strategic Use of Routine Events, Accidents and Scandals, *American Sociological Review*, Vol. 39 pp 101-112

Murdock, Graham (1981) Political Deviance: The Press Presentation of a Militant Mass Demonstration, in Cohen, Stanley and Young, Jock (eds) *The Manufacture of News: Deviance, Social Problems and the Mass Media*, London: Constable pp 206-225

Poole, Elizabeth (2002) *Reporting Islam: Media Representations of British Muslims*, London: I.B. Tauris

Poole, Elizabeth and Richardson, John E. (eds) (2006) *Muslims and the News Media*, London: I.B. Tauris

Richardson, John E. (2004) *(Mis)Representing Islam: The Racism and Rhetoric of British Broadsheet Newspapers*, Amsterdam: John Benjamins

Robinson, Piers et al. (2006) *Media Wars: News Media Performance and Media Management during the 2003 Iraq War*, ESRC Research Report No. RES-000-23-0551, Swindon: Economic and Social Research Council

Rojecki, Andrew (2002) Modernism, State Sovereignty and Dissent: Media and the New Post-Cold War Movements, *Critical Studies in Media Communication*, Vol. 19, No. 2 pp 152-171

Simonson, Karin (2003) *The Anti-war Movement: Waging Peace on the Brink Of War*, Geneva: Centre for Applied Studies in International Negotiations

Tumber, Howard and Palmer, Jerry (2004) *Media at War: The Iraq Crisis*, London: Sage

van Dijk, Teun A. (1991) *Racism and the Press*, London: Routledge

van Zoonen, Elisabeth A. (1992) The Women's Movement and the Media: Constructing a Public Identity, *European Journal of Communication*, Vol. 7 pp 453-476

Part III:

Military Communication of War

CHAPTER TEN

WESTERN AND TERRORIST WAYS OF WAR

MARTIN SHAW

For over seven years the United States has been occupying the lands of Islam in the holiest of places, the Arabian Peninsula, plundering its riches, dictating to its rulers, humiliating its people, terrorizing its neighbors and turning its bases in the Peninsula into a spearhead through which to fight the neighboring Muslim peoples...All these crimes and sins committed by the Americans are a clear declaration of war on Allah, his messenger and Muslims. And ulema have throughout Islamic history unanimously agreed that the jihad is an individual duty if the enemy destroys the Muslim countries.

Statement by Osama Bin Laden and others, 23 February 1998

The deliberate and deadly attacks, which were carried out yesterday against our country, were more than acts of terror. They were acts of war...We'll be focused, and we will be steadfast in our determination. This battle will take time and resolve, but make no mistake about it, we will win.

President George W. Bush, 12 September 2001

Our war on terror begins with Al Qaeda, but it does not end there. It will not end until every terrorist group of global reach has been found, stopped and defeated.

President Bush, Address to a Joint Session of Congress and the American People, 20 September 2001

Your democratically elected governments continuously perpetuate atrocities against my people all over the world, and your support of them makes you directly responsible, just as I am directly responsible for protecting and avenging my Muslim brothers and sisters. Until we feel security, you will be our targets, and until you stop the bombing, gassing, imprisonment, and torture of my people, we will not stop this fight. We are at war, and I am a soldier. Now you too will taste the reality of this situation.

Mohammed Sadiq, London suicide bomber on 7 July 2005, in Al Qaeda video shown on Al Jazeera television, 1 September 2005

The contested language of 'war' in the early 21st century

A specific conflict, or 'war', between Al Qaeda and the United States can be traced back almost a decade, to the 1998 bombings of the US embassies in Nairobi and Dar-es-Salaam, and in a sense longer, to actions earlier in the 1990s in which Osama Bin Laden was implicated. In the minds of Bin Laden and his associates, the US had clearly provoked their 'jihad' with its military presence in Saudi Arabia and other 'aggressions' against Muslims. However, the US did not recognize this as 'war' until 9/11 prompted Bush's declarations. Since then this war has been mutually recognized, and the global 'war on terror' has been largely accepted as reality in the world's politics and media.

Yet it is striking that at every stage of this recent conflict the protagonists have felt the need to justify the idea of 'war', and there is a sense in their statements of pushing beyond the manifestly legitimate uses of the word. It is certain that the US never made the 'clear declaration of war on Allah, his messenger, and Muslims' that Bin Laden claimed. In 1991 it was defending the government of one Muslim country, at the latter's invitation, and its people, from the government of another Muslim country however illegitimate the resulting military presence appeared to some Saudis.

Clearly Al Qaeda did inflict the 9/11 atrocities as an act of war, and to that extent Bush was correct. Yet it was not clear how – except in the political impact and size of the death toll – these acts differed from other 'acts of terror'. In virtually all 'terrorist' campaigns, the bombers see themselves as waging war, but states usually *refuse* this label: for them 'terrorists' are normally criminals, not warriors. The fact that 9/11 manifestly constituted terrorism (in the sense of an armed campaign designed primarily to achieve its political goals by creating fear in a civilian population) and was criminal in US and international law, meant that Bush's labeling involved a radical *choice* of response, opting for 'war' over law enforcement as the defining framework of the US campaign.

Moreover Bush's targeting of 'terror' in general – not just Al Qaeda – made his war remarkably open-ended. The uncertainty of this designation remains; indeed it deepened once the global 'war on terror' was extended to the overthrow of the Saddam Hussein regime which, despite its many crimes, was hardly connected to global Islamist terrorism. That uncertainty remains on the Al Qaeda side, too, is reflected in the London suicide bomber's need to insist that he is a 'soldier', at 'war', since that claim would hardly seem credible to most Londoners on the receiving end of the attacks or, indeed, to many Muslims worldwide who would recognize it as an attack on civilians.

The ideologies of 'war' asserted by both Al Qaeda and the US administration remain, therefore, sharply contested despite the apparently mutual recognition (after 9/11) of the conflict's military character. Most Muslims reject the idea that their faith is involved in a generalized war with the US, and many elements of the population in Western states, including the US itself, are highly ambivalent about -- if not opposed to -- the global 'war on terror'. Major Western governments such as those of France and Germany opposed its extension to a conventional campaign against the Iraqi regime, while neither the Spanish nor even the British government responded to the terrorist attacks on their capitals by accentuating 'war' on terror. On the contrary, official responses in both countries designated the bombers as criminals and centered on police investigations. The latter were, in fact, quite successful in quickly apprehending those immediate perpetrators who had survived: in both countries, 'terrorists' were arrested, tried and convicted for their parts in these atrocities (as, indeed, was the one surviving perpetrator of 9/11).

Nevertheless, both Al Qaeda and the US persist in waging global 'wars' against each other. This fact obliges us to take seriously both the military character of the conflict and the highly contrasting – in the jargon, 'asymmetric' – forms of the two campaigns. Al Qaeda has not reflected publicly on the historic significance of its methods of war, although clearly they are a radical extension of those waged by many insurgent groups over the last century or more. Bush (2001), however, noted from the outset the novelty of this war for the US: 'This war will not be like the war against Iraq a decade ago, with a decisive liberation of territory and a swift conclusion. It will not look like the air war above Kosovo two years ago, where no ground troops were used and not a single American was lost in combat.' Although in a sense this statement was correct – clearly a campaign against a terrorist network had to be different in significant respects from one against a state – it also now appears ironic in that the 'war on terror' became a framework for a new war against the Iraqi state.

In reality both sides are operating within the common framework of global surveillance warfare that shapes all wars in the early twenty-first century, regardless of such secondary differences. Through examining how the new 'terrorist' and 'Western' ways of war respond to these changing general conditions of warfare, I shall argue that the terrorist way is, in the short term at least, *better adapted* to the new conditions than the Western. In the light of this argument, I shall question whether Bush, Tony Blair and others were wise to embrace 'war' as the answer to 'terrorism'.

The global surveillance mode of warfare[1]

To define a general framework within which to understand all warfare in the current period might seem ambitious. The range of armed actors seems enormous -- from the sole superpower lavishing trillions of dollars on ever more sophisticated weapons systems to local armed groups brandishing Kalashnikovs, with many gradations in between. After the Cold War, many accounts emphasized the development of 'new wars' centered in non-Western regions and involving fragmenting local states and militia (Kaldor 1999; Duffield 2001). Western involvement was seen primarily in terms of 'humanitarian intervention' in its many forms. Western *wars*, however, such as the Gulf War of 1991, seemed to be different. Yet these were not two different types of war. 'New wars' often led to Western 'interventions' which sometimes became 'new Western wars' (as over Kosovo). Likewise Western 'wars' generally required 'interventions' (policing, humanitarian aid, reconstruction) in their aftermaths and these, if unsuccessful, led to further messy phases of 'new war' (guerrilla war and counter-insurgency).

Western and non-Western warfare took place within the same environments: the same zones of war, the same social and political spaces in which armed force was used, and a common global political-military-media environment. And, as 9/11 showed, a minimally armed movement – a small group using knives to hijack civilian airliners – could launch a devastating attack on a superpower, turning the heart of its greatest city into a war zone. Thus it became clear that ultimately war is globally equalized: however asymmetric its modalities, the same conditions apply to all actors, only not in the same way.

The general conditions of warfare in a given era concern not just the types of armies, armaments and strategies that are adopted, but the type of relationships between military power and social relations in general. The rise of industrial capitalism in the nineteenth century gave rise to the mode of *industrialized total warfare* in the first half of the twentieth. This was based on direct, extensive mobilization of society for war, through mass conscription, labour-intensive war economies, state direction and totalizing ideologies. Mass media – newspapers, cinema, radio and later television – played crucial roles as mobilizing instruments, often directly state-controlled and utilized in a crudely instrumental and propagandistic way. The corollary of this form of mobilization was direct, extensive civilian targeting, as those whose labour and ideological support sustained the production of warfare also became its victims.

This mode of warfare became attenuated after the Second World War. However, as the development of nuclear and other high-technology weapons (many of them of mass destruction) made the mass mobilization side of total warfare increasingly redundant the mass targeting of civilians increased exponentially in the nuclear arms race. But this nuclear culmination of industrialized total warfare was also a dead end, since instantaneous total and mutual destruction was politically self-defeating. Nevertheless at lesser levels of destruction and in non-Western regions, total war conditions continued to have some purchase throughout the Cold War period, as indeed they have to some extent even today.

In general, however, there has been an increasing shift from direct mobilization to *indirect participation* by society in warfare. Increasingly armed actors rely on relatively highly trained, specialist forces rather than mass-participation or conscript armies. Instead of direct mass participation, popular war-participation is generally limited to the indirect legitimation of military leaders through elections, opinion polls, and other manifestations of support. And while in total war both combatant states and guerrilla movements achieved near-monopolies of surveillance in the territories they controlled, today all organized protagonists are subjected to much more *extensive and intensive, complex, multi-dimensional surveillance*, increasingly even within their 'own' territories – if they control any, which is not always the case with terrorist movements – and, even more, in the wider arenas of global society and politics. Global surveillance operates at a number of levels, through states, international institutions, international law, non-governmental organizations and social movements. All of these levels of surveillance, at global, regional, national and often local levels, operate to simultaneously *constrain and enable* new forms of war. Yet the most extensive forms of surveillance occur through globally diffused media coverage, and all the other forms of surveillance depend on media for much of their substance. It is through mass-mediated information that other elite institutions frame much of their own surveillance. By consuming television, press and Internet sources of news and opinion, too, wider populations participate in the surveillance of warfare.

Global surveillance in both these senses depends on the *transformations of media* in the twenty-first century. Contemporary media sources are typically competing and overlapping, through national, regional and global networks. Media as a whole can no longer be mobilized as vehicles for one-sided propaganda, as they often were in the twentieth century. Propaganda continues through partisan interventions and media (not least, the websites of states and armed organizations), but audiences increasingly have access to multiple and divergent sources. In these conditions, armed protagonists can no longer simply *produce* media coverage to conform to their political and military objectives; instead their principal concern is media *management*, influencing rather than controlling the content of a range of (more or less autonomous) media outlets.

In the conditions of any general mode of warfare, different armed actors practice distinctive *ways of war*. In conditions of total warfare, for example, democratic states, totalitarian states and guerrilla movements mobilized and targeted in distinctive ways, and individual armed actors were further distinguished. In conditions of global surveillance warfare, the same is true. The constraints on and possibilities for warmaking by democratic states, authoritarian states, local armed movements and global armed networks are radically different. The same general conditions impose different parameters on armed actors depending on how they are located within the global state system and global society and, of course, in the regional and national structures of these global arenas. The two types of actors with which we are concerned in this chapter – global terrorist networks and Western states – have both adapted more radically to the new conditions than have other actors such as major non-Western states and nationally based armed movements.[2] However terrorists and Western states are affected by the new conditions in more or less opposite ways. Examining each of their ways of war in turn will illuminate the asymmetric war in which they are involved, the strategic strengths and limitations of the two sides and the significance of media in contemporary warfare.

The new terrorist way of war

Since terrorism is distinguished from other forms of military action by the methodology of producing fear in civilian populations, it has always depended on spreading awareness of its actions (which directly affect relatively small numbers) among a larger target population. Certainly the production and magnification of fear – often among civilians as well as the armed enemy – are components of many military strategies, including those of the West. But in the hands of terrorists they become the sole, or at least predominant, method during a particular campaign.[3] And while knowledge of atrocities, and the resulting fear, spread very effectively even by word of mouth, mass media magnify them so much more quickly and effectively. Terrorism as we know it is pre-eminently a strategy of the age of mass media. Having first developed along with the press in the late nineteenth and early twentieth centuries, terrorism has reached new levels of both murderousness and symbolic impact in the twenty-first century age of global media.

Today it is possible for the actions of small groups of militants against a few hundred civilians to spread fear among hundreds of millions – not just in one country but across the emerging global society, across time as well as space. Since 9/11, almost every air passenger and resident of a capital city or other site of symbolic importance continues to experience, at some level, the fear generated by the attacks carried out by 19 militants on that autumn day in 2001. This fear has been reinforced by only a small number of further successful attacks. New York and Washington (2001), Istanbul (2003), Bali (2002 and 2005), Madrid (2004), London (2005): these sparingly distributed major atrocities of Islamist terrorism (to which must be added, however, the attacks on Western civilians in Iraq and the numerous plots against Western countries that have been thwarted) have spread their effects worldwide. What is striking about these actions – considered as the military acts that they are claimed to be – is their perpetrators' brazen embrace of murderousness against the unarmed. While Western militaries disavow violence against non-combatants – and even 'ethnic cleansers' routinely deny their genocidal violence – Islamist global terrorism spectacularly embraces civilian-killing, obliterating the distinction between combatant and non-combatant. In language that echoes the most extreme manifestations of fascism, it defines its war as a conflict of peoples rather than states or armed movements. Thus Ayman Al-Zawahiri (2005), Al Qaeda's second in command, hailed 'the blessed London raid, which came as a slap in the face to the conceited crusader British arrogance, and made it drink from the same cup from which it had long made the Muslims drink':

> This blessed raid, like its glorious predecessors in New York, Washington, and Madrid, brought the battle to the enemy's soil after long centuries in which the enemy brought the battle to our lands and after its legions and forces have occupied our lands in Chechnya, Afghanistan, Iraq, and Palestine, and after centuries in which it occupied our lands, while being secure in its home. Rejoice, oh peoples of the crusader coalition, in the calamities brought upon you and which, Allah willing, will be brought upon you by the policies of Bush, Blair, and those who follow them. Oh peoples of the crusader coalition, we have warned you, but it appears that you want us to make you taste the horrors of death. So taste some of what you made us taste.[4]

Certainly, closer inspection shows that these perpetrators still *understand* the civilian category, and consequently the need to *justify* its amalgamation into the armed enemy. Thus al-Zawahiri continued:

> We say to them that these civilians are the ones who pay taxes to Bush and Blair, so they can equip their armies and give aid to Israel, and they are the ones who serve in their armies and security services. They are the ones who elected them, and even those who did not vote for them consider them legitimate rulers who have the right to give them orders and must be obeyed, and who also have the right to order strikes against us, killing our sons and daughters, and to wage war in their name, and to kill Muslims on their behalf. Moreover, they consider disobeying their orders a crime punishable by law.

Yet such justifications are not advanced to convince the target populations. Islamist political strategy does not seek to persuade Western peoples ideologically, but through indiscriminate violence and its threat. The method of spectacular violence aims only to produce fear and disorientation that will in turn destabilize the enemy Western regimes.

Even in relation to the global Muslim audience, Islamist terrorists seek to persuade only a minority that is prepared to countenance this extreme violence against non-combatants, and these more complex justifications must be understood as produced for their benefit. For radical Islamism is an elitist, not a democratic, ideology. As long as there is a significant section of the Muslim population that will support – or merely condone – violence against Western civilians, thus providing ideological reinforcement and continued funding and recruitment for the armed groups, it does not really matter to Islamist terrorists if the majority continues to hold back from mass murder.

Its confidence in speaking for the truth of its tradition enables it to embrace slaughter, and its terrifying global media-political effects, where other equally death-producing late modern practices equivocate. In the long run, this approach may limit radical Islamism's political success; in any situation in which it needs more genuine majority support, even among Muslims, terrorism will be found wanting. Islamists will need to adapt their strategies and politics to succeed (rather as the Provisional IRA has done), if they are ever to appeal to majorities of Muslims. In the short term, however, spectacular slaughter creates an impressive illusion of power, at least among the minority of predominantly young men whom the movement needs to sustain its operations. This power is validated by the enormous effects that even relatively small actions have in the mass media – both the national media of affected states and the global media through which every terrorist action is comprehensively magnified and diffused to sympathetic minorities among Muslims everywhere. In this context it does not matter at all that these actions are almost universally condemned – this too is backhanded confirmation, easily picked up by sympathizers, of their power. Nor does it matter that the results of the actions are, literally, atrocious. Nothing is more symbolically powerful in the era of global human rights than bloody images of civilian massacre.

The new Western way of war

On the surface, the contemporary Western way of war is far better adapted to complex global surveillance than that of Islamist terrorism. Where the latter echoes the amalgamation of civilians and armed enemies that the West partly embraced in the era of total war, today's Western militarism is politically correct, adopting the post-1945 distinctions of international humanitarian law. Neither Iraqis nor Afghans as such were *enemies* for the Western armies that bombed and invaded their countries in 2001 and 2003 respectively. On the contrary the US and its allies claimed, with some credibility, to be *liberating* civilian populations from the repressive Taliban and Saddam Hussein regimes, just as in the 1990s they had helped liberate (predominantly Muslim) Bosnians and Kosovo Albanians from the grip of Serbian power.

In the new Western way of war, civilians are acknowledged as being killed or dying only through 'collateral damage' from bombs and other weapons targeted on strategic positions, or 'accidentally' as a result of targeting errors. Yet because Western wars are driven simultaneously by domestic political considerations as well as international objectives, greater priority is given to protecting the lives of Western military personnel than of civilians in war zones. Believing (after Vietnam) that electorates will tolerate only limited casualties among Western forces, governments tailor strategy towards 'force protection' rather than civilian protection. This leads to systematic, understood and in that sense intended transfers of risk from Western soldiers and aircrew towards the very civilians whose rights and liberties are proclaimed as one of the reasons for military action. In the world of global-surveillance, mediated warfare, the Western way of war can be defined as *risk-transfer war* (for further discussion, see Shaw 2005, especially Chapter 4).

This concept helps to explain the paradox that while US and other Western troops are directed to avoid predominantly civilian targets, and to discriminate between combatants and non-combatants in battle zones, substantial civilian casualties are a normal result of Western strategy, and its Achilles' heel in the ideological conflict with Islamism. In the 1991 Gulf War, for example, the numbers of *direct* civilian casualties from bombing was low relative to previous wars in which comparable amounts of explosive were dropped. Indeed the US was proud of its casualty record:

> The combination of stealth technology, PGMs [precision-guided missiles], and satellite-aided navigation allowed precision attack as never before. Despite dropping 88,000 tons of bombs in the 43-day air campaign, only 3,000 civilians died directly as a result of the attacks, the lowest number of deaths from a major bombing campaign in the history of warfare. A key factor in explaining this low number was that US pilots abided by strict rules of engagement that required them to return with their bombs if unable to positively identify their military targets. As the commander of the operation, General Norman Schwarzkopf said: 'We have been very, very careful in the direction of our attack to avoid

damage of any kind to civilian installations. It's going to happen; it's absolutely going to happen; there's no question about it, but we're doing everything we can to avoid it' (Rizer 2001).

Subsequent advances in 'precision' weaponry and strategy meant that even the more direct assault on the Iraqi capital in 2003 produced hardly any more immediate civilian casualties. However, in the context of the shorter campaign, as Carl Conetta pointed out (2003), the casualty *rates* for both military and civilians were higher than in 1991. Moreover the *perception* of low civilian casualties in the 1991 war rested on a very limited field of vision. There *were* large numbers of civilian dead, but these were *indirect* results of the US-led campaign: the results of the destruction of electricity supply, which in turn damaged water and sewage facilities; and of Saddam's repression of the Shi'ite and Kurdish rebellions precipitated by the US victory (for estimates of casualties, see Daponte 1993). In Iraq in 2003, the character of the US campaign meant that there was a greater tendency to produce direct civilian casualties: even in the 'major combat' phase, 'the portion of war fatalities that were civilian non-combatants may have been twice as great…almost 30 percent…versus almost 15 per cent' in the Gulf War; and at least as many if not more Iraqi non-combatants were killed, although the war lasted only 21 days compared to 42 in 1991 (Conetta 2003).

These outcomes were due to the objective for which the invasion was carried out: regime change. This dictated a much greater role (relatively speaking) for ground power and for combined arms warfare. And it dictated fighting in and near cities, producing at least two thousand non-combatant casualties in Baghdad alone. It also set the most demanding goal possible for ground forces and cast them into a conflict where the adversary's resistance was bound to be desperate. Thus 'although Operation Iraqi Freedom was supposed to exemplify the new warfare, it provides no unambiguous support for the hypothesis regarding civilian casualties. … the promise of a "low casualty" warfare will not be realized in practice if US strategic and operational objectives escalate in tandem with the advance of the new capabilities. Nor will the new warfare capabilities lead to an era of reduced conflict deaths if their promise serves as a rationale to wage more wars' (Conetta 2003).

After the years of inconclusive – even escalating – guerrilla war that have followed the US invasion of Iraq, this conclusion from 2003 seems like a serious understatement. Continuing US operations, not only in high-profile incidents like the clearing of Fallujah in 2004 but in countless smaller armed policing actions, have killed many thousands more civilians. The invasion, far from ending the threat of 'terrorism' in Iraq, opened the door to Islamist fighters who along with local armed 'resisters' based in the Sunni population have launched widespread direct attacks on the Shi'a and Kurdish civilian populations, as well as on US and new Iraqi forces. These attacks eventually resulted in extensive counter-attacks on Sunni civilians by Shi'ite armed groups. By the end of 2006, Iraq Body Count had recorded around 50,000 Iraqi deaths since 2003; although these may have included some combatants, many civilian deaths had also gone unrecorded.[5] A study based on excess mortality compared to the period before 2003 (Gilbert Burnham et al. 2006) estimated no fewer than 655,000 deaths. Although this study's methodology was criticized[6] it suggested increasingly catastrophic levels of casualties as a result of the many-sided war that followed the 2003 invasion.

Much of this 'body counting' in Iraq has been, I have argued, an attempt to intervene in the 'risk economy' of the war, to make civilian risks count.[7] And yet in the end it is not the statistics that matter most. In the mediated global surveillance environment of the war, individual incidents count more than overall figures. Just as terrorist spectaculars in Western cities, like the Madrid and London bombings, unsettle the whole political environment, and repeated terrorist massacres in Iraq constantly emblazon the US failure on global television screens, so the cases in which US forces are *seen* to harm civilians are most significant in dramatizing the moral and political credibility of their campaign.

Of course, the US military themselves understand this problem and civilian killings by occupation forces are under-filmed, under-reported and dwarfed in their Western political significance by terrorist massacres of civilians as well as killings of US and Iraqi troops and police. Terrorist attacks on journalists – more have been killed in Iraq than in any other recent war – also inhibit the reporting of US failures. Interestingly, compared to the Gulf War, in which the Ameriyya shelter bombing of 13 February 1991 was a high-profile example of the USA's killing of civilians, and the Kosovo War, in which the bombings of a train in southern Serbia and a refugee convoy in Kosovo (12 and 14 April 1999) itself were particularly embarrassing incidents for NATO, the Iraq War that began with the 1990 invasion of Kuwait has produced few really defining incidents. Even the two bombardments of Fallujah, in 2004 and 2005, failed to decisively damage the benign self-image of the US campaign in the eyes of its domestic public opinion.

Only the Abu Ghraib scandal of 2004, which concerned cruelty and torture rather than killing, comprehensively and unequivocally had this effect, magnified internationally by huge critical media coverage. Ironically it was still images supplied by the hand-held cameras of over-confident military perpetrators – rather than the efforts of professional reporters and photographers – which contributed this single most important 'blowback' to the US occupation.

The deeper irony of contemporary Western militarism is that its nominal embrace of civilian protection – in ideologies of liberation and human rights – opens the US and its allies to these contradictions. Both Islamist terrorists and Western forces practice small massacres – incidents involving tens and hundreds of victims (rather than the tens and hundreds of thousands of the ghastliest incidents of total war). But the Islamists who embrace mass murder, justifying it to their constituency, have an easier time than the Western leaders who regret and even (on occasion) apologize for it. As we have seen, Islamist terrorists obliterate the distinction of combatant and non-combatant, so that 'enemy' civilians are as much the enemy as any armed personnel. They can then celebrate their murders, the ideological calibration accentuating the shock of the attacks themselves, and providing a narrative that reinforces the visual impact of the televised results of their violence. Western leaders, on the other hand, can only hope to hide the victims of their violence, disconnect the harmful results from their intentions, and obfuscate the lines of responsibility. Having proclaimed the standard of liberation, rights and 'cleaner' war, they are fair game for any evidence to the contrary.

Moreover Western political and military institutions are much closer to the centers of global political, legal and media surveillance of war. For this reason their actions are liable to be scrutinized far more critically than those of their opponents. Even if the more craven sections of Western mass media evade this task and apologize for their governments, there are plenty in the more critical 'quality' press and public television arenas who will at least open up the issues. And for the burgeoning regional media of the non-Western world, on Al Jazeera and other channels, the mismatches of Western values and practices are easy targets. Moreover, Islamist propagandists are explicit in exploiting these contradictions. Simultaneously with their equation of military and civilian targets, they make an equation of their own and the West's civilian victims, justifying their own intentional killing of civilians by reference to the (however 'unintentional') killing of civilians by the West: 'If you don't stop your injustices, more and more blood will flow and these attacks will seem very small compared to what can occur in what you call terrorism.'[8]

For the practitioners of this way of war, intentions are of little relevance: what matters is that the West killed innocent members of their people. Deaths, whether accidental or intended, ended lives: and in the global media age they all add up to pictures of dead and mutilated bodies, which can be readily invoked by nationalist, Islamist and other ideologies to justify counter-killing. Thus are the 'accidental' civilian victims of Western bombing and counter-insurgency in Iraq, Afghanistan and elsewhere invoked by Osama Bin Laden and others to justify their own more deliberate killing of Western civilians.

Conclusion: the limitations of warfare for the contemporary West

The conventional wisdom of the global 'war on terrorism' is that the brutal, explicitly murderous strategy of global Islamist terrorism requires an equally brutal, determinedly military response. And certainly we need to be clear-headed about the seriousness of the threat to capital cities, civil aviation and some other arenas of contemporary Western society. However, my discussion suggests that *war* against this enemy is difficult to sustain. In the conditions of global media, political and legal surveillance, Western military action has become, and is always likely to be, embroiled in impossible contradictions. Arbitrary, 'accidental' killings of civilians are inevitable in modern war, especially given the preference of Western militaries for high-altitude and long-distance bombardments that reduce risks for their own personnel.

Certainly the failure to protect Western soldiers themselves may have more damaging short-term political consequences than any amount of harm to non-Western civilians. The figure of 3,000 US military deaths in Iraq was much more damaging to the Republicans in the November 2006 mid-term elections than the much larger (but uncertain) number of Iraqi civilian dead. Yet the remorseless, even if routinized, coverage of civilian casualties had created an overwhelming impression of the futility of the US role and therefore brought into question the value of US troops' own sacrifices. Thus risk-transfer war had shown itself capable of exposing Western leaders to political *risk-rebound*, while its role in legitimating Al Qaeda's assaults on Western cities threatened even more serious damages.

Yet the moral and political consequences for the West of its casual attitude to civilian casualties are still more profound. In the era of global media surveillance, war and human rights can be *seen* not to go together. States that attempt to combine them will neither win wars nor be credible upholders of human values. The West can follow the path of war – or if it really values humanity it must find other ways of upholding democracy and global order. It should leave war, along with the authoritarianism and brutality that generally belong with its practice, to its enemies who embrace them.

Notes

[1] This chapter relies heavily on Shaw (2005), Chapter 3
[2] In this chapter, therefore, I leave on one side the 'ways of war' of authoritarian and semi-authoritarian, often quasi-imperial states (such as China) and of local, including genocidal, armed movements. Although these are also increasingly affected by the conditions of global surveillance warfare I regard them as less thoroughly adapted, and generally still more influenced (than global terrorism or the West) by the old conditions of total warfare. See Shaw (2005: Chapter 3)
[3] However, organizations that practice terrorism are not necessarily *exclusively* terrorist. Thus Hamas's armed campaigns inside Israel, using suicide bombers against civilians, are clearly terrorist; yet it is also a political actor inside Palestine. Al Qaeda's armed campaigns inside the West are terrorist; but fighting alongside the Taleban in Afghanistan it is a more conventional guerrilla force
[4] Ayman al-Zawahiri (2005), comments on London bombings. Available online at: http://www.memri.org/bin/opener_latest.cgi?ID=SD97905, accessed 2 September 2005
[5] See http://www.iraqbodycount.org, accessed 17 November 2006
[6] For example, http://www.iraqbodycount.org/press/pr14.php, accessed 17 November 2006
[7] See my *The New Western Way of War*, Chapter 5, for further discussion
[8] Statement by the military spokesman for al-Qaida in Europe, Abu Dujan al Afghani, Associated Press, 14 March 2004. Available online at: http://www.nytimes.com/2004/03/14/international/europe/14WIRE-QATAPE.html?ex=1081483200&en=e4cd73006599e6dc&ei=5070, accessed 7 April 2004

References

Bush, George W. (2001) Address to a Joint Session of Congress and the American People, 20 September. Available online at: http://archives.cnn.com/2001/US/09/20/gen.bush.transcript, accessed 17 November 2006

Burnham, Gilbert et al. (2006) *The Human Cost of the War in Iraq: A Mortality Study, 2002-2006*, Baltimore, Maryland: Bloomberg School of Public Health, Johns Hopkins University

Conetta, Carl (2003) *The Wages of War: Iraqi Combatant and Non-combatant Fatalities in the 2003 Conflict*. Project on Defense Alternatives Research Monograph #8. Available online at: http://www.comw.org/pda/0310rm8.html, accessed 21 November 2003

Daponte, Beth (1993) A Case Study in Estimating Casualties from War and Its Aftermath: The 1991 Persian Gulf War', *Medicine and Global Survival*, Vol. 3, No. 2

Duffield, Mark (2001) *Global Governance and the New Wars*, London: Zed

Kaldor, Mary (1999) New and Old Wars: Organized Violence in a Global Era, Cambridge: Polity

Rizer, Kenneth (2001) Bombing Dual-Use Targets: Legal, Ethical, and Doctrinal Perspectives, *Air and Space Power Chronicles*. Available online at: http://www.airpower.maxwell.af.mil/airchronicles/cc/Rizer.html, accessed 10 September 2003

Shaw, Martin (2005) *The New Western Way of War: Risk-Transfer War and its Crisis in Iraq*, Cambridge: Polity

Chapter Eleven

Dimensions of Perception: Shaping the British Approach to Information Strategy During Military Operations

Angus Taverner

> Perceptions are real. If you're playing to win they have to be favorable. Your ability to persuade people to listen to you, understand what you are saying, and support you, will determine whether you win or lose!
>
> Lord Bell, Chime Communications Former Communications Advisor to Margaret Thatcher

British military doctrine now requires all operations to be planned and conducted in line with a 'manoeuvrist approach'. This emphasizes the requirement for a clear understanding of the desired end-state from the outset while the aim should be to achieve an outcome by changing attitudes and behavior; if necessary but not always, by use of force. An 'effects-based approach' embraces a range of options from subtle influence, largely in the fields of traditional and defense diplomacy, through coercion and deterrence to the total physical destruction of an enemy. Effectiveness is dependent upon the communication of information, options and intent. Target audiences are deemed likely to react in a variety of ways; either complying with the intent, possibly ignoring it or belligerently reacting against it.

Over the past decade in the UK, information strategies have been designed to address all aspects of 'soft' engagement with an opponent, an adversary or a designated target population. Moreover, they recognize that target audience perceptions are largely responsible for shaping people's attitudes and behavior. To add further complexity, the impact of intervention and military action will change perceptions across the board. It may be argued, therefore, that it is important to consider the information dimension in the context of the overall strategic campaign plan rather than as an isolated entity, as has traditionally been the case.

'Perception' has rarely been considered formally at the core of the military strategic planning process. But recently in the UK, the concept of 'information campaigning' has been developed in parallel to support strategic and operational plans. However, it has been largely left to the Ministry of Defense's media and communication staff to determine how best to manage the communication of policy and to manage news as it develops, largely in isolation from other planners.

It is now largely accepted, in most areas of human activity, that perceptions shape behavior and attitudes. Accordingly, for the military getting this right is arguably an essential element of their 'effects-based approach' to strategic planning. It is also important to acknowledge that perceptions are not confined to a single adversary audience but that diplomatic and military freedom of manoeuvre is likely to be constrained by adverse perceptions amongst wider national and international audiences. This chapter focuses on 'perceptions' and 'soft effects' as key elements in broader strategic planning, both within the MoD and across government more generally. It is also important to note that it is now accepted doctrinally that information should not be regarded as a distinct 'instrument of national power' but, instead, is intrinsic to the three other instruments: diplomacy, military and economic.

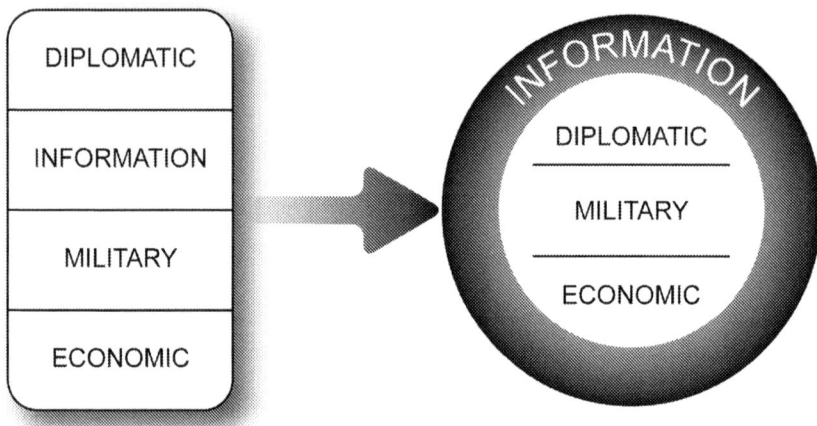

Figure 11-1: DIME Model versus the DME Model

Understanding Target Audience Perceptions

Unless engaged in a war of national survival, UK military operations are primarily intended to influence a particular leadership, audience or group in support of government policy. Target audience receptiveness to the government's intent is invariably a function of how they *perceive* the UK's objectives and the actions that are being taken to achieve those objectives. Considerable academic and commercial research has been dedicated to the subject of perception. Tim Bell's widely quoted statement, at the top of this paper, in many ways summarizes the prevailing wisdom in terms of a Western approach to marketing and public relations. Arguably, people's view of their world is shaped through a series of external filters rather than through direct experience. Shaping target audience perceptions is, therefore, central to determining people's attitudes and how people behave.

Over the past decade, British operations have highlighted a number of examples of success, and sometimes failure, as the result of getting perceptions right or wrong. OP PALLISER, Sierra Leone 2000, is often cited as an example of a Peace Support Operation (PSO) that was planned from the outset to achieve campaign success by influencing the perceptions of a number of key audiences, both within the country and beyond. Operational and tactical activity was shaped to send clear messages to the people of Sierra Leone, the insurgent rebels, other governments in West Africa, the international community and the British public. This was not simply a matter of presentation. Rather the information dimension was brought to the heart of the planning and decision-making process and the desired end-state was successfully achieved.

In contrast, arguably, the operation in Afghanistan in 2001, OP JOCANA, which committed 3 Commando Brigade to fight insurgents in the Tora Bora mountains, did not give the same prominence to perceptions. The result was 'a militarily success' but it fell short of achieving the overall desired effect because the outcome of the operation failed to match public expectation.

Recent international terrorist activity provides a number of examples of how 'received perception' rather than judgment based solely on direct experience, determines popular behavior. This leaves people vulnerable to asymmetric manipulation of their own perceptions of events – for instance, electing not to fly post-9/11, more fearful for their personal security because of media coverage of terrorist attacks, or buying in emergency supplies because of a perceived increase in the threat to their well-being. The reality these people experience in their daily lives in most cases does not change – their trains run normally, coffee is still available in their favorite café, their children go to school and colleagues appear at work each day. However, their exposure to media coverage that highlights how other people are behaving, sometimes in a different country, prompts them to behave accordingly, even if this seems irrational when viewed objectively.

This phenomenon is largely related to the increasing reach and breadth of the media (not just news but brand-led marketing, entertainment, the world-wide web and advertising) and a growing tendency to be guided by second-hand opinion rather than lessons drawn from direct experience. Moreover, this seems to be as much the case in less sophisticated societies as it is in the developed world – even though the dominant media there may not be television but local radio, the mobile telephone, word on the street, rumor, or simply gossip.

Moreover, it is generally agreed that people's views of the world are no longer constrained to their immediate community, locality or even state. A tsunami occurs in the Indian Ocean and a worldwide reaction is evoked resulting in billions of dollars of aid. It has become a commonplace to talk about the 'global village' – but conversely individuals do not feel they have an influential voice in this village. Increasingly, this is as true for a Tuareg tribesman as it is for a banker on Wall Street. Against this backdrop, it is argued that the UK's current approach to strategic planning does not encourage popular perceptions to be considered formally in the politico-military planning process, nor does it have in place appropriate mechanisms to ensure that this is co-ordinated properly across government.

'Soft effects' and political-military planning

It may be argued that the development of strategy and operational planning should be conducted on a cross-government and, ideally, cross-coalition basis. A 'conceptual model' that maps the 'effects-based approach' in terms of audience perceptions is set out below. It is designed to show the linkage between where perceptions are at the outset, how they might be and where they need to be. Arguably, perceptions can be measured in a number of different ways from the hard measurement of observed behavior to focus groups and opinion polling. Whatever method is employed, the model highlights the need to maintain a clear understanding of the desired campaign end-state and objectives, while taking account of the wider campaign context. It suggests the need to evaluate a target audience's perception of its current state and the likely impact of proposed courses of action in terms of target audience behavior, as well as attitudes towards our desired end-state. Analysis can highlight the gap between prevailing perceptions and where perceptions need to be.

In turn, the process should identify the effects that need to be achieved to reach the end-state. This would initiate a cycle of planning and action which can be evaluated periodically to determine progress.

It may also be suggested that different people are likely to perceive that end-state in different ways:

- Some will embrace it for what it is.
- Some will embrace the aspiration but misunderstand it.
- Some will understand the desired intent and oppose it.
- Some will *mis*understand it and oppose it.
- Some will choose to fight it vigorously.
- Some may not care.
- Many are unlikely to understand the end-state but still have positive or negative perceptions about the likely outcome.
- Some may not care about the outcome but just support or oppose the engagement.

Clearly, each of these involves different perceptions and as a first step, it is probably important that these are understood and evaluated in terms of how easy or difficult it is likely to be to change them.

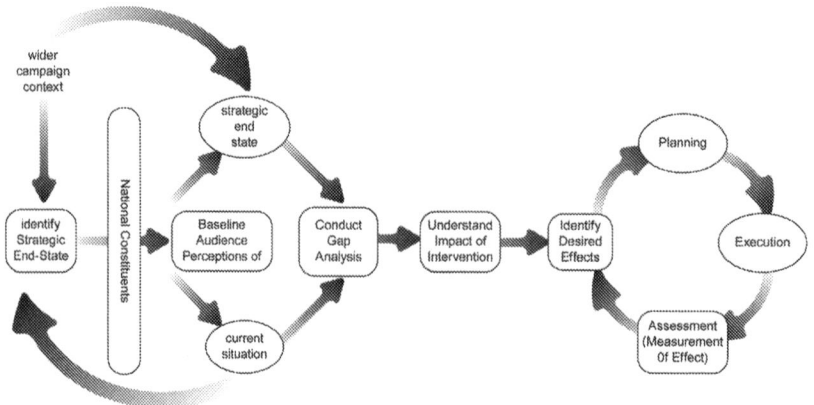

Figure 11-2: An Effects-Based Approach to Measuring the Effectiveness of Information Strategy: 'A Conceptual Model'

Changing perceptions

The key to the model lies in acknowledging that individuals and communities perceive matters in different ways and the suggested 'gap analysis', if done objectively and with honesty and rigor, would highlight how far perceptions need to change if a desired end-state is to be achieved. This is likely to be challenging – particularly if the end-state desired, is outside the cultural, historical and understood compass of a target audience.

From this basis, strategic planning would need to be supported by more broadly-based intelligence assessment that addresses not only the physical strengths and weaknesses of an enemy, and leadership intentions, but also analysis of how the general population perceive their lives and how they view the prospect of external intervention. For example, a UK force may see its involvement as a 'force for good' but others may perceive it as aggressive and unwarranted interference.

Input to decision-making and campaign planning

If this premise is accepted, then two deductions can be drawn. First, it should be an essential part of the planning process to develop a proper and robust understanding of how a particular population views the world from its perspective. Especially, how it views the prospect of external intervention – garlanded liberators or foreign aggressors? Secondly, perceptions rarely match reality. This requires attention to effective ways of communicating intent, not only internationally but also within operational theatres. Arguably, the process needs to focus not only on leaderships but also on populations generally, in order to understand both how they are likely to react during war-fighting operations and how they are likely to behave in the post-conflict stabilization phase once the initial mission has been completed.

It may be further argued that if perception is accorded a central place alongside the political and military dimensions of strategic planning, then this may have a considerable impact on the manner in which future strategic decisions are taken and campaigns planned.

Planning – tactical to strategic coherence

If the importance of understanding perceptions and getting them right is to be included in the strategic and operational planning process, some changes in the structure and conduct of strategic campaign planning process are also likely to be required. At the highest strategic level, it is suggested that effects-based planning needs to embrace a co-ordinated, cross-government information strategy. The outline of this would be agreed across government departments to ensure clarity of intent, a clear statement of ends, and an expression of the means that would be made available to achieve the aim. This would enable other government departments to understand more fully the roles they are required to play and a timeline against which to do so.

The information strategy would form part of the strategic planning process and not be left simply to the communication staff to interpret. This could then be expressed in terms of four broad audiences: UK national, international, regional and regime (this accepts that there are always likely to be sub-divisions within each audience group). In turn, this would enable strategic planners to articulate more clearly the means by which they hope to make an effect on each of these audiences. Arguably, it would also expose knowledge gaps about the perceptions amongst each of these audiences and then allow further refinement of the optimum ways and means, not only of achieving the desired effect upon the target audience but also of sustaining the widest support for doing so.

As part of the development of the information strategy, key themes and messages would need to be developed for each audience and these should arguably be set on a timeline related to the strategic phasing of the operation, the interim criteria, decision points and the campaign end-state. These could also be represented in a flow chart to show 'what ifs', depending on the paths taken by the identified audiences.

Measures of Effectiveness (MoE) would also need to be agreed from the outset so that the success or otherwise of the perception dimension of a campaign could be monitored and adjustments made as operations progress. To achieve this, it would be important for planners to agree what constitutes success in a manner that is measurable and readily understood – for example, numbers of displaced people returning to their homes, numbers of attacks on security forces, percentage of the population expressing agreement with a coalition's aims or even the levels of popular support for what is being achieved by the general public in the UK. An effects-based approach suggests that the measurement process needs to be agreed at the outset and that military planning ought to be focused accordingly.

Structures, process and resources

If it is accepted that 'soft effects' should be a central feature of any effects-based approach, then this implies that the structures and process, both within defense ministries and more widely across governments, should be re-aligned. If planners continue to separate responsibilities, this will perpetuate a view that 'perception' is not central to campaign planning and, while it will be ever present at the back of any successful commander's mind, it will not merit the formal attention that other elements of the campaign planning process attract.

It is suggested that this neglects an important dimension of strategic planning. An effects-based approach suggests that this needs to start with a clear expression of the desired end-state. This ought to be expressed in terms, not only of physical change and observable changes in an adversary's behavior, but it should also be defined in terms of where audience perceptions need to be, if the end-state is to be both achieved and sustained. It almost certainly needs a defeated adversary or former warring factions to support the end-state once it has been reached.

Trying to understand how enemies, insurgents and even allies view the world has always been a challenging part of the military art. In an age when information has increasing potency, it has never been more important, yet command and control structures are arguably poorly organized to ensure that this crucial dimension is fully thought through. To achieve this balance between 'kinetic' and soft planning, it is suggested that an 'effects policy group' should be established. This probably ought to be a cross-government forum focused on clearly delineating and articulating the desired end-state.

Conducting operations – the commander's role

In implementing this effects-based approach, the role of the commander at all levels remains key. Commanders, particularly senior ones, become identified not only with the men and women they lead but also as the individual manifestations of that force. The names of familiar foes echo down the centuries: Wellington versus Napoleon, Montgomery versus Rommel, even Schwarzkopf versus Saddam. Similarly, eighteenth and nineteenth century historians were fond of associating successful commanders with the places of their most notable triumphs and occasional failures: Clive of India, Woolf of Quebec, Gordon of Khartoum springing readily to mind. This trait was not pure whimsy but a demonstration of the psychological impact these commanders made on their adversaries and the places they fought.

It is, perhaps, notable that the attritional twentieth century did not produce so many publicly acknowledged commanders. Perhaps only Field Marshal Montgomery of Alamein has achieved a similar status to his famous predecessors. And he is significant as a role model for the effects-based commander because, while he took a largely traditional approach to the use of overwhelming force and manoeuvre to overcome his opposition, he believed that a commander should have a public face – particularly if he was going to break the perception that the German enemy was unbeatable. Deliberately cultivating his image, Montgomery came to be seen as the British general who could beat the enemy. Not only did this significantly raise both the morale of his troops and the wider British public but it also had an effect on his German adversaries. As Montgomery put it: 'I would define leadership as the will to rally men and women to a common purpose, and the character which inspires confidence.' Whether Montgomery was the best British commander of World War Two remains debatable; many soldiers and historians giving that accolade to Field Marshal Bill Slim or Field Marshal Alan Brooke. Nevertheless, Montgomery's deliberately cultivated image delivered psychological effect. Even today, he remains the single World War Two commander that most people can still recall.

At the beginning of the twenty-first century, commanders have largely buried themselves in concrete bunkers, at the heart of large tented cities or in the citadels of capital ships. The cult of the commander is less fashionable and 'face time' on television is not encouraged – often, it is suggested, by politicians. Commanders who do allow themselves public exposure have sometimes been pilloried by their peers, accused of 'grandstanding' or seeking the limelight. General Sir Charles Guthrie, when he was Chief of Defense Staff between 1999 and 2001, was frequently criticized both for being too overtly involved in the 'political game' and for developing a media profile. General Sir Michael Rose, while commanding UNPROFOR in former Yugoslavia in 1994, was also criticized for making too many public appearances and, therefore, playing to the gallery. However, if the commander is to be seen as the embodiment of the forces under his command and the struggle, perhaps, as a contest between two commanders then it may be argued that not only is this sensible but should be positively encouraged.

In a similar vein, individual units and formations should be encouraged to exploit their reputations. In Iraq in both 1991 and 2003, it was easier to explain the role of 'The Desert Rats' rather than the more anonymous sounding 7th Armoured Brigade. The Parachute Regiment has been uniquely successful in developing the 'Para' brand – aggressive, heroic and indomitable – in a manner that most other military units have not.

It is probably not entirely coincidental that, despite their light, agile role, the Parachute Regiment and Royal Marines are the forces of choice for most operations. It appears to take some effort to persuade political leaders that other, less glamorous, units are militarily just as capable and may be better suited to deliver the desired effect. Politicians recognize the message they are delivering when they send in the Marines or Special Forces. It reassures the domestic audience and sends a clear message of intent to the warring factions in the country in question. It is hardly surprising, therefore, that any British prime minister and his or her secretary of state for defense, seeking to achieve a political result using military force will promptly suggest the early deployment of units which have a track record of success and whose reputation resonates ahead of them.

In the commercial world, hard-won reputations are carefully nurtured and jealously protected. The comings and goings of high-profile business leaders can add or subtract substantial values to the share price of a company. The primary reason for this is the effect these individuals are perceived to have on a company's ability to make profits. While stock market sentiment may sometimes seem idiosyncratic, it provides a close analogy to the effect that successful generals may have upon the enemy and similarly the reputations of the units they command.

From this discussion, a number of key elements can be identified that make the planning and execution of perception-orientated operations different from more traditional military approaches. First, the conduct of such operations needs to remain focused throughout on achieving an agreed end-state. This is not necessarily about breaking an enemy's will through the destruction of his forces and thus his continuing ability to resist – although arguably this may be the effect that a commander may want to achieve. In most cases, effects-based operations are planned to influence an adversary into pursuing a course of action that is not of his choosing. The approach emphasizes the psychological dimension of warfare to achieve desired ends over the physical dimension. It may involve little or no fighting and those conducting effects-based operations are taught to understand that success is not measured in US General Westmoreland's infamous Vietnam 'body count', nor is it measured in hectares of ground taken and held. Instead, effects-based operations are assessed in terms of adversary reactions and whether he is going to bend or not – arguably a political judgment as much as a military one.

As part of this effects-based approach it is argued that a commander's mission should be distilled and clarified in terms of perception as much as physical activity. Yet traditional factors such as terrain or an assessment of balance of forces may be given precedence to identifying the level of popular support an adversary enjoys and assessing the psychological vulnerability of the key leadership figures. From this type of analysis it may become obvious that the leadership of a rogue state is deeply unpopular, exercising control through fear and terror rather than enjoying widespread support and consent.

Tactical execution

In developing an effects-based tactical plan that is also sensitive to the perception dimension, a commander must be especially alert to higher levels of intent. He must be conscious of the limitations on his freedom of manoeuvre, particularly the likelihood of causing collateral damage – each civilian death or destruction of a building offering a propaganda opportunity to his adversary. He should also probably think about how to use weapon systems to emphasize his intent rather than in terms of attrition of the enemy's capability.

The UK 1st Armoured Division's operation to secure Basra in southern Iraq, in early April 2003, presents a good example of the effects-based approach in action at the tactical level. As the commander, Major General Robin Brims, said at the time: 'I am a patient man, I am not in the business of creating another Stalingrad.' Conscious of the need to avoid civilian casualties and minimize the impact of the civilian infrastructure, he devised a concept of operations which encouraged probing sorties into the city without trying to take or hold ground. Rather akin to aggressive patrolling, these enabled the British division to demonstrate intent, taking out enemy resistance as it was encountered, without exposing the force unnecessarily. After nine days of these probing operations, Brims's will had been exerted over the enemy and they had fled leaving Basra open to coalition forces.

The information campaign had been central to the division's success. Intelligence had revealed that Iraqi forces were demoralized and largely paralyzed without a chain of command. Without orders the Iraqis feared to use initiative. By interdicting the command and control capabilities of the Iraqi forces, orders could not be disseminated – except in the end by paper and runners. Orders as they were received proved merely confusing, often days out of date and impossible to implement. Crucially, the coalition also targeted the principal Iraqi commander in Basra, Saddam's cousin, Ali al Majeed – so-called 'Chemical Ali'. Feared and apparently loathed by the population, reports of his demise after a precisely targeted air attack on the house in which he was believed to be living, seemed to release the final reservations in the civilian population regarding coalition intent; it also sent a clear message to the Iraqi forces that further resistance was probably futile.

Conclusion

In many ways, it is suggested that taking account of perception at all levels of military planning seems to represent the opportunity to deliver a full flowering of Clausewitz's thinking on warfare. By focusing on a desired end-state it forces practitioners to consider the optimum ways of achieving political results rather than simply how to defeat a military adversary. Arguably, it offers the thought that physical defeat of an adversary may not achieve the ultimate strategic goal. Instead, by placing greater emphasis on the importance of perception, it allows political leaders and military commanders to examine more widely the means at their disposal to achieve desired outcomes. To be successful, all the levers of state power need to be closely co-ordinated to maintain cohesion between sometimes widely disparate elements. This requires closer political involvement, often below the military strategic level, to ensure that different elements are mutually reinforcing rather than discordant.

History is full of examples of military effects that have achieved wider political or diplomatic results. However, they have rarely been planned as such. Today, the combination of precision weapons designed to limit physical damage to an 'acceptable minimum', network-enabled capability allowing the instant passage of information, the acknowledgement that a military response does not have to be the act of last resort, and broader recognition of the psychological dimension of war, certainly offers a strategic approach that makes military involvement more 'useable' and possibly, therefore, more probable.

An approach to military planning that includes the important dimension of perception arguably must embrace a government and coalition-wide information campaign, identifying the key audiences to be targeted, both physically and psychologically, ways in which they can be engaged and clearly articulating the 'measures of effectiveness' by which targeting should be assessed. Targeting must be intelligence-led with a stronger emphasis on psychological influences than has traditionally been the case. Moreover, since perceptions are shaped by all lines of development and not just by military activity, shaping perceptions across all audiences should be a co-ordinated effort across government.

Chapter Twelve

A Century of Psyops: Psychological Warfare from the First World War to Lebanon

Ron Schleifer

Psychological warfare, known also as psychological operations (psyop), seeks to advance the cause of victory in wartime by targeting specific audiences with a variety of specially crafted messages. A strategic weapon, invaluable both on the battlefield and home front, psyop can add significantly to its user's military power if used correctly. Its success depends on whether it is of sufficient breadth, scope and depth; whether it is tailored to the user's military and political objectives and whether it is used consistently throughout any conflict – that is before, during and after. This, in turn, demands the establishment of a highly professional psyop organization, working in constant and close co-operation with the relevant military and political authorities.

While such an elaborate set up may, in the short term, prove expensive to put into place, it is, in the long run, well worth investment. Not only is psyop more economic than conventional weapons, but the advantages accruing from a properly waged campaign far outweigh its costs. Nor can psyop's moral aspect be ignored. After all, given that it rarely results in the loss of life or property, while its overarching aim is to bring the fighting and killing to an end as quickly as possible, there is little doubt that, as a rule, psyop is a considerably more ethical, tactical and strategic weapon than its standard counterparts[1].

Psyop's current basic operating principles were laid down during the First World War. An integral part, albeit to varying degrees, of most 20th century wars and conflicts, psyop appears set to take on an even more central role in 21st century warfare in the light of its proven track record combined with the continuing revolution in communications technology. This chapter will present an overview of the main developments in psyop over the last hundred years. Drawing on examples from wars of varying intensity, it will begin by defining psyop's operational principles. It will then offer a brief review of the changes in the use of psyop over the years and conclude with some general remarks on the future of psychological warfare in the 21st century.

Psyop's basic principles

Psyop's basic operating principles, which, as noted, first emerged during the First World War – the division into three main target audiences and the definition of several overarching themes and messages – remain largely intact today. The means used to convey them, as shall be seen, are the main novelty of modern psyop (Taylor and Sanders 1982).

Target audiences

War routinely triggers among its participants – be they private individuals, states or communities – a range of quintessentially primeval emotions including hatred, self-sacrifice, fear and revulsion. Psyop draws upon these feelings, channeling and exploiting them to advance well-defined military and political goals (Linebarger 1957: 153-157).

The home audience

Of the three psyop target audiences, the home audience is the most important of all. Wars often demand a huge sacrifice on the part of the local population who must be convinced that it is well worth making. Accordingly, the public, soldiers and civilians have to be persuaded that they are facing a justifiable existential threat and that the goals they are fighting for are vitally important and morally just. Leaders who fail to achieve this will have little chance of winning their wars. It is in this context that psyop plays a crucial role.

A properly waged psyop campaign must also strengthen the population's self-belief and conviction that, despite present hardships, they can and will emerge victorious. This is particularly true during long, drawn-out conflicts that engulf the home front as well, as was the case in the First World War. This was why in 1915, with the number of casualties rising daily and with no hope of victory in sight, the British government set up the National War Aims Committee in an attempt to boost the population's waning enthusiasm for the war. And, while the First World War was admittedly a high-intensity war, this principle holds equally true of low-intensity conflicts such as between the Palestinians and Israelis.

The enemy audience

The second target audience is the enemy whose soldiers and civilian population must be persuaded they have absolutely no chance of winning the war, thus concluding that the sooner the war is brought to an end the better. One way of achieving this is to flood the enemy with details of one's military power and expertise, past and present. In 1917, for example, the United States, having finally joined the war, began bombarding the German frontline with leaflets detailing its vastly superior industrial-military capabilities. Smaller, weaker sides, like the Vietcong, tend, by force of circumstance, to point out that military clout alone does not win wars and that the human factor is of greater consequence, particularly one's fortitude, resolve and, above all, one's willingness to sacrifice everything for the cause.

Psyop directed at enemy audiences often begins even before the outbreak of war. By pointing out to the enemy that: (a) it is fighting for a lost cause and (b) its defeat on the battlefield is a given, psyop hopes to convince enemy audiences to come to terms rather than go to war. During the First World War psyop efforts targeting the enemy were primarily aimed at the soldiers serving on the front as the civilian population were difficult to reach given the limitations of the available media at the time.

One of psyop's basic assumptions is that wars can be won not only by physically pounding the enemy's fighting forces, but by pummeling their psyche as well. By fermenting unrest among the rank and file, psyop strives to make enemy soldiers hesitate before pulling the trigger, if not abandon the battlefield altogether. The wider aim, however, is to force the opposing side's leaders to reconsider, in light of the above, whether or not they are capable of continuing the war at all. In the targeting of enemy civilian populations, psyop seeks to undermine faith in the legitimacy of a war's cause or convince the population of the futility of continuing to fight in a battle that is clearly lost – as was evident in the United States' targeting of Japanese soldiers in 1944-5 (Sandler 1999: 220).

Neutral audiences

The third target audience consists of neutral countries, organizations and individuals. Though not directly involved in the fighting, these audiences are considered worth lobbying in order either to win their support or, at worst, prevent their backing the enemy. The British psyop efforts in the United States during the First World War provide a good example of the former whilst the German campaign an example of the latter. But while Britain, which unleashed a massive, finely-tuned and well-coordinated psyop campaign, ultimately secured American support, Germany failed to achieve its objectives, not least because of the almost total lack of co-operation between its military and political authorities (Lasswell 1927: 3; Macdonald 2001).

Messages

A review of psyop messages used throughout the 20th century reveals the presence of several archetypal psyop themes. For example, domestic audiences, like neutrals, are generally deluged by messages that either demonize the enemy or emphasize the justice and morality of one's own cause. The enemy audience, on the other hand, is repeatedly told that it is fighting a losing battle whilst being subjected to a continuous barrage of messages provoking strong feelings of guilt. Both themes come to the fore most clearly when directed at the enemy's soldiers. The latter are bombarded with messages underlining the futility of their efforts in an inane, felonious and doomed war. These messages are intended to make them waver on the eve of battle, or, better still, desert and/or surrender altogether. On the whole, psyop messages can be divided into seven generic themes:

Victory is inevitable

Directed at domestic or neutral audiences and designed to mobilize the former and gain the support of the latter, messages within this theme stress in particular one's own side's ability to win the war. Such messages can also be directed at enemy audiences, and are often accompanied by others underlining the enemy's inability to win the war. The aim, in both cases, is to undermine enemy morale. It is a theme commonly used by revolutionary movements, hoping to compensate for their comparative lack of resources *vis-a-vis* the opposing side, as the FLN did in its battle against the French colonial government in Algeria (see Fanon 1968).

Legitimacy

Messages of legitimacy – whether targeting domestic, neutral or enemy audiences – emphasize the justice and legitimacy of one's own war aims, while underlining the degree to which enemy objectives are iniquitous, immoral and illicit: something the North Vietnamese consistently did in the course of their battle against the United States. The aim, of such messages is, once again, to garner support while weakening enemy resolve. When directed at neutral audiences there is the additional bonus of nipping in the bud any possible aid and succour for the enemy.

The futility of continuing the war

Targeting the enemy, messages rooted in this theme attempt to bring the war to a quick end. They do so by arguing – as Nazi Germany pointed out to Britain following the fall of France in 1941 – that the conflict could easily be resolved if only the opposing side would see it, or by insisting that the enemy is fighting a losing battle – as Nazi Germany tried to persuade Churchill's government in 1941, the year Britain stood alone. In either case, the objective is to scupper enemy morale by convincing them there is no point in continuing such a senseless war: precisely what Hizbollah achieved in 2000 during the war against Israel in southern Lebanon (Wehrey 2002).

Demonization

As its name suggests, demonization essentially seeks to depict the opposing side as evil. Extremely manipulative and inflammatory, demonization messages are largely directed at home audiences, giving rise to feelings of almost irrational revulsion, outrage and hatred. They are considered particularly effective in encouraging one's own soldiers to overcome any fighting inhibitions by divesting the enemy of any vestige of humanity. During the First World War, the British launched a well-orchestrated atrocity campaign in an attempt to demonize the Germans by describing them as being little different from their barbarian Hun ancestors in their savage conquest of Belgium when, it was claimed, they plundered churches, raped nuns, and generally brutalized the population, regardless of age or sex (Roetta 1974) .[2]

Demonizing the enemy is also an effective way of gaining neutral support. The Americans, during the First Gulf War, swamped the media with images of the environmental damage caused by Saddam Hussein's flooding the Gulf basin with oil. The heart-rending pictures of a dying cormorant with its wings fused together and flapping helplessly on the beach did much to blacken Saddam's name in the eyes of world. Little was said about the fact that this specific bird was suffering as a result of an oil sleek from a tanker attacked by the US army (Knightley 2004: 497).

Driving a wedge

Based on the age-old adage of divide and rule, the 'driving a wedge' theme also aims to cripple enemy morale by playing up the differences between various groups in its camp. In particular, it exploits the differences between the government and public at large, and the soldiers serving on the front line and civilians in the rear, as well as officers and enlisted men. Religious and national minorities are, naturally, considered prime targets for such messages. In 1917, Britain sought to drive a wedge between the Austro-Hungarian government and its various minorities by exploiting the Austro-Hungarian Empire's multi-national character. Noting that the Austro-Hungarian army was divided into ethnically homogeneous units, it played Czech music to Czechs units and Slovak music to Slovak units to galvanize national sympathies while undermining each ethnic group's loyalty to the Empire (Roetter op cit: 75).

Sixty years later, in an effort to spread dissent within enemy ranks, North Vietnam called attention to the fact that the number of Afro-Americans serving in the army far outweighed their numbers in American society.[3] The Americans drew on the same theme during the Iraqi war when, hoping to divorce the Iraqi people from its leadership, they bombarded the former with messages insisting that the United States had no quarrel with the people of Iraq, only its corrupt and iniquitous regime by underlining the threat the regime posed to Iraqis, the region and the world at large.[4]

Guilt

Directed at the enemy and seeking to evoke feelings of self-reproach and wrongdoing, guilt has proved to be one of the most effective psyop themes of all and goes to the root of psyop's rationale. War, by its very nature, is an ugly affair and psyop seeks to impress upon enemy just how horrific it actually is. Describing at length and in graphic detail the damage wrought by enemy action, particularly on the civilian population, the 'guilt' theme prays upon the enemy's conscience, hoping to shatter its soldiers' fighting instincts while undermining support for the war at home. Guilt-inducing messages were repeatedly used by the North Vietnamese through organized press field trips to bombed out civilian residences.

From asset to liability

This theme is devoted to impressing upon the enemy the high military, economic and political price it will pay should it continue to fight, or in the case of an occupying force, should it fail to relinquish its hold on the occupied territory. Emphasis is placed upon the fact that this price will far outweigh any possible gain. Routinely used in low-intensity conflicts, such themes came to the fore during the Vietnam War and the Palestinians' campaign against Israel where the Palestinians took every opportunity to stress how destructive the occupation of the West Bank and Gaza was to Israel and Israeli society.[5]

Psyop techniques

One commonly used psyop technique, employed to reach both enemy and neutral audiences, is that of establishing front organizations. Such organizations became especially popular during the Cold War. The Soviet Union mastered this technique during the 1920s establishing numerous such organizations in Western Europe designed to promote Soviet politics (Shultz 1984). Contrary to common perceptions, psyop does not as a rule deal in lies. This is not for any moral reasons, but simply because credibility is key to any psyop campaign's success. This does not however mean that psyop messages consist simply of unadulterated truth. More often than not, they give part of the facts or offer a particular take on the reality.

Black psyop, however, unlike its more commonly used alter-ego, white psyop, does trade in lies. Yet, given that credibility is psyop's greatest asset, there is a need, when employing it, to distance the source of the message from the message itself. Evidence of lying just once is enough to bring a carefully constructed psyop edifice crashing to ground. And, it is here that front organizations may come into play. Spreading disinformation by means of a third party means they will become the target for any flak should the truth come to light, thereby limiting the damage to one's psyop campaign's credibility.[6]

Front organizations are also an effective way of adding credibility to a psyop offensive, a credibility which would not be so forthcoming if the target audience were to be aware of a messages' actual source. This was why, in the months leading up to Second Gulf War, in 2003, the United States launched Radio Tikrit, supposedly run by indigenous Iraqis. Having initially lauded the Iraqi regime, the station soon began to reprove – albeit mildly – Saddam Hussein and his regime. Once fighting broke out, having established its credentials, the station then broadcast messages condemning Iraqi leaders.

Another commonly used psyop technique that made its first appearance between 1914-1918 consists of manufacturing events and/or exploiting opportunities on the ground. In some cases wartime incidents are deliberately orchestrated for psyop effect, in others existent events are exploited for psyop purposes. For example, in 1915, in an attempt to further their anti-German campaign in the United States, the British took advantage of the fact that Germany was issuing a medal in celebration of the sinking of the Lusitania in which 128 Americans died. Thousands of metal copies of the medal were distributed in the US together with a leaflet denouncing the barbarian Germans' joy over the enormous loss. That the medal was a private not government initiative was glossed over. Crucial to the effectiveness of exploiting events as a pysops technique is the need for a never-ending stream of events to utilize that not only overwhelm the enemy in quantity and speed, but also disable any opportunities for them to launch a psyop counter-attack.

Methods of conveying messages

During the First World War most countries set up information bureaus. Their purpose was to persuade the public at home and abroad that the war was just and would be won even if the battle proved to be long and arduous. To disseminate these and other messages, extensive use was made of the popular press, films, pamphlets, newspapers, booklets and books. But if, in 1914-18 reaching one's home audience or even neutrals was a relatively easy affair, gaining access to the enemy proved to be a much more difficult. Then, as now, this demanded creative thinking with regard to message conveyance. In response, the British used airplanes, artillery rockets, even hot air balloons to bombard enemy lines with leaflets emphasizing the evils of Germany's cause. Difficult to target, enemy civilians were relatively neglected. Since then, a range of increasingly sophisticated means of communication have developed in the field of pysops.

Developments in the field of psyop

Focusing on a number of global and regional conflicts this section will touch upon some of the principal developments in psyop since the First World War. While little has changed in terms of target audiences, themes and techniques, there have been revolutionary changes in the methods of delivering and distributing psyop messages owing to advances in the field of communications technology. It is on these that the following brief review will centre.

The Second World War (1939-1945)

It is hardly surprising that Nazi Germany unleashed a well-orchestrated psyop campaign well before the outbreak of war in 1939, both at home and abroad given that propaganda was key to Hitler's political manoeuvrings.[7] Headed by Josef Goebbels, Hitler's minister of information, the Nazi propaganda machine proved a highly effective tool and one reason why German support for the war was strong until its end. Well aware that credibility was of great importance, Goebbels rarely told outright lies, though he did become expert at spreading half-truths.

One exception to this rule, however, was the Big Lie technique that was based on Hitler's insight that if a lie was told often enough and with sufficient conviction it would eventually be accepted as the truth. The Big Lie was used to hammer home anti-Semitism, including the claim that Jews were involved in a global conspiracy aimed at taking over and subverting the world for their own iniquitous purpose. The other Big Lie was the claim that Germany had always been abused by its neighbors and, therefore, needed much larger territorial space (*Lebensraum*).

Once the fighting began, both the Allies and Nazi Germany devoted a great deal of time, money and effort to honing their respective propaganda machines. Both made extensive use of the radio, a relatively new and very popular medium, to reach audiences at home and, more importantly, deep within the enemy camp, something that had been virtually impossible to do previously. At the start of the war French soldiers manning the Maginot Line listened to German radio transmissions that claimed French staff officers were enjoying a 'cushy' life as opposed to the sheer awfulness of the reality of the front line (Roetter op cit: 109-110).

During the war, Britain's clandestine radio broadcasts were eagerly awaited and listened to by many in conquered Europe as a source of both succour and inspiration (Balfour 1979: 431-436). Black propaganda also flowered, with the Allies and Axis powers each disseminating black psyop under the cover of bogus and third-party radio stations. In 1944-5, seeking to lower German morale, the Americans created the

National Union of German Women, an organization of alleged lonely German women promising to console soldiers or officers on leave. Consequently, soldiers at the front were led to wonder about the loyalty of their spouses at home.[8]

The Vietnam War – North Vietnam (1961-1973)

The North Vietnamese victory in Vietnam was in no small part due to their elaborate psyop offensive. Hanoi realized early on in the campaign that the key battle in the war was the battle for American public opinion, and that this would not take place not in the paddy fields of Vietnam but on the streets of New York and Washington. As such, North Vietnam's psyop tactics aimed to convince the American public, and ultimately the US government, that the situation in Vietnam was futile. Playing on themes like 'divide and rule', the North Vietnamese fuelled the growing debate within the United States over the morality of fighting in a distant country that posed no real threat to American security. In so doing, Hanoi helped drive a wedge between various sectors in American society. Additionally, the North Vietnamese attempted to persuade Americans that the huge human, political, economic and moral losses generated by their country's involvement in Vietnam far outweighed any possible gain.

Drawing inspiration from communist North Korea's psyop experiences in the 1950s, North Vietnam's contribution to the waging of psychological warfare proved both innovative and long-lasting. Hanoi courted the Western media, taking advantage of the growing number of reporters, photographers and film crews who swamped the country as the war dragged on. Celebrities, too, were considered important, with Jane Fonda's (*Hanoi Jane*) visit to North Vietnam becoming one of the North's more striking psyop coups. Journalists, like celebrities, were furnished with visas, invited to press conferences, taken on organized field trips. North Vietnam was able to penetrate the American political debate exposing harrowing images of the devastation caused by US military action. If the first helped further ignite the moral debate in the United States over the war, the latter induced feelings of horror and guilt. Both served to increase pressure on the Nixon government towards a withdrawal from the Vietnam.[9]

The First Gulf War – The United States (1991)

The First Gulf War proved to be a watershed in the use of psyop. Following a barrage of US Army messages, mainly by air dropped leaflets, assuring Iraq's soldiers that no harm would come to them should they capitulate (the alternative being, it was emphasized, a cruel death in battle) well over 70,000 Iraqis downed arms and surrendered. Broadcasts and leaflets guaranteeing the Iraqis safe conduct convinced many, particularly following the carpet bombing of Iraqi army columns, that it would be far better to surrender than die. Upon surrendering, many Iraqi soldiers were found clutching these leaflets indicating some proof of psyop's effectiveness. Moreover, it offered incontrovertible evidence of the value of a carefully thought-out, well-coordinated psyop campaign in its ability to save Iraqi and American lives through the distribution of cheap radio transmitters and several tons of paper.

The First Gulf War was also turning point in the astute manipulation of the media. The United States began to prepare for a psyop campaign months before the outbreak of war. Assembling a team of articulate, media-savvy experts to fashion and spread its psyop messages, the United States began almost immediately to put into practice various new wartime strategies regarding the relationship between the government, army and media, constantly refining them in the process. In essence, both the government and the army laboured to keep the media in a happy, co-operative frame of mind. Taking advantage of the media's insatiable craving for information in the era of 24 hours news channels, reporters were inundated with facts, figures and daily briefings. Nor did the United States neglect the correspondents' creature comforts, housing and feeding, in an impressive and expensive logistical effort (Taylor 1998).

Hizbollah and Southern Lebanon (1985-2000)

Hizbollah's ultimately successful psyop campaign to bring about Israel's withdrawal from Lebanon was a master-class in the use of psyop in low-intensity wars. Hizbollah's potent blend of guerrilla and psychological warfare played a crucial part in convincing Israel to abandon the south of the country. Using the from 'asset to liability' theme, Hizbollah first persuaded the Israeli public and then its government that the price paid for staying in Lebanon far outweighed any possible security gains.

As part of its psyop campaign Hizbollah developed a new strategy, summed up in a phrase 'a battle unfilmed is a battle unfought'. This entailed having a camera operator accompanying and videotaping Hizbollah operations. Given that video, by its very nature, offers only a partial, selective view of reality, it allowed Hizbollah to focus on specific incidents within the operation, thereby suggesting they had significance way beyond their actual battlefield worth, for instance with the planting of a Hizbollah flag on an Israeli army post. The fact that the guerrillas were almost immediately killed and the flag taken down within minutes was ignored.

Broadcast on Hizbollah's television station, Al-Manar, these tapes were eventually picked up by the Israeli television networks. Although of extremely low quality, they were often the only visual record of what was happening, or seemed to be happening in Lebanon. Hence, Israelis watched with a mixture of horror and fascination pictures as Israeli units were ambushed by Hizbollah fighters or IDF army vehicles were blown up by road mines.[10] In addition, the Internet proved another extremely successful useful means of infiltrating Israeli households. Logging on to Hizbollah's websites, Israelis were confronted with appalling images chronicling the war in Lebanon with Hizbollah's anti-Israeli operations at the forefront (Maura 2003). There is little doubt that the cumulative psychological effect of these images resulted in belief in Hizbollah's military prowess. that ultimately led to Israel's withdrawal from Lebanon.

The Iraq War – The United States (2003)

One of the main challenges facing the Bush administration in the run-up to the 2003 Iraq War was to convince both American and world public opinion of the need to go to war at all. To this end, it launched a media-driven psyop campaign stressing that Iraq was on the verge of developing weapons of mass destruction. Combined with Saddam Hussein's close contacts with radical Islamist and terrorist organizations, this meant that Iraq posed a direct threat to the United States and the world at large.[11] Having exploited psyop to garner support for the idea of going to war, the United States – assuming that victory depended, to a large degree, on deepening that support – devised a strategy designed to achieve precisely that.

It embedded journalists in various fighting units, hoping, at the very least, to gain a degree of control over the way war was reported.[12] Advantage was also taken of various new, and by now easily available, technologies, such as satellite networks, the Internet, videophones, to broadcast to homes across the globe pictures from the war. The fact that these images were transmitted direct from the battlefield and in real time gave them a degree of authenticity that supported the US Army's interest of presenting an image of successful military operation (McLane 2004).

The Iraq War proved crucial in highlighting the importance of one frequently neglected aspect of psyop: 'consolidation psyop'. This is used mainly to convince a conquered or liberated population that, because its interests mesh with those of the occupying force, it has nothing to lose and all to gain by co-operating with the campaign's aims.[13] While the United States did make a few desultory efforts in the direction of consolidation psyop, such as enabling free press, distributing mine-awareness leaflets and providing medical services, on the whole it failed to win the heart and minds of the Iraqi public with notably dire consequences.

Conclusion

There have been no significant changes in the basic principles, themes or techniques of psychological warfare over the last hundred years. However, the means of conveying psyop messages has developed significantly. Technological advances have meant that psyop messages can be broadcast with growing ease and cunning, and, no less importantly to wider audiences. Whilst initially psyop was limited to targeting domestic and neutral audiences, it is now able to reach the enemy at home. By the close of the 20th century, thanks to technological gadgets like beepers, palm tops and blackberries, psyop operators have been able to target not only the public *en-mass* but individuals as well. Traditional channels of communication remain important, however. Indeed, leaflets, radio broadcasts and even graffiti remain powerful psyop delivery channels. It would appear that this pattern of combining the old with the new is set to continue well into the 21st century.

Psyop's proven success record – particularly during the First Gulf War – combined with improvements in communications technology that mean virtually anyone, private individual, organization or state can distribute information quickly, easily and cheaply to any number of people almost anywhere in the world, heralds a significant increase in the use of psyop in the 21st century. The world seems set to move from large-scale wars to low-intensity conflicts in which psyop reigns supreme in accordance with the notion that, as the intensity of the war declines, the importance of audience persuasion rises. This suggests that more resources will be devoted to the development of new and better psyop programmes in the future.

This is particularly true given the current rise in the number of radical states and organizations, which exploit psyop to gain crucial political and military advantage. Conversant with Western culture, and technologically proficient, these often small and weak entities, mostly but not exclusively Islamist, are becoming extremely adept at fashioning and distributing highly effective psyop messages. Enterprising, creative and unorthodox – at least in the field of psyop – as well as lacking in any bureaucratic and often moral constraints, they are able to exploit all that psyop has to offer as a cheap, accessible and effective weapon.

And it is here where the main psyop challenge to the West lies. For if the West hopes to prevail it must rise to the challenge, transcending any administrative, though not moral limitations, and strengthen and refine its psyop capabilities, allocating psychological warfare a greater role in its overall military and political strategies.

Notes

[1] For a detailed introduction to psyop, see Daugherty, William E. and Janowitz, Morris (1958) *A Psychological Warfare Casebook*, Baltimore: Johns Hopkins University Press pp 2-4. Also, US FM -33 -1 PSYOP. Available online at:
http://www.fas.org/irp/doddir/army/fm33-1/. Examples of the successful deployment of psyop can be found in Johnson, Richard, D. (1997) *Seeds of Victory: Psychological Warfare and Propaganda*, Atglen, PA: Schiffer Publishing

[2] Roetter, Charles (1974) *Psychological Warfare*, London: B.T.Batsford, ch. 2

[3] See http://www.psywarrior.com/VCLeafletsProp.html, accessed on 12 December 2006

[4] For a comprehensive description of the psyop leaflets used during the First Gulf War, see Johnson, *Seeds of Victory*

[5] On Palestinian psyop, see: Efaw, Jamie, *Palestinian Psychological Warfare: the First Intifada*. Available online at:
http://www.unc.edu/depts/diplomat/item/2006/0103/ca_efaw/efaw_intifada.html, accessed on 12 December 2006

[6] If in black psyop the signature appended to the messages differs from that of their true author, in white psyop the two are one and the same. There is also a third category known as grey psyop, which consists of messages whose point of origin is loosely camouflaged as the case of www.all4lebanon.org

[7] At this point in time the term psyop had not yet come into use. As a result, the line between what is now known as psychological warfare and propaganda was often blurred and the two terms were often used interchangeably

[8] Mauch, Christof (2003) *The Shadow War Against Hitler: The Covert Operations of America's Secret Intelligence Service*, New York, Columbia University Press. See also www.psywarrior.com which contains a digest of numerous covert operations

[9] The question of whether, and if so to what degree, the media was responsible for the US withdrawal from Vietnam is another question and one which is still the subject of much controversy

10 Interviews with soldiers who had served in Lebanon, conducted May 2003

[11] President Bush Outlines Iraqi Threat, Office of the Press Secretary, 7 October 2002. Available online at http://www.whitehouse.gov/news/releases/2002/10/20021007-8.html, accessed 12 December 2006

[12] This tactic was first used, albeit to a limited and tentative degree, by the British in Northern Ireland. See Curtis, Liz (1984) *Ireland, The Propaganda War: The Media and the Battle for Hearts and Minds*, London: Pluto Press

13 On consolidation psyop, see:
http://www.iwar.org.uk/psyops/resources/us/jp3_53.pdf, accessed on 12 December 2006

References

Balfour, Michael (1979) *Propaganda in War 1939-1945: Organizations, Policies and Publics in Britain and Germany*, London: Routledge and Kegan Paul

Fanon, Franz (1968) *Wretched of the Earth*, New York: Grove Press

Lasswell, Harold (1927) *Propaganda Techniques of the First World War*, London: Kegan Paul

Linebarger, Paul M. A. (1957) *Psychological Warfare*, NY: Arno Press pp 153-157

Macdonald, Bill (2001) *The True Intrepid: Sir William Stephenson and the Unknown Agents*, Vancouver: Raincoast Books

Knightley, Phillip (2004) *The First Casualty: The War Correspondent as Hero and Myth-Maker from the Crimea to Iraq*, Washington: Johns Hopkins University Press

McLane, Brendan. R. (2004) Reporting from the Sandstorm: An appraisal of embedding, *Parameters*, Spring pp 77-88

Maura, Conway (2003) *Cybercortical warfare: The case of Hizbollah.org*. Paper prepared for presentation at the European Consortium for Political Research (ECPR) Joint Sessions of Workshops, Edinburgh, 28 March-2 April 2003. Available online at: http://www2.scedu.unibo.it/roversi/SocioNet/Conway.pdf, accessed on 12 December 2006

Roetta, Charles (1974) *Psychological Warfare*, London: B.T. Batsford

Shulz, Richard H. and Godson, Roy (1984) *Dezinformatsia-Active Measures in Soviet Strategy*, Washington: Pergamon-Brassey's

Sandler, Stanley (1999) *Cease Resistance, It's Good for You: A History of US Army Combat Psychological Operations Command*, Washington: United States Army Special Operations Command. Directorate of History and Museums

Taylor, Philip M. and Sanders, Michael. L. (1982) *British Propaganda During the First World War*, London: Macmillan

Taylor, Philip. M. (1998) *War and the Media: Propaganda and Persuasion in the Gulf War*, Manchester: Manchester University Press

Wehrey, Frederic. M.A, (2002) Clash of wills: Hizballah's psychological campaign against Israel in South Lebanon, *Small Wars and Insurgencies*, Vol. 13, No. 3 pp 53-74

CHAPTER THIRTEEN

KIDNAP VIDEOS: SETTING THE POWER RELATIONS OF NEW MEDIA

MAKRAM KHOURY-MACHOOL

The political communications of wars have changed radically since the occupation of Iraq in 2003 by the Anglo-American military powers. First, the introduction and increased availability of new information communication technologies (ICT) has allowed disparate resistance groups greater access to new global media. In addition, formerly marginalized groups are now to a certain extent able to narrate and represent themselves. Though various groups are acting underground and in *ad-hoc* conditions under military occupation, such groups understand that they can only really be present in the war if they produce and transmit political communications of their own. In some cases, these groups have succeeded to counter and perhaps triumph over the media power of the occupying forces.

Thus, as a result, the political communications of the occupying Western powers no longer control the media nor dictate and dominate the global discourse of 'sanitized' war coverage. By utilizing low-cost video productions and disseminating them via the new media, Iraqi resistance and, particularly, kidnapping groups have managed even to supersede the direct address of US military officials, for the first time since the 'Gulf War' of 1991. This chapter argues that the videos of kidnapping groups should be viewed as a form of political communication in their own right, and thus considers these texts within broader political, cultural-linguistic and socio-religious contexts.

'Preferred' forms of punishment

In his *Discipline and Punish: The Birth of the Prison*, Michel Foucault (1977) opens with a graphic description of the public execution in 1757 of Robert-François Damiens, who had attempted to assassinate Louis XV. Alongside this, Foucault presents a prison timetable from just over eighty years later, enquiring how such a change in French society's punishment of convicts could have developed in such a short time. Foucault then offers two snapshots of contrasting 'technologies of punishment'. The first type, 'monarchical punishment', involves the repression of the populace through brutal public displays of executions and torture, while the second is 'disciplinary punishment', a 'preferred' form of punishment which Foucault claims is practiced in the modern era.

Albeit a low technology of communication, it was photography that provided graphic images of war in the past, unlike today. Executions or beheadings conducted by Western occupation forces and documented by camera as 'memories of war' did reach the media, though they were not originally destined for viewing by the public. One remarkable example is the British army's 'trophy' picture that generated such outrage in 1952 when the communist newspaper, the *Daily Worker*, devoted its entire front page to a photograph of a Royal Marine commando in the Malayan emergency holding aloft two severed heads. The London mainstream press on Fleet Street initially ignored the image, while the government even denied its authenticity. Yet, the colonial secretary later admitted before the House of Commons that the picture was, indeed, genuine.

Foucault's 'preferred' model of 'disciplinary punishment' has yet to be implemented in occupied, 'modern' Iraq. Here, a proxy culture of executions has begun directly and indirectly to be conducted and mediated by the various parties involved under this most technologically advanced of occupations. Perhaps the first symbol of public execution in occupied Iraq came on 9 April 2003 in Baghdad, when a US soldier placed an American flag as a hood around the neck of the statue of President Saddam Hussein, an image that became an international media event. Since contemporary media from Iraq is becoming what Thompson describes as a 'reworking of the symbolic character' (2001: 11) of military, economic and social life, military power and coercion have thus been able to produce symbolic forms in the shape of executions.

The international political embarrassment, even though brief, caused to the Iraqi government and the occupying forces through the airing of Saddam's execution by hanging in December 2006, was also evidence of the role of low-cost communication technology, such as the mobile telephone, in military conflicts mediated in modern times. Similarly, footage of the decapitation of Saddam Hussein's cousin, Barazan al-Tikriti, obtained due to political access to his execution chamber, may be seen to be an intertextual reference to the videos of hostages displayed by Iraqi resistance groups, which will be discussed in further detail below.

Located within the wider paradigm of political communications, the following case study examines the utilization of low cost video productions and their dissemination by Iraqi kidnap and resistance groups via the new media. It analyzes a number of Iraqi kidnap and hostage videos, all of which were aired on the Internet or, chiefly, by Arab satellite channels and later as selective footage in the global media, between March 2004 and March 2006. A methodological framework was devised to obtain quantitative and qualitative data that would support the hypothesis that the political communications of kidnapping groups in Iraq should be seen within the frame of counter-hegemonic relations to the occupation's hegemonic media. Furthermore, it is argued here that the low-cost videos produced and circulated through advanced communication technology display symbolic forms choreographed to serve the political purposes of these groups, and to grant them global symbolic power, albeit by utilizing a culturally specific new media production.

For the purposes of this study, thirty kidnap videos were analyzed, all of which were located freely on the Internet. The entire sample was transcribed to aid the subsequent content analysis. The coding frames were designed to reflect the recurring patterns initially apparent in the transcripts, and units of data were measured either in seconds, such as in the time each group was visually present on screen, or by the rate of recurrence, such as the citation of key terms or phrases, or symbolic imagery.

From mediated media to direct media

The 1991 'Gulf War' was 'a showcase for Western image technologies' (Robins 1996: 64) and can arguably be seen as a war between the watchers and the watched. Among Western audiences, by and large, there was a separation between knowledge and feeling. Under such circumstances, the victim was psychologically invisible, a phenomenon that can be described as 'sanitized' war coverage. Killing was done at a distance, through technological mediation, and without the shock of direct confrontation and violence. This was necessary to break the causal link and for the enemy to be depersonalized as a faceless 'other'. High-tech strikes were played repeatedly on Western networks, and were watched and re-watched, like video games, sometimes at private screenings. Even though the 1991 Gulf War coincided with the emergence of international satellite television, such as CNN, and was the world's first televised war (Taylor 1992: 7), some material was edited before its airing.

This formula was challenged dramatically in the 2003 'War on Iraq', a challenge that had begun in the Middle East some three years earlier. The first 'cyberwar' in the context of the Middle East, which had utilized the Internet as a form of political lobbying, was that waged following the outbreak of the second Palestinian *Intifada* (uprising) on 28 September 2000 (Khoury-Machool 2007). Though kidnappings and hostages videos were not characteristic of the Palestinian resistance, signs of Israeli losses in the cyber domain began to appear when Israeli 'hacktivists' demanded a truce in this so-called cyberwar (Khoury-Machool 2002: 70-83). In Iraq, following its occupation in 2003, political communication went one step further, to make full use of cutting-edge, modern technology in what was to be the first fully web-based war. This led to the introduction of direct media or unmediated political communications, aired directly to audiences without mediation by any media organization.

Media resources as power

A prominent feature of Iraq's 2003 occupation is the seizure by the Anglo-American military powers of the economic resources of one of the world's biggest oil reserves. Hence, the economic power and dominance of the occupying forces have facilitated further the production, reproduction and circulation of symbolic power and forms, and have made it difficult for resisting groups to respond. Ostensibly, this predicament reflects an imbalance between the occupier and the various resisting groups, and is twofold in nature: first is the imbalance between the occupying armies and the local armed factions; second is the imbalance between the media arm of the occupying forces and the supposedly less powerful media wings of the resistance or kidnapping groups.

For example, budgetary allocations indicate that, in the case of both Iraq wars, Bush Sr, Bush Jr and their respective advisors believed the media had tremendous influence on the public as a political communications tool during times of war. US governmental data suggests that, on 16 February 2006, US President George W. Bush sent a $72.4 billion emergency supplemental funding request for the fiscal year 2006 to Congress, to pay for the ongoing 'war on terrorism' (USINFO 2006). By winter 2006, his administration had spent $1.62 billion on advertising and public relations contracts, spanning a period of two and a half years. The US Department of Defense has spent more than any other government agency on media-related contracts, paying $1.1 billion for recruitment campaigns and other public relations efforts, according to a report by the Government Accountability Office (GAO), an investigative, non-partisan arm of Congress.

At the time of the 1991 Gulf War, investment in media communication to increase coverage and electronic newsgathering was high, compared with today's low cost technology. In 1991, CNN paid $200,000 for a special communications system in Baghdad, giving reporter Peter Arnett a direct line to its headquarters in Atlanta (Arnett 1997: 3). The subsequent advancement of and increased access to ICT, however, has given marginalized and small oppositional groups the possibility to act as political players, to gain recognition through the media, and to participate and react immediately to any political message communicated to them via the international media. Through such communications, these groups have been able to negotiate with and apply pressure on foreign or occupying governments, or to call for policy change *vis-à-vis* strategies for occupied Iraq. Hence, for the first time, the occupying superpower has lost its dominance in setting the agenda for everyday life in occupied Iraq. Now, counter-hegemonic groups share in contributing to the construction of Iraq's political reality and Western technological supremacy is being decisively challenged.

It should be stressed, however, that Western occupying forces and Iraqi resistance groups have contradictory aims, or at the very least a conflict of interests, with regard to the media and their use. Whilst the occupying powers attempt to present a sanitized representation of events through their media teams and the thousands of journalists who have covered Iraq since the beginning of the occupation (Löwstedt 2003: 3), activities in the arena of political communications by resistance and kidnapping groups have tended to draw on few resources. With many 'non-embedded', and hence 'not trusted', journalists working alongside the occupying forces, cameras are fast becoming vital weapons for many different local resistance groups. With no embedded journalists amidst them, these groups use vans with two holes drilled in the back: one for the camera and another for the weapon. Along with others, such modest resources are the 'means which enable them to pursue their aims and interests effectively' (Thompson 2001: 13).

For as long as killings *en masse* take place but are not aired, these then enter the frame of 'what the eye doesn't see, the heart doesn't grieve'. However, as a result of the uneven coverage enforced in the main by US media organizations, Iraqi resistance groups have now become the 'unofficial' producers of media products to end-users. The techniques employed in this electronic resistance have led to the premise that the greater the proximity between the executor and his victim, as represented visually through camera and on screen, the more effective will be the message conveyed to audiences regarding the sufferings of the occupied, and the more emotive will be the viewer's response.

Hostage videos: multi-faceted audiences

In the process of the production and dissemination of hostage videos, local, regional and international dimensions are present simultaneously. In producing these low-cost outputs, resistance groups active in Iraq keep in mind a multitude of audiences: the Arab-Islamic audience (both inside and outside Iraq), those of the occupying nation-states, their governments and publics, and the rest of international public opinion. The Arabic language is almost exclusively employed, having the power to reach out to potentially 300 million Arabs worldwide. In the case of Arab-Islamic audiences, it may be argued that the producers of these videos assume that these productions will offer gratification to certain viewers, due to widely held expressions of sympathy towards Iraqis, and as 'morale boosting' exercises in the face of occupation.

Emergence and characteristics

The phenomenon of resistance groups producing and circulating videos from Iraq of their kidnap victims is a development of the utilization of the low cost production and distribution model made possible by the advancements and availability of new media. In view of the heavy military presence of the occupying armies, and in order to minimize risk to themselves, resistance groups began to employ ICT to bypass so-called 'undesirable areas' (Castells 2002: 144), such as heavy military checkpoints. Thus owning 'symbolic power', these groups have been able to produce symbolic forms in the shape of language and visuals without significant financial input, giving credence to the view that symbolic power 'requires no financial investments' (Lull 2000: 161).

The advent of the Internet has provided anyone in a war zone with access to a computer and an Internet connection the necessary resources by which to create counter-hegemonic content, and to place it within a public arena accessible by a global audience. Because of the Internet, control of the media and particularly its content has proven harder than ever before, and has served to undermine the role of embedded journalists and the newsworthiness of their stories. The versatility of new media has also been beneficial to resistance groups: it is not a 'static' media, but is interactive and updateable, while text, music and video can be distributed all at once.

The Iraq case demonstrates that opportunities for political communication are no longer rigidly controlled by a military superpower, capitalist state or elected government. Furthermore, the phenomenon of the global viewing of the kidnapping of hostages and their execution, suggests that 'the globalization of crime further subverts the nation-state' (Castells 1997: 259). The use of ICT in contemporary Iraq has meant that the Internet has now become central to the life of the occupiers as well as the occupied, signifying the former's diminishing ability to impose censorship on the latter.

The first kidnappings in Iraq took place in March 2004, almost one year after the country's occupation. Between 2004 and 2006, more than 200 foreign nationals were kidnapped in Iraq, though Iraqi nationals, in fact, have been more exposed to kidnapping than any other national group. Furthermore, the number of Arabs and Muslims executed thus far is significantly higher than that of citizens of the countries participating in the occupation. As an adjunct to this form of psychological warfare, hundreds of kidnap videos have been produced. Despite these videos, kidnappers have tended not to conduct long political communications dialogues with Arab governments via their Arab hostages, and the result for such hostages has invariably been death. In addition, kidnappers have tended not to invest significantly in such productions, though one notable exception is the kidnap video of Egypt's ambassador to Iraq, Ihab el-Sherif, who was taken hostage in July 2005.

Through a repeated pattern of production, dissemination and the posting of video clips, kidnap groups have established a process of 'accumulation of prestige' (Thompson 2001: 16). The globalization of media and ICT has afforded these groups the ability not only to produce this news, but also to circulate it immediately and at speed. The visuals of the hostages are invariably sufficiently graphic to convey the desired political message, the basic message of which may be supplied by translation services, even if distorted and without full interpretation. Though professionalism in terms of production is not paramount, the ability to produce and distribute these videos under constant conditions of risk is an indication of the symbolic capital these groups possess. After their airing, we see evidence of what Thompson describes as the 'respect accorded to certain producers or institutions' (ibid) in the form of comments posted secretly or openly on the net through chat rooms, thereby ensuring that the spectator is fully engaged in the process of this production.

Genre

Of the several hundred hostage videos that have been produced, we may see various shared characteristics, identifying them as a distinct war-media genre. Chiefly, the videos under discussion are a hybrid of both the 'constructed world' of Hollywood cinema and the low budget, primitive nature of documentary making. The sequences that appear within these videos share neither the verisimilitude associated with Hollywood productions, nor the 'observational' stance of documentary films. They are neither false depictions of reality, nor are they compatible with what can be described as a consciously neutral, 'fly on the wall' style of documentary film-making. Production-design is one of the major areas of difference between these media texts and the unobtrusive surveillance of documentaries. Whilst documentaries record the environment and (as their name suggests) 'document', rather than create, their subject, these hostage videos take place within pre-mediated, 'constructed' scenes.

Occasionally, depending on the group that has conducted the kidnapping and produced the video, costume, scenery, props, the positioning of 'actors' and the use of colors within the frame are all considerations taken into account by the producers before filming takes place. This controlled environment is what is conventionally adhered to by Hollywood, and yet is conversely unexploited by traditional documentary-makers.

Logistics

In the volatile context of occupied Iraq, the heavy presence of Arab satellite channels has also been significant in breaking Western media dominance of news production and definitions of reality. Among Arab audiences, the Western media was 'often seen as gloating over Arab defeat' (Hallin 1998: 215). Thus, highly newsworthy hostage videos, the 'end product of a complex process' (Hall et al. 1987: 53), have tended to be delivered to Arab satellite channels when logistically possible. Such videos generally begin in the domain of a counter-military operation conducted by surveillance and force; the process of preparing for the kidnapping is never shown, nor are post-kidnapping logistics revealed.

The movement of the media crew usually follows the kidnapping operation, and ends in the location where the set-up and filming takes place. In some cases, the production takes place in the same location as where the captives are being held. In other cases, production takes place in more professional 'studios'. Live, filmed performance is a key component of these productions. Consequently, they tend to be improvised, and presented in public-free theatres such as shelters, cellars, lofts and stores. In some videos, the *mise en scène* appears to have been set up for the performance in advance, whereas in others, it appears as though the performers have simply transported a banner and head-coverings with them, to the site of filming.

Cultural specificity

Arguably, there are recurrent and pertinent elements and rituals in kidnap videos from Iraq. What Price (1998: 89) describes as 'the supra-sentential nature' of these communiqués forces their producers to devise content that is somehow vaguely understandable to the viewer, regardless of his or her cultural, social, linguistic or political beliefs. Thus, the communicational construction of these videos is purposefully basic, as will be shown below, and is designed to propagate a political message of fear. Major aspects relate to background detail, which display prominent, yet culturally specific, symbolic forms borrowed from different sets of circumstances, such as banners and Arabic calligraphy (*al-khatt al-'arabi*); the element of sermonizing (*khutba*); the use of colour in the costume of kidnapper and kidnapped; the body language of participants; and the use of weaponry.

Background detail: banners and calligraphy

Being skilled in the use of and fully aware of the role played by new media in the war in Iraq, kidnapping groups have realized that their military and symbolic power cannot be effective without the production of symbolic forms. When considering how the background of these videos has been set up for political communicational purposes by the producers of the media product, certain salient motifs emerge. It should first be clarified, however, that some of the videos studied are exempt from this particular evaluation, since they were filmed outdoors and thus were not always provided with a background suitable for examination.

The Arabic language appears to be the most vital symbol in these productions, which disseminate a particular version of Iraqi-Arab-Islamic culture as a form of counter-hegemony. The banner or signboard (*yafita*) is probably the most recurrent element in the *mise en scène*. On every banner, there are two main elements, the first being the *basmala*: 'In the name of Allah, the most gracious, the most merciful', along with the name of the organization. The second most prominent element is the frequent use of the Islamic declaration of faith, or *shahada*: *la ilaha ila allah wa Muhammadun rasulullah* (There is no God but Allah, and Muhammad is his messenger).

In 74 per cent of the productions studied, the banner is a dominant feature mounted on the background wall. Though variable in size and shape, the flag consistently shares two traits: it is black (though in one instance it is both white and black), and it contains a text or message written in Arabic. Texts and messages are presented in Arabic *khatt* (calligraphy), be they in the *mise en scène* itself during filming, or inserted during the production process. These productions appropriate and make conscious use of rooted cultural-religious elements in Arab culture. The cultural significance of calligraphy is twofold: given the sacred nature of writing in Islam, as bearer of divine revelation, calligraphic inscriptions have emerged in Islamic art and religious architecture as the most important means of decoration, with *mihrabs* (prayer niches) and *minbars* (platforms) bearing Qur'anic inscriptions (Schimmel 1970: 3-4). Furthermore, as it was in Iraq that Arabic calligraphy first developed as a professional art, it comes as little surprise to find that its use is still an important element of modern Iraqi publishing, and also of new media. Amongst the *sitta* (six) styles used in these videos are: *Thuluth, Naskh, Rihan, Muhaqqaq, Tauqi' and Riqa'*.

In 18 per cent of instances where a banner appears within the production, part of their design incorporates a round yellow symbol in the middle of the banner, a color that traditionally indicates the sacred. Thus, it can be argued that the producers are embedding the text with certain intended meanings *vis-à-vis* the use of background within the frame. The Arabic text immediately informs the viewer of the group's Arab-Islamic heritage, while the use of color indicates that the group believes it is performing the sacred will of the Prophet Muhammad, and that their actions are sanctioned by divine power, expressed in the *basmala*.

Religious symbols: adaptation of the khutba

Another symbolic form used in the hostage videos is the *khutba*, a form of oratory or rhetorical mode of public speaking, entailing eloquence, style, cogency and grace. According to the *Lisan al-'Arab*, 'the *khutba* in Arab culture is the name for the words in a speech, normally in rhymed prose'; furthermore, it 'is like a letter with a beginning and an end. It also gives a lesson in good manners – *tahdhib*' (Ibn Mandhur 1955). *Khutba* predates Islam and can be social, political, secular or religious. More specifically, *khutba* is an Arabic term referring to the Islamic sermon delivered both before the Friday *salah* (prayer) and after the prayers of an *eid* (feast). The person who delivers the *khutba* is called the *khatib*, usually the *imam* (prayer leader), though sometimes these roles are played by two different people. There are no requirements of eligibility to become a *khatib*, though the person must be a male who has attained the age of puberty. It is also required that the *khatib* be in a state of physical purity. The audience at a *khutba* should be quiet and attentive; many scholars suggest that they refrain from everything (even performing *salah*), and that they give the *khatib* their undivided attention.

Elements of the *khutba* are alluded to throughout all of the kidnap videos studied. The *khutaba'*, or orators, make their *khutba*s short on occasion (i.e. one to five minutes, in accordance with the Prophet Muhammad's saying: 'Make your *salah* long and your *khutba* short'), whereas on others, where the motive of political communication predominates, *khutba*s can be lengthy. Kidnap videos do not feature an 'official' orator, presenter or mediator between the kidnapping group and its audiences. Rather, a (necessarily unidentified) front man is selected, who acts as spokesperson for the group. The process of inviting journalists for briefings or visits is clearly considered too risky; hence, due to security considerations, no mediation process exists.

Inevitably, *khutba*s in these videos are highly rhetorical, containing strong elements of religious and/or nationalist discourse. Most of the time, the *khutba*s are written and then read aloud by the *khutaba'*. Most are speeches conveying a political stance, while others articulate a party platform or make various demands of different authorities. *Khutba*s are frequently pronounced by the leader of the group, who is presented cinematically as a central, heroic figure, or by the group member possessing the most radiophonic voice. A variety of language games and allusions are employed, revealing meanings derived from the fact that the kidnappers aim in part at an audience with an Islamic religious education, possibly in the hope of gaining their sympathy, granting them gratification, or generating further recruitment to their cause. At the end of the *khutba*, and before the *salah*, the *khatib* and the audience make their supplications aloud.

Color in the costume of kidnapper and kidnapped

In the material analyzed, all of the kidnappers wear balaclavas, predominantly black, whilst 71 per cent wear primarily black items of clothing. The use of balaclavas has a dual purpose: it hides the identity of the participant whilst also evoking the association of balaclavas with acts of violence, terrorism or guerrilla warfare. This signifies to the audience that these men are violent and dangerous; furthermore, the resulting lack of identification decreases empathy with the activist, whilst enhancing empathy with the hostage, whose face is exposed.

The dominant use of black has many symbolic connotations (Barthes 1993), which may be taken in an ethnic or theological perspective reconcilable with that of religion. Its use here can be seen as one of cultural appropriation and borrowing: it has been argued that the symbolism of the color black in Islam was transmitted through the Copts of Egypt, in turn from the traditions of ancient Egypt, where Anubis, the Greek name for the ancient Egyptian god of embalming or lord of the dead, was depicted as black. In Arab pre-Islamic times, the black flag was a sign of revenge; it was also the color of the head-dress worn when leading troops into battle. In the Islamic period, black became the ritual color of the Prophet Muhammad (Feisner 2000: 126), and later of the Abbasid dynasty, itself centered in Iraq, and of the Shi'ites when mourning the death of Husayn at Karbala.

Yet the use of black also has many universal psychological significations; most specifically, it is recognized as a color representing authority, power, anger and death. Thus, through the pre-meditated selection of color, it may be seen how the creators and producers of these films intend to communicate messages of power, danger and revenge. The producers' use of black, especially when combined with the Arabic text, demonstrates an attempt on their part to integrate Arab-Islamic motifs and signifiers into their productions, and to underscore the 'Islamic' nature of their activities.

Another color used in the context of costume is orange. In 18 per cent of the material reviewed, the hostages are dressed in bright orange clothing, evoking that worn by the prisoners at the Guantanamo Bay detention camp in Cuba. This instantly evokes an ironic understanding of the relationship between kidnapper and kidnapped, whilst also drawing a distinction between the legitimacy of these 'terrorists'' treatment of their 'prisoners', and the opposing, 'lawful' US government's treatment of its detainees at Guantanamo Bay. It is to be noted that, from the films analyzed, the ritual use of orange dress relates solely to non-Muslim American and European hostages, especially those nationals of countries involved in the war, such as the US, Britain and Italy.

Body language of participants

On every occasion where the kidnappers make an appearance in the footage, they are standing, while the hostages are sitting or kneeling 89 per cent of the time. When the kidnappers appear on screen with the hostage in an establishing shot, the hostage is always sitting or kneeling, and is constantly positioned either directly in front of a single guard or in the middle of the group if more than one kidnapper is present. In this way, the hostage becomes the focus of the framing. This is a fundamental, instinctive demonstration of the relation of power between hostage and hostage-taker. Through the most basic and obvious use of body language possible, the video makers are conveying to their audiences the message that the kidnappers are in control: they stand, while the obedient hostage is forced to sit or kneel. In the opening sequences of the videos, the hands of 41 per cent of the hostages are bound, whilst 26 per cent are also blindfolded. This further embellishes the hostage-takers' complete dominion over and 'possession' of their captives, with the hostage being seen as a product of ownership by the organization, and one with whom they are free to do as they see fit.

The use of weaponry

The visual presentation of pistols and guns is apparent in 70 per cent of these video productions. Yet, out of the 70 per cent featuring a firearm, this was used to kill the hostage in only 30 per cent of the footage. On 48 per cent of occasions, a bayonet or knife appears within the film, and is used to kill the hostage every time. Clearly, there is a strong indexical meaning conveyed by weapons as powerful as blades and guns; the gun, in particular, being the successor to the blade in its use in warfare, is the most advanced signifier of violence available to the producers of the film. In addition, the mere appearance of such weaponry connotes a strong message to the audience concerning the kidnap group's power, and the inherent danger it presents.

Narrative structure and technical features

There is a certain 'narrative' structure observed when viewing the majority of kidnap videos that end with the hostage's death. In such instances, the chronological composition follows a distinctive pattern: the opening, 'establishing' shot introduces the hostage, who then makes a statement and/or the hostage-taker makes a statement. The hostage is then executed, and the clip ends with a careful close-up of the hostage's dead body (occurring in 75 per cent of the videos surveyed). This specific sequence of events conveys a particular message through the action portrayed: you will pay attention to our cause, or you have not paid attention to our cause, thus violence will happen, and the blame and its ramifications lie with you. Considering the political context of these videos, the 'you' should be considered to be the government responsible for the citizen featured therein.

The 'establishing shot'

The 'establishing shot', a term described by Bordwell and Thompson as one which 'shows the spatial relations among the important figures, objects and setting in a scene' (2004: 502), has been modified here to describe the 'establishment' of setting (locale, scenery, weapons etc) and principal participants, namely the hostage(s) and activist(s), within the footage, by use of a static middle-shot. At the beginning of 93 per cent of the texts examined, an establishing shot was used, while on the 70 per cent of occasions when a kidnapper appears within the film, they are framed within the establishing shot, armed and guarding the hostage as mentioned above.

If the establishing shot is used to give immediate context to the scene, then the final framing of the hostage's dead body is used to emphasize the extremity of the scenario. It is the view of the present author that, in cases such as the beheading of Western hostage victims such as the Briton Kenneth Bigley and US nationals Jack Hensley and Eugene Armstrong, their executions are presented as a substitute for regicide against Blair and Bush respectively. The purpose of the close-up adheres to the cinematic convention of encouraging empathy, by allowing the spectator to maintain eye-level contact with the subject, the most natural form of communication between humans. In the case of kidnap videos, it is used to serve as the culmination of the message delivered by the producers: you have not listened to our message or obeyed our command, and here is the result.

Editing

Editing, in its most basic form, is the selection and joining of separate camera shots. To illustrate the multitude of potential motives behind editing within film, Bordwell and Thompson (2004: 502) define editing as 'the selective control of the flow of information'. By editing a film, the potential exists to alter radically the perception of spatial and temporal dimensions, to change the narrative or remove it completely. Within this scenario, we have another example of how the text of the kidnap video operates within a 'constructed world', which the creators of the footage have carefully designed in a pre-meditated manner, to present their chosen perspective and narrative to the audience. This is how the 'plot' of hostage videos is enabled, and thus it has the most direct influence on how the audience consumes the information presented therein.

Some 67 per cent of the kidnap videos examined contained editing, with the remaining 33 per cent shot in one long take from start to finish. The immediately noticeable effect of the 'long take' versus the edited versions is that they appear much more amateurish and rushed, less professional and thus less authoritative. In 50 per cent of videos that use editing, non-diegetic graphics are used, from text appearing across the screen, to visual wipes (an overt, ostentatious transition from one shot to another which varies between lines moving across the screen to the shot moving away in a 3-D block, then coming back with a 3-D block of the new shot). Such manipulations of footage increase the perceived proficiency of the filmmakers, and thus conclude with a more memorable, distinctive impression left upon the viewer.

Voiceover and music

In a number of the kidnap videos, the voiceover is given in imitation of hymns (*tawshihat* or *ibtihalat diniyya*), accompanied by phrases and sound bytes from anthems, marching and rallying songs, including the phrase '*La budda an yubada*'. ('It is inevitable; he will be exterminated.') These are different from other modes of voiceover presentation, which attempt to reproduce *tajwid* (recitation of the Qur'an), or poetic genres such as Andalusian *muwashshahat*. Non-diegetic music is used in 28 per cent of footage featuring editing; this increases the professional appearance of the footage whilst also encouraging sympathy with the victim. Non-diegetic music of a seemingly sympathetic nature is sometimes played over shots of executions, creating a strange juxtaposition as those who killed the subject now seemingly encourage the audience to empathize with the murdered hostage. This further stresses that blame for these deaths should be laid upon those governments who did not respond to the kidnappers' commands. Such music suggests they are saying: 'This tragedy would not have happened had our demands been met.'

Conclusion

Taking the 2003 occupation of Iraq and subsequent hostage-taking as an example, the above has attempted to demonstrate that, in today's world, the political communications of wars have transformed exponentially. The introduction of ICT and its availability has allowed Iraqi resistance and, notably, kidnapping groups to have almost unlimited access to new global media. The kidnap videos phenomenon demonstrates that the political communications of the occupying powers no longer dictate and dominate the global discourse of war coverage, as was the case during the first Iraq war in 1991.

The political communication process as displayed in Iraqi kidnap videos concerns political power (who will govern a future Iraq?), economic power (who will control Iraq's oil?) and military power (who possesses it?). Though aired in the public sphere, the messages of these videos refer to a particular geographical area, and tend to convey the message of liberation and the ending of Western occupation. Whether these kidnap videos have an impact on citizens and viewers in the occupiers' countries is a subject beyond the remit of this study, though it should be pointed out that, on occasion, *khutba*s in these videos have directly addressed the citizens of these countries, asking them to place more pressure on their governments to withdraw from Iraq.

The availability and possession of cheap, advanced technology in addition to the skills to operate it, has meant that, for Arabs and Muslims, this is not only an 'open war' (McNair 1995: 170), but also a constant, live media war on all fronts. In the 1991 Gulf War, Iraqis, Arabs and Muslims owned no communication technology, hence their version of reality could neither be heard nor seen. The subsequent coverage of pan-Arab satellite channels has given unlimited access to Arab news and views, with this information now flowing from the Arab world, as a counter-centre of information, towards the West. Thus Arabs themselves have become a source of information, which in itself has become appealing to Western media organizations. Furthermore, the launch of Arab websites in non-Arab languages, namely English, means that information about Arabs has now become available from Arabs, but in English. Thus self-narration on a variety of levels has been achieved through the proliferation of ICT.

Media products such as hostage videos have not only countered the media war propaganda of the occupying forces, but even challenged them repeatedly, by supplying responses to stories and footage regarding Western soldiers or compatriots. Simply put, traditional disinformation by the Western occupying powers may be seen to have diminished after 2003, due to the ability of the other side to supply powerfully symbolic counter evidence.

George W. Bush's declaration of the end of the 'War on Iraq' in 2003 appears not only to have been militarily wrong. 'Ending' the war has been militarily impossible, since counter-campaigns against the occupation are being launched by resistance and kidnap groups on an almost daily basis. In addition, the 'war' has persisted through the use of counter-propaganda by Iraqi resistance organizations. Arguably, web-based counter media campaigns in the form of kidnap and other videos may be seen to have contributed to the deterioration of the political image of both Bush and Blair, both of whom have achieved their lowest popularity ratings since the occupation of Iraq was implemented.

If Iraqi kidnapping groups had solely the equipment to produce these videos without the means to disseminate them directly, they would have needed to deliver their tapes to television channels. Clearly, to approach foreign journalists in hostile territory is not considered to be the best option, since many are embedded and branded part of the occupation's propaganda machine. The availability and credibility of some Arab news channels has since provided a more secure channel by which to deliver these videos, a method adopted by Osama Bin Laden. As this study has shown, however, Iraqi kidnapping groups have now recognized that, by bypassing the intermediary, they are afforded the most direct means of delivering their videos and the messages they contain – in an uninterrupted form and according to their own terms and conditions.

References

Arnett, Peter (1997) *The Media and The Gulf War: An Eyewitness Account*, United Arab Emirates: ECSSR
Barthes, Roland (1993) *Mythologies*, London: Vintage
Bordwell, David and Thompson, Kristin (2004) *Film Art: An Introduction,* New York: McGraw-Hill
Castells, Manuel (1997) *The Power Of Identity*, Oxford: Blackwell
— (2002) *The Internet Galaxy: Reflections on the Internet, Business and Society*, Oxford: OUP
Feisner, Edith Anderson (2000) *Color: How To Use Color In Art And Design*, London: Laurence King Publishing
Foucault, Michel (1977) *Discipline and Punish: The Birth of the Prison*, London: Allen Lane
Hallin, Daniel C. (1998) The media and war, in Corner, John, Schlesinger, Philip and Silverstone, Roger (eds) (1998) *International Media Research: A Critical Survey*, London and New York: Routledge pp 206-231
Hall, Stuart, Critcher, Charles, Jefferson, Tony and Clarke, John (1987) *Policing the Crisis: Mugging, the State and Law and Order,* Basingstoke: Macmillan Education Ltd
Ibn Mandhur (1955) *Lisan al-'Arab*, Beirut: Dar Sadir
Khoury-Machool, Makram (2002) The globalisation of media: the first cyberwar in the Middle East, in Singer, Caroline (ed.) *The Middle East in London*, London: Stacey International pp 70-83
— (2007) Palestinian youth and political activism: the emerging Internet culture and new modes of resistance, *Policy Futures in Education*, Vol. 5, No. 1 pp 17-36
Löwstedt, Anthony (2003) *Caught in the Crossfire: The Iraq War and the Media – A Diary of Claims and Counterclaims*, Vienna: International Press Institute
Lull, James (2000) *Media, Communication, Culture: A Global Approach*, Cambridge: Polity
McNair, Brian (1995) *An Introduction to Political Communication*, London and New York: Routledge
Price, Stuart (1998) *Media Studies*, London: Longman
Robins, Kevin (1996) *Into the Image: Culture and Politics in the Field of Vision*, London and New York: Routledge
Schimmel, Annemarie (1970) *Islamic Calligraphy*, Leiden: E. J. Brill

Taylor, Philip M. (1992) *War and the Media: Propaganda and Persuasion in the Gulf War*, Manchester and New York: Manchester University Press
Thompson, John B. (2001) *The Media and Modernity,* Cambridge: Polity

Chapter Fourteen

Pat Tillman and The Military-Media Complex

David Altheide

War is not healthy for children and other living things.

Anti-war poster, 1960s

. . . the safety of the children of the world depends on it.

President Clinton's comment about bombing Iraq, 1998

The military let him [Pat Tillman] down. The administration let him down. It was a sign of disrespect. The fact that he was the ultimate team player and the watched his own men kill him is absolutely heartbreaking and tragic. The fact that they lied about it afterward is disgusting.

Pat Tillman's mother, Mary

This chapter examines how military propaganda covered up the cause of death of Pat Tillman, a promising young professional football player, who was killed by his own men in Afghanistan on 22 April 2004. Tillman, according to his father, was a 'poster boy' for the military and the Bush administration's prosecution of unpopular wars in Iraq and Afghanistan. The role of the military in covering up the details of the blunders that led to his death is part of a broader story about its growing relationship with the mass media since the end of the Vietnam War, as well as the first Persian Gulf War.

The military/entertainment complex

Entertainment is a crucial component in any propaganda campaign. For instance, during the 1991 Gulf conflict, it was used to win public support for 'troops' even if the war was not widely supported. On 28 March 1991, it was reported (*Arizona Republic*: A2) that National Football League (NFL) Films were 'putting together highlights of the Persian Gulf War for a documentary co-produced by the Pentagon'. A spokesman for NFL

Films stated: 'I don't want to say that war is the same as football, but our talent as film makers can very easily be transferred to this sort of venture.'

But not all aspects of war receive media attention. Significantly in 2003, journalists were not permitted to view and film the coffins of dead soldiers as they were returned from Iraq to Dover Air Force Base. The military argued that this was necessary to protect the privacy and dignity of family members, although another interpretation that received little attention from news agencies was that this was part of a propaganda effort to avoid publicity and visuals of dead soldiers. Instead, local and national TV news shows carried photos of 'fallen heroes' night after night. An exception was when the names and photographs of dead American soldiers were read and displayed on the late night news show, Nightline, on 30 April 2004. The show had to be expanded from 30 to 40 minutes to cover all the US soldiers killed in the war. The American Broadcasting Company was severely criticized by politicians and organizations that viewed this as critical of the war effort, including the Sinclair Broadcasting Group, which prohibited its eight stations from carrying the telecast.

Numerous writers have documented how the media easily fell into line with the propaganda effort during the 2003 Iraq invasion (Kellner 2003 and 2004; Altheide 2006). The propaganda was so controlled that even 'big city' newspaper editors were reluctant to print critical pieces, even when it became apparent that the US was torturing prisoners in violation of the Geneva Convention as well as the military code of conduct (Umansky 2006). Indeed, after a British journalist, Carlotta Gall, working for *The New York Times*, uncovered the murder of prisoners by US officials, her editor was still reluctant to prominently display the story.

The story ran on page fourteen under the headline 'US Military Investigating Death of Afghan in Custody'. (It later became clear that the investigation began only as a result of Gall's digging.) Gall attributed the delay to the reluctance to 'believe bad things of Americans' post-9/11. 'There was a sense of patriotism, and you felt it in every question from every editor and copy editor,' she says. 'I remember a foreign desk editor telling me: "Remember where we are – we can smell the debris from 9/11"' (Umansky 2006: 18).

The military/industrial complex

While arms manufacturers still benefit from military build-ups and wars, so do the news media. (Altheide and Snow 1978; Smith 2006; Sperber 2000; Stone 1972). Throughout the last century, business, advertising, and 'show biz' joined in the promotion of war (Halberstam 2000; Hallin 1986; Hertsgaard 1988; Hess 1996). Jackall and Hirota's (1994) provocative account of George Creel and the role of the Committee on Public Information (CPI) at the start of World War 1, and the amazing transformation of the role of public relations in public life led them to conclude that '… the rationalization of advertising and public relations in the twentieth century was largely a product of war'.

Yet the military-industrial complex was essentially a creation of the Cold War era. Congress, the mass media and public took for granted that the Soviet threat was immense and required massive military expenditures to combat the 'communists' as well as the regimes they supported. In general, the mass media were a minor – albeit a supporting – player in the rules and strategies of national and international dominance. Print and movie media served governmental interests, often as explicit propaganda outlets for hot and cold wars until the 1960s. Reliant on governmental licencing and regulations, the television industry lacked the markets and the infrastructure to challenge governmental initiatives.(Barnouw 1990; Halberstam 2000; Hertsgaard 1988).

The military-industrial complex changed when the Soviet Union capitulated to capitalism and its champion, the United States. Notwithstanding the perceived role of a strong military in achieving 'victory' over the Soviets, members of Congress and others argued that the military budget could be reduced, and many claims-makers, who championed other social causes for more government funding, agreed. If the 'external' enemy would be less of a threat in the future, there were still domestic problems to be reckoned with, including crime, drugs, and gangs. The major networks' television schedules promoted 'domestic' threats and sources of fear, with a number of 'reality' shows emphasizing crime, violence, fear and danger (Fishman and Cavender 1998).

Sociologist C. Wright Mills joined President Dwight D. Eisenhower in the 1950s in urging caution over an emerging military-industrial complex. Their concern was that the military and big weapons manufacturers were pursuing common interests to the detriment of the political process. The connections were managed as high-ranking retired military personnel found lucrative jobs as lobbyists and advisors with major aircraft and arms manufacturers (Domhoff 1990; Mills 1956).

Kicking the Vietnam syndrome

The debacle in Vietnam seriously damaged the US's military credibility and it took more than two decades of Hollywood movies and entertainment to bolster claims that the US actually *won* that war, or *would have won* it had it not been for the 'political defeat' at home, referring to the domestic protests and the reluctance of politicians (such as Lyndon Johnson) to 'hit 'em with everything we had'. Many people blamed the mass media, particularly television journalism, for the eventual US withdrawal. It would take a number of military 'victories' against adversaries such as Grenada (1983), Panama (1989) and Iraq (1991) to redefine losses as victories and restore the military's influence on politics and its reputation with the public (Altheide 1995).

An adversarial relationship with the military was apparent in some media outlets until the 1980s when government censorship and restrictions first separated and then 'reintegrated' the media (Der Derian 2001; Knickerbocker 2002). Indeed, the Gulf War in 1991 was enthusiastically supported by most media outlets, with celebratory coverage of well-orchestrated, although often invalid, visuals of dramatic success and 'kills' (for instance, coverage gave the impression that most Patriot missiles hit their targets – though this was false (Taubes 2002).

Several developments in the media and information technology fields were critical for the resurgence of American military in foreign policy. One was the expanding use of satellites for military and commercial purposes (e.g. surveillance and communication). Another was the rise of cable TV, particularly that of the '4th network' – CNN – and 24 hour news. During the 1990s the 4th network was followed by a 5th (Fox), as well as conventional networks' expansion (e.g. MSNBC). With costs rising for the big three networks, ABC, NBC, and CBS sliced news staffs, relying on satellite feeds, as well as the work of 'stringers' throughout the world rather than fully staffed foreign bureaus (Lowry 1998: F1). As a result, international reporting declined, except for reactive 'crisis' coverage, which was often 'live' (Wasburn 2002; Wu 2000).

Resurgence of the military after 1991 Gulf War

The Gulf War of 1991 was important for the resurgence of the military and the military-media connections (Altheide and Snow 1991). Despite initial proclamations by media pundits and some academics about media control and censorship, this war contributed to the shared use of entertaining visuals by the Pentagon and the major networks in the US and throughout the world. Generals and journalists joked as they led global audiences in viewing bomb-sight videos of explosions, 'hits', complete with 'oohs' and 'ahs' and occasional laughter when, as in one case, a motorist crossed a bridge just moments before it exploded. CNN's round-the-clock live coverage of the missile and aerial bombardment of Baghdad helped establish its future role as an important player in international affairs and coverage.

CNN's Gulf War coverage is significant in several other ways. First, it operated in enemy territory, but with the full co-operation of the 'enemy', the highly 'demonized' Saddam Hussein. 'Both sides' appreciated the role of the media and gave it privileged status in order to promote and use key visuals – a 'dramatic hit' or 'civilian casualties' – for their own purposes. Despite having its movements restricted, CNN became the signature network of the Gulf War, and over the next few years would add other campaigns to its resume. Second, the 'real time', round-the-clock coverage meant that viewers associated it with 'live' and 'actual' coverage. Indeed, top Pentagon and governmental officials were told to 'tune in CNN' to find out the latest about the Gulf War (Altheide 1999; Lowry 1998).

Third, the technology of warfare combined the use of 'target cameras' that could broadcast flight toward a target, as well as sophisticated aircraft cameras that could follow a missile and record its 'hit'. This made spectacular dramatic visuals that are the foundation for the entertainment format of television. Such visuals contributed to the changing role of military press briefing. Fourth, the journalist's role shifted to commenting on the visuals being seen, and the technical aspects of weapon systems, rather than rationale and strategy for the entire operation.

The sophisticated obfuscation of Iraq War news did not happen immediately. The military learned to handle the press. As Seymour Topping reported (1998: 58): 'After watching some 600 of his troops float down with Russian MIG fighters flying cover above them, the U.S. commander, General John Sheehan, remarked: "It really is a different world." The general was referring to the new relationship with former Cold War opponents, but he could very well have been speaking of the changed relationship between the American military and the media.'

News values and the military

In addition, news organizations and their military sources increasingly shared similar views on news values. As Army Major Bob Hastings explained to the *Washington Post*'s Steve Vogel (1998): '. . .information officers must be ready to take advantage of "media moments" from gauging a reporter's perspective on a story to brushing dandruff off the general's shoulders and, most important, knowing how to get out the "command message": the information or story angle that commanders want the public to know.'

This media-military partnership included shared information technology as well as perspectives on the 'story', emphasizing weapons and strategies, which required military experts to narrate visuals. 'Air time' or what was allocated to broadcast, emphasized the visuals of armaments, as did newspaper photographs. The dominant frames and themes of the coverage were about technology and weapons. *Los Angeles Times*' correspondent George Black (1991 M7) noted that news media treated the initial phase of Desert Storm exactly in the way the military wanted, 'a blur of meaningless press conferences, video-game images…and the illusion of news'.

Traditionally, experts were used on a case-by-case basis, but the nearly eight month planning for coverage of the Gulf War suggested a more permanent relationship between sources and journalists. Black (ibid) reported: 'To fill in the gaps left by the Pentagon, every network producer has a Rolodex full of military analysts and retired officers, many of them highly paid shills for the arms industry.'

Following the Gulf War, numerous military officials and spokespersons became reporters, correspondents, and consultants to the networks (e.g. Pete Williams, Tony Cordesman, Chuck Horner, and Norman Schwarzkopf). General Schwarzkopf, who gave lectures for fees of $50,000 and sold his autobiography for $6 million, was given his own television show. In later years he would be interviewed by former subordinates who also worked for the networks. Most of the discussion about impending war would focus on strategies, military goals, and weapon systems. Seldom would lengthy analysis occur about the legitimacy of an operation or its foreign policy implications.

War is now communicated as a routine part of everyday life. It is incorporated as part of broadcast and news formats. Other network coverage further normalized war. With a fireplace in the visual background, media consultant Schwarzkopf was asked what a difference the missiles that were used in the attack on Iraq might have made in the Vietnam War. With a smile, he said that the politicians then might not have permitted the military to use them against Hanoi (Altheide 1999).

The Tillman Story: death of a hero

Tillman, like thousands of other US soldiers, was killed after President Bush landed on an aircraft carrier and declared victory on 1 May 2003. Tillman was a sports celebrity – a National Football League player – who displayed independence and character in many of his personal and professional choices. A former standout linebacker for the Arizona State University Sun Devils, Tillman went on to join the Arizona Cardinals, who also played in Sun Devil stadium. He and his brother, Kevin, who was a minor league baseball player – and who was serving with Tillman the day he died – enlisted in the army and became Rangers to fight for their country. Their highly publicized enlistment was a godsend for the military, which was having difficulties recruiting young men and women to fight in a controversial war begun under false pretenses. More citizens were becoming aware that a major justification for attacking Iraq – to destroy Weapons of Mass Destruction – was false since these weapons did not exist. This posed a major problem for US propaganda.

The Tillman story illustrates how propaganda has become fused with the entertainment format and media logic (Altheide and Snow 1979; Altheide and Snow 1991) in forging a renewed relationship between news and entertainment, the major networks and the military, and foreign conflicts and domestic policy. This was important for the Tillman case since he was a celebrity, a football star. Sports, especially televised sports, incorporated all the major elements of the entertainment format (Altheide and Snow 1979).

Sport is a great vehicle for propaganda, and sports personalities are ideal sources to help fans identify with the propaganda message. Audiences recognize and identify with individual athletes, who are associated with familiar sports. Propagandists, such as government officials, seek to link athletes and others, who are well known, with values, causes, and justifications for a particular war (Jackall 1994). The positive link is forged through heroism. Like bridge construction, forging heroic identity for an audience takes creative work; unlike building bridges, social constructions rely on symbolic meanings of words and images. One construction by the military-media complex involves the death and significance of Pat Tillman, a 27-year-old promising professional football player, who walked away from a multi-million dollar contract with the Arizona Cardinals, to join the Army and serve as a Ranger in Afghanistan where he was killed by fellow Rangers on 22 April 2004.

Dominant cultural symbols

The media representation of Pat Tillman was constructed through news reports to reflect dominant values about cultural symbols (e.g. patriotism and God bless America), masculinity (e.g. sports), and the War with Iraq. Positive vocabularies of motive and intention (Mills 1940) were attributed to Pat Tillman by major sports organizations (e.g. the National Football League) including nationally prominent politicians (e.g. Senator John McCain).

Tillman's death essentially provided a 'face for the war' particularly for Arizonans. Another Arizonan, Lori Piestewa, a Hopi mother of two, who was killed by enemy troops in combat in Iraq in March 2003, was a very different 'face' of the war for Arizona. Piestawa went 'missing' on the same day (24 March) as Jessica Lynch, who would later be rescued and featured on numerous television shows for her heroism (House 2004). Partly because she was believed to be the first Native American women killed in a foreign war, Lori was heralded as a hero, her family was fêted, and highways and a mountain were named for her in Arizona. Little was written about why a young single mother with two children would join the army. One account stressed her uniqueness:

> Piestewa, 23, had been the focus of spots on programs as varied as Hardball With Chris Matthews and Good Morning America. Dozens of other programs, from Inside Edition to the Oprah Winfrey Show, pursued interviews with family members. German- and Spanish-language television stations sought to tell her story...She came from the same environs that produced the famed Navajo Code Talkers of World War II, who have enjoyed a recent renaissance in the public spotlight because of last year's movie Windtalkers. And, with the number of US war dead in Iraq at just over 100, the media focus on the victims was concentrated and intense, especially on those with unusual backgrounds like that of Piestewa (House 2003).

Others saw her service, like that of many poor Americans, as an opportunity to obtain some income, escape the grinding poverty of reservation life, and provide an opportunity for her children. But it had been more than a year since Piestawa was killed, and until her death, she was unknown outside her community.

Tillman: white, male and successful

Tillman was different: he was male, white, successful and a rich professional athlete, who had clear local reputation and a national identity as a professional football player. There were few like him in this war or any US war for the last 30 years (Smith 2006). He was a prime icon and there was an essential story line waiting for him: a courageous, patriotic, strong, successful, wealthy professional athlete, who put it all aside to defend his country while bravely defending his comrades. As we shall see below, most of these points resonated with the patriotic narrative, except for the disquieting discovery that his own men killed him.

Like many high profile college and professional athletes, Tillman was popularly regarded as exceptional. He was an intelligent, aggressive, outstanding football player at Arizona State University. He was also white. He played football for four years at ASU, where he received numerous recognitions for his aggressive defense play and perseverance (Smith 2006). Rule violations that may have been treated as unacceptably deviant by another athlete – and certainly another student – apparently did not hinder Tillman's success at ASU. In addition to serving 30 days in jail for a violent beating he administered shortly before hitting campus, he was also given to climbing the 200-foot light towers at ASU's Sun Devil Stadium to 'meditate'. A photograph of Tillman in a light tower accompanied several media reports about his death. The caption in the *Sports Illustrated* report read: 'Solitude: When in need of his own space in college, Tillman climbed to the top of Sun Devil Stadium' (Smith 2004: 46). Nothing was said about this being a rule violation.

Tillman was unlike other athletes (ibid), never really seeking the limelight, interested in ideas, and stating that life was just too easy. Following the hijackings and attacks on several buildings on 9/11, Tillman and his brother, Kevin, were reported (ibid) to have been very upset. They joined the army six months later, aiming for the Rangers, and Pat and Kevin Tillman gave up, respectively, a $3.6 million dollar contract with the Arizona Cardinals, and a minor league baseball career. This action was interpreted as turning away from fame and fortune in favor of patriotism and duty to country (Smith 2006). The Tillman brothers received the Arthur Ashe Courage Award at the Espy Awards ceremony on 16 July 2003 after their enlistment. While it was reported that Tillman also left his new bride of a few months to join the Rangers, the departure was told from his vantage point – listening to an 'inner voice'. (ibid). Thus, the sense of selflessness – forsaking fame, fortune, and living with his wife – were part of the character and commitment statement that would be told about Tillman after his death.

The initial report: the manufacture of the myth

The military, like all organizations, promote themselves by providing dramatic performances of their members, including the use of false information. The initial report was that Tillman and his Ranger patrol were ambushed, and that Tillman showed initiative that saved the lives of several comrades. According to the Army report issued within days (30 April) of his death:

> Tillman's platoon was split into two sections for what officials called a ground assault convoy. Tillman led the lead group. The trailing group took fire, and because of the

cavernous terrain the group had no room to maneouvre out of the 'kill zone'. Tillman's group was already safely out of the area, but when the trailing group came under fire he ordered his men to get out of their vehicles and move up a hill toward the enemy. As Tillman crested the hill he returned fire with his lightweight machine gun. Through the firing Tillman's voice was heard issuing fire commands to take the fight to the enemy on the dominating high ground. Only after his team engaged the well-armed enemy did it appear their fire diminished. As a result of his leadership and his team's efforts, the platoon trail section was able to maneuver through the ambush to positions of safety without a single casualty (Rand 2004: 10).

Numerous publications, including the quickly published book (Rand 2004), carried the Army's account of Tillman's death. For instance, the *Arizona Republic* reported:

As Tillman and other soldiers neared the hill's crest, the Army reported, Tillman directed his team into firing positions and was shot and killed as he sprayed enemy positions with fire from his automatic weapon (House, 29 May 2004).

A *Sports Illustrated* account provided graphic details of his death:

Dusk fell...the shadows twitched with treachery...the Rangers scrambled out of their vehicles as they came under ambush and charged the militants on foot. Suddenly Pat was down, Pat was dying. Two other US soldiers were wounded, and a coalition Afghan fighter was killed in a firefight that lasted 15 or 20 minutes before the jihadists melted away (Smith 2004: 42 and 46).

Largely based on these false accounts, Tillman was awarded a Silver Star and a Purple Heart and was posthumously promoted to Corporal on 30 April 2004. The top American officer in Iraq, John Abizaid, knew that it was a lie on 29 April 2004, although Tillman's parents, his widow, and his brother, who fought alongside him, were not told the truth for another month (Rich 2006). His parents, devastated by the loss of their son, were outraged at the dishonorable way that his death was covered up by the military. His mother, Mary, noted:

Pat had high ideals about the country; that's why he did what he did. . . The military let him down. The administration let him down. It was a sign of disrespect. The fact that he was the ultimate team player and he watched his own men kill him is absolutely heartbreaking and tragic. The fact that they lied about it afterward is disgusting (White 2005).

Pat and Mary Tillman became even more upset as more details of the cover-up emerged over the next several months. Mary denied President Bush an opportunity to star in a 'cameo role' during a memorial service one memorial service, and later added:

They could have told us upfront that they were suspicious that it was a fratricide but they didn't. They wanted to use him for their purposes. It was good for the administration. It was before the elections. It was during the prison scandal. They needed something that looked good, and it was appalling that they would use him like that (Rich 2006).

The military performance: the Big Lie

On 8 May, some 800 people attended a memorial service for Pat Tillman at Sun Devil Stadium. They included professional athletes, students, coaches, Governor Napolitano, as well as ASU President Michael Crow, who, along with former coach, Larry Marmie, quoted stories of Pericles about warfare and heroes. Marmie added that Tillman was 'all about truth' and an elementary school teacher was reported to have said that 2nd and 3rd grade students had been writing narratives about Tillman (Collom 2004).

Several weeks after the memorial services a different story appeared to challenge the heroic tale of his death. Tillman and his Rangers were not ambushed, but rather, a mine exploded, and in the confusion, he, like numerous comrades in the last two US wars, was shot by his own men in an act of 'gross negligence' (White 2005).

When it became apparent the military covered up the circumstances surrounding Tillman's death, Arizona Senator John McCain ordered an investigation. Over the next 18 months more details emerged about how his ranger unit, split into two parts, suffered miscommunication, ultimately mistaking Tillman for an enemy and fired repeatedly without verifying the target.

The soldiers in Afghanistan knew immediately that they had killed Tillman on 22 April 2004, and quickly began the cover-up, including burning his uniform and body armor (Smith 2006). As noted above, army officials insisted that they did not know the truth, but later investigations revealed that a general was informed of this within the next ten days (Rich 2006). The army and other participants in the military-media complex benefited from Tillman's nationally televised memorial service on 3 May 2004. Tillman's parents did not learn how he died until weeks later, and even then many details were not disclosed (Staff 2005). Patrick Tillman, Sr., an attorney, decried the 'botched homicide investigation', adding:

> After it happened, all the people in positions of authority went out of their way to script this. They purposely interfered with the investigation, they covered it up. I think they thought they could control it, and they realized that their recruiting efforts were going to go to hell in a handbasket if the truth about his death got out. They blew up their poster boy (Staff 2005).

The politics of fear needs heroes

The politics of fear needs heroes to hold up to audiences members as role models, who not only do 'heroic things' but more importantly, support the political order without question, including dying for it (Altheide 2006). Heroes are propaganda products and reflect the mass media construction process, particularly the creative work of the military-media complex. This includes the use of media logic and entertainment formats (Altheide and Snow 1979). The politics of fear shrouded Pat Tillman as a subject and an object. As a subject, his 'self' was communicated through an artful construction of moral and patriotic ideals.

He was presented as an idealized object, icon-like, to be valorized, emulated, and connected to the military causes in Iraq and Afghanistan. He was used for various purposes, and this use was constituted through mass media coverage, publicity, and the entertainment format. He became a product of the politics of fear, a guardian of claims about legitimacy of war, and a defender against those who might question the legitimacy of the war against 'terrorism'. Such questions were not part of the military-media script.

References

Altheide, David (2006) *Terrorism and the Politics of Fear*, Lanham, MD: Alta Mira Press
Altheide, David L. (1995) *An Ecology of Communication: Cultural Formats of Control*, Hawthorne, N.Y.: Aldine de Gruyter
— (1999) The Military-Media Complex, *Newsletter of the Sociology of Culture* Vol. 13, No. 1
Altheide, David L. and Snow, Robert P. (1978) Sports versus the Mass Media, *Urban Life* 7 pp 189-204
Altheide, David L. and Snow, Robert P. (1979) *Media Logic*, Beverly Hills, CA: Sage
Altheide, David L. and Snow, Robert P. (1991) *Media Worlds in the Postjournalism Era*, Hawthorne, New York: Aldine de Gruyter
Barnouw, Erik. (1990) *Tube of plenty: The evolution of American television*, New York: Oxford University Press
Black, George (1991) Rolodex Army Wages a Nintendo War: TV's Deskbound Generals Tune Out on the Crucial Issues: Morality, Economics, Values, *Los Angeles Times* 27 January
Der Derian, James (2001) *Virtuous war : mapping the military-industrial-media-entertainment network*, Boulder, Colo /Oxford: Westview Press
Domhoff, G. William (1990) *The power elite and the state: How policy is made in America*, New York: Aldine de Gruyter
Fishman, Mark and Cavender, Gary (1998) *Entertaining crime: television reality programs*, New York: Aldine de Gruyter
Halberstam, David (2000). *The powers that be*. Urbana, University of Illinois Press.
Hallin, Daniel C. (1986) *The 'uncensored' war: The media and Vietnam*, New York: Oxford University Press
Hertsgaard, Mark (1988) *On Bended Knee: The Press and the Reagan presidency*, New York: Farrar Straus Giroux
Hess, Stephen (1996) *International news and foreign correspondents.*, Washington D.C.: Brookings Institution
House, Billy (2004) Tillman killed by friendly fire, *Arizona Republic,* 29 May 2004 p. 1
Jackall, Robert (ed) (1994) *Propaganda*, New York: New York University Press
Jackall, Robert, and Hirota, Janice M. (1994) America's First Propaganda Ministry: The Committee on Public Information During the Great War in Jackall., Robert (ed.) *Propaganda*, New York: New York University Press pp 137-173
Knickerbocker, Brad (2002) Return of the 'military-industrial complex?' *Christian Science Monitor*, 13 February p. 2
Lowry, Brian. (1998) Brave New World for Iraq Coverage; Television: There are Now Three All-News Cable Channels, Creating a Difficult Environment for Network News Operations, *Los Angeles Times*, 19 December: Calendar (F)1
Mills, C. Wright (1940) Situated Actions and Vocabularies of Motive, *American Sociological Review* 5: 904-913. Available online at: http://pubpages.unh.edu/~jds/Mills%201940.htm, accessed on 14 October 2006
Mills, C. Wright (1956) *The power elite*, New York: Oxford University Press

Rich, Frank (2006) The Mysterious Death of Pat Tillman, *The New York Times*, 6 November 2005. Available online at:
http://www.truthout.org/docs_2005/110605Z.shtml, accessed 14 October 2006

Smith, Gary (2004) Code of Honor: Pat Tillman 1976-2004, *Sports Illustrated*, 3 May pp 40-46

— (2006) Remember His Name:Pat Tillman's Road: From 9/11 to Afghanistan, *Sports Illustrated* 11 September pp 86-101. Available online at:
http://sportsillustrated.cnn.com/2006/magazine/09/05/tillman0911/index.html, accessed on 14 October 2006

Sperber, Murray A (2000) *Beer and circus: How big-time college sports is crippling undergraduate education,* New York: Henry Holt

Staff. (2005) Tillman's parents lash out at Army, *Washington Post*, 23 May 2005. Available online at:
http://www.eastvalleytribune.com/index.php?sty=41825, accessed on 22 September 2006

Stone, Gregory Prentice (1972) *Games, sport and power*. New Brunswick, New Jersey Transaction Books

Taubes, Gary (2002) Postol vs the Pentagon, *Technology Review* pp 52-61. Available online at:
http://www.hfxpeace.chebucto.org/_reference/BMD/TechnologyReviewPostolProfile_March2002.pdf#search=%22patriot%20missile%20hoax%22, accessed 22 September 2006

Umansky, Eric (2006) Failures of Imagination:American journalists and the coverage of American torture, *Columbia Journalism Review,* September/October 2006. Available online at:
http://www.cjr.org/issues/2006/5/Umansky.asp, accessed on 22 September 2006

Vogel, Steven (1998) Military Trains a Special Corps of Public Relations Troops; 3,500 Journalists a Year are Schooled at Brand-New Center at Fort Meade, *Milwaukee Journal Sentinel*, 25 October p. 6

Wasburn, Philo C. (2002) *The social construction of international news: We're talking about them, they're talking about us*, Westport, Conn. and London: Praeger

White, Josh (2005) Army withheld Tillman details: New report shows top officials knew death was from 'friendly fire' days before memorial, *Washington Post* 4 May. Available online at:
http://epaper.aztrib.com/Repository/ml.asp?Issue=EVT/2005/05/04&ID=Ar00700&Mode=HTML, accessed on 22 September 2006

Wu, Denis H. (2000) Systematic Determinants of International News Coverage: A Comparison of 38 Countries, *Journal of Communication*, Vol. 50 pp 110-130

Chapter Fifteen

The Military, the Media and Mimesis

Neal Curtis

'Juba' is the name that US troops in Iraq have given to a sniper who claims to have killed 37 soldiers as of November 2006. Nothing is known about this person, or even if this person is, in fact, a collective body of snipers or a sequence of copycat attacks. What is known is that the sniper fires only once, and leaves an empty bullet casing together with a note at the presumed site from where the shot was fired. Whoever Juba turns out to be his activities are indicative of the ways in which insurgents and those we call terrorists are waging war through the use of new technologies that are central to the revolution in military affairs (RMA) regularly referred to as Information War. The significance of Juba's killings lies not only in the sapping of morale amongst soldiers, but in the fact that each shooting is videoed and quickly uploaded on to an insurgent website. Here, Juba's achievements have become legendary and are part of a concerted propaganda campaign against the occupation.

The videos perfectly capture Paul Virilio's argument in *War and Cinema* (1989) that eyeshot has finally got the better of gunshot. In his analysis of what he calls the logistics of military perception, Virilio outlines how seeing equates to killing, or how, in the fantasies of military speculators, 'full spectrum dominance' equates to the global control of hostile movement. In this information environment Juba's eyeshot, repeated endlessly every time the insurgent website is visited, makes a mockery of the US military's fantasy of control. In this sense, each video can be said to both mimic the logic at the heart of the RMA and counter it at the same time by showing the gaping holes in the US military's 'strategy of *global vision*' (Virilio 1989: 1). As the bullets enter soldiers through the gaps in their armour – the neck, the lower spine, and under the arm are reportedly the preferred targets – so the videos expose and record the weakness and hubris of the military panopticon. In response to the new planetary surveillance technologies of the US military, Juba trains his sight on them: Juba watches and the insurgency watches with him.

The manner in which the methods of information war have been turned against both the US military's rhetoric of invincibility and the US government's rhetoric of freedom no longer surprises us. There are, of course, those catastrophic moments of auto-immunity, such as the photographs that came out of Abu Ghraib, in which the weapon of choice for the new digitized military, namely cyberspace, turns against its greatest advocate and threatens to bring down an administration, or least threatens the careers of the architects of war. In this instance the very networks that were to produce the ultimate military organism carried the images that attacked the tissue of that organism. The British, of course, did not escape this pathology of Information War. They too suffered from this auto-immunity when a 'secret home video' shot by a British soldier showing the brutal and apparent indiscriminate beatings of Iraqis near Basra in February 2006 also found its way into cyberspace.

But aside from these instances of auto-immunity, the enemy are also increasingly using new technologies to their advantage. From the initial surprise that the 'primitives' against which we were fighting were actually knowledgeable in the use of new media and were as well versed in the power of visual culture as any advertising executive, we no longer consider their technical sophistication as anything out of the ordinary. We are now accustomed to seeing grainy images from jihadist websites that display kidnap victims, the last words of suicide bombers, and beheadings, all of which aim to counter the propaganda of the US and British governments.[1] While these websites function within a conventional understanding of propaganda, it is the move of the insurgents and so-called terrorists into the area of 'soft' entertainment media and their use of popular cultural products such as computer games and music videos that is especially interesting.

Der Derian and the MIME-Net

This move towards 'soft' entertainment media is in keeping with a process that James Der Derian has most fully analyzed in his book *Virtuous War*. Here he addresses the now familiar innovations in the RMA pertaining to the use of computers, the Internet and other mobile technologies associated with digitization, but he also reports on how links between the military and the entertainment industries are becoming much stronger, reproducing the rhetoric and the spectacle of warfare even during peacetime, and diffusing it throughout the culture of contemporary life. The relationship between the military and the entertainment industries documented by Der Derian compels us to rethink our understanding of the military-industrial complex that Eisenhower warned about in 1961. In light of the new partnerships and shared interests that go far beyond those of the powerful arms manufacturers, Der Derian argues that we now need to think of this complex in terms of what he calls the Military-Industrial-Media-Entertainment Network, or MIME-Net for short.

The acronym speaks of the relations of imitation or mimesis through which the culture industry reproduces a militarist worldview. The MIME-Net, according to Der Derian, 'runs on video-game imagery, twenty-four-hour news cycles, multiple modes of military, corporate, university, and media power, and microchips, embedded in everything but human flesh (so far)' (2001: 126). His research aims 'to study up close the mimetic power that travels along the hyphens', allowing 'the virtual tail [to wag] the body politic' (Der Derian 1999: 61). In what follows I will briefly set out Der Derian's account of the MIME-Net and propose that research of this kind also needs to take account of the ways in which the imagery and products of the culture industry now regularly used by the military are appropriated, borrowed or imitated by the enemy producing what can only be called a Counter-MIME-Net.

What is most significant for Der Derian is that the emerging MIME-Net produces a qualitatively new form of power that can 'seamlessly merge the production, representation, and execution of war' (2001: xx). While the MIME-Net cannot be said to have a monopoly over the generation and circulation of information, it is significant that this network has an increasing foothold in the varying divisions required for a successful war machine. Its industrial actors develop the weapons; its actors in news and entertainment circulate the representations most suited to an increasingly militarized world, while its military and governmental actors execute the warfare itself.

The MIME-Net and its multiple vectors are, thus, akin to what Philip Graham and Allan Luke (2003) call an autopoietic system, continually producing and circulating meanings for the purpose of legitimating itself. Regarding the relationship between violence and forms of entertainment they argue that 'militaristic production values are direct, strategic and purposive. The Center for Defense Information (CDI) details almost a century of direct and conscious involvement by the military in the production of movies[2] – a practice, which [...] began with [George] Creel' (ibid: 162). They go on to note how this is a two-way relationship with movies becoming useful reference points for politicians and their handlers who are adept in the semiotic art of intertextuality. Their recent example is Bush's *Top Gun* style media stunt on the deck of an aircraft carrier in 2003 announcing victory in Iraq.

The mimetic circuit of legitimacy

Another very good example of how the film industry has contributed to this mimetic circuit of legitimacy can be found in Lynda E. Boose's analysis of Vietnam films. She argues that two contrasting versions of the Vietnam film mirror the conflict at the heart of American society. The Vietnam War, she argues, brought the American people 'as close as they ever have to considering America's global guilt in the promotion of war' (1993: 71). Films such as *The Deer Hunter*, *Apocalypse Now*, and *Born of the Fourth of July* retold this loss of military, masculine and moral authority. However, a second type of Vietnam film represented by the excessive militarism of Arnold Schwarzenegger and the muscularity of Sylvester Stallone helped recapture that authority and tentatively restore the US military confidence that was to be completed in actuality by the success of the First Gulf War. In Stallone's *Rambo* series, for example, she argues that 'the unjustly rejected Vietnam vet goes back to the scene of America's loss to rescue the figural representation of a "missing" American masculinity embodied on-screen as the emaciated and emasculated versions of maleness who are imagined as having been left behind' (75). While anti-war films continued to portray small, vulnerable men, right-wing films 'used the megabodied male to articulate the vision of an invincible America that did not "lose" the war so much as it was prevented from winning it' (76), an argument that may well return in neo-conservative accounts of Iraq.

By using Walter Benjamin's (1979) analysis of the mimetic faculty[3] Der Derian seeks to map the ways in which the various actors in the MIME-Net, which includes film producers and directors, varying levels of military personnel, computer game designers, politicians, diplomats, corporate executives, academics, novelists, script writers, news presenters, journalists, arms dealers, TV producers, advertisers and computer scientists mimic and reproduce the discourse and spectacle of war and thus legitimize its logic. In the context of the war against terror, films such as *Pearl Harbor* and *Black Hawk Down*, focusing on the disastrous US intervention in Somalia 1992-1993, exemplify the mimetic functions that Der Derian is trying to trace. For Cynthia Weber *Pearl Harbor* is of interest because of the place Pearl Harbor has in the American imaginary. Re-releasing it after the events of September 2001 was an attempt to align the newly announced war against terror 'with a time before America questioned its moral purity, i.e. before America dropped the nuclear bomb on Hiroshima' (2003: 192).

In turn *Black Hawk Down* in the context of the 'war against terror' seeks to portray America as both willing saviour and absolute victim. According to George Monbiot, Ridley Scott's film mimics the post-9/11 rhetoric of civilization versus barbarism. 'The Somalis in *Black Hawk Down* speak only to condemn themselves. They display no emotions other than greed and the lust for blood. Their appearances are accompanied by sinister Arab techno, while the US forces are trailed by violins, oboes and vocals inspired by Enya. The American troops display horrific wounds. They clutch photos of the loved ones and ask to be remembered to their parents or children as they die. The Somalis drop like flies, killed cleanly, dispensable, unmourned' (2002).

Beyond this well-known complicity between Hollywood and the military the vectors of mimesis are as numerous as the actors within the network in the sense that mimesis may take the form of the dominant discourse of realism that assumes all human actors are competitive 'self-maximizing unit[s]' (Der Derian 2001: 44). This discourse is, of course, central to the military worldview, but is also commonplace amongst diplomats, neo-liberal economists, journalists and filmmakers. It also reappears as a veiled social Darwinism in all manner of television programmes that privilege possessive individualism and survival of the fittest. Other vectors include the technologies of simulation and virtuality developed by the military, computer games manufacturers and cinema special effects teams. Here computer games such as the US military's own *America's Army*, plus a host of other games including *Ghost Recon*, *War on Terrorism*, *War on Terrorism 2*, and *Full Spectrum Dominance* are exemplary of the mimetic process. Similarly, advertisers, TV news editors, security advisers and weapons manufactures all mimic and reproduce the vector of fear that ensures people both arm themselves and consume beyond their needs, a point made exceptionally well by Michael Moore in *Bowling for Columbine*.

Another element in the functioning of the MIME-Net can be seen in the long-standing concern regarding the nature of news itself that privileges war and violence as being especially newsworthy. This is even more the case when considering television news with its emphasis on the drama of pictures. As Daya Kishan Thussu has put it, 'news is largely about conflict, and conflict is always news' (2003: 117). This is especially the case with 24-hour news services such as CNN, Fox and Sky. Because these companies operate in a competitive commercial market they are constantly chasing ratings, and as Thussu notes, 'good news does not make compelling television, which instead thrives on violence, death and destruction…In fact, it has been argued that the rolling news networks have to be conflict-driven or else they will cease to operate as successful businesses' (ibid: 123-124).

To secure ratings these networks also mimic the aesthetics of virtual environments such as the Internet and computer games, creating an aesthetic synergy between entertainment, news and military communications. As Armand Mattelart argues, the success in public relations terms of the ideology of the new cyberwarriors 'resides in the way they have moulded themselves to the imaginary of mass culture' (1994: 118). He continues: 'They were, of course, aided by the "new aesthetics of arms", which means that arms manufacturers are more and more attentive to the creative forms circulating in post-industrial society. It is as if, in the very design of the killing machine projected onto the TV screen, were now incorporated its dimension of media exhibition, its "desiring" dimension, its "communicating" value.' Through this attention to and deployment of the creative forms currently circulating in consumer culture a visual complementarity between military, media and entertainment domains begins to be established.[4]

'The angry global hive of real-time TV'

In this scenario images of conflict, violence and instability are constantly played, securing viewers *and* reproducing the narrative of an infinitely insecure world from which we must protect ourselves at all costs. 'The technical reproducibility of war,' Der Derian notes, 'has produced a kind of global swarming' (2001: 49); neither New World Order nor global village, just 'the angry global hive of real-time TV'. And for these issues of foreign policy to remain a ratings-winner the story must be told with as little deliberation as possible, avoiding historical events that brought us to a particular juncture, and presenting what President Richard Nixon called the drama of 'Good and Evil' as personalized stories of individual wickedness and immorality. Thus we end up with villains like Saddam Hussein and Osama Bin Laden whose photographs appear as wanted posters from classic westerns, with Bush famously asking for Bin Laden 'dead or alive'. Indeed, the persistence of this rhetorical and visual vocabulary from Hollywood's version of the winning of America has lead John Brown (2006), a former Foreign Service officer, to argue that in the mind of leading neo-conservative intellectuals such as Robert Kagan and Max Boot the 'Indian wars' are not yet over, and that the bombing of Afghanistan of 2001 and invasion of Iraq of 2003 are equivalent to 'taming the frontier'.

Beyond the news services, television schedules more broadly, also tend to mimic the discourse that dominates the current mindset. Increasingly, in the wake of the September 2001, the 2003 invasion of Iraq and the 7 July 2005 terrorist attack in London, television companies offer a steady diet of documentaries detailing the effects of a terrorist attack, as well as countless dramas narrating similar threats, all of which, according to Der Derian, contribute to the 'serial murder of the imagination by worst-case scenarios' (2001: 46). Here we could name successful shows in the US such as 24, and the British intelligence drama Spooks, but it is worth giving the recent Fox TV production Sleeper Cell a special mention. The series' website reads:

> Shadowy, unseen terrorist threats readying to unleash 'dirty' radioactive bombs...chemical weapons...germ warfare agents...fertilizer-fuelled explosives...all are scenarios evolving as fast as what an amateur chemist can concoct in a home-garage. Color-coded warnings and emergency response drills are things our governments are doing to prepare us, but even veteran anti-terrorism government officials know the most effective weapon – against home-grown terrorist 'cells' – is getting an 'operative' on the inside...The drama melds current events and pertinent political developments into its contemporary storylines as it explores the personal and professional side of committed agents combating the greatest and most concealed threat to the world today.

The programme's opening scene starts with an image of a white mosque against a cloudless blue sky. As the camera pulls back it is revealed that this is only a picture of a mosque stuck to a wall. Pulling further back we become aware of bars to a cell through which the picture is being viewed. Finally, from the bottom of the screen the head of a Muslim man appears as he arises from his prayer mat. The message is a simple one: Islam equals unfreedom and criminality. What is more, this is an American prison and the enemy is within, and presumably ready to break out at any moment. For Der Derian, the US media are replete with such images, and in response to this daily diet of threat and danger the 'technological exhibitionism' (Mumford, 1964: 342) of American military might acts like Prozac, Der Derian argues, for an American public drip-fed stories of bogeymen. It is a 'technopharmacological fix for all the organic anxieties that attend uncertain times and new configurations of power' (2001: 114).

In this regard, the functioning of the MIME-Net fits very well with James Carey's ritual model of communication. Carey argues (1992) that the ritual model is indebted to religion because it takes on a liturgical function that binds a community together through the projection of an identity and a world to which that identity corresponds. This projection, he writes, 'creates an artificial though nonetheless real symbolic order that operates to provide not information but confirmation, not to alter attitudes or change minds but to represent an underlying order of things, not to perform functions but to manifest an ongoing and fragile social process' (ibid: 19). From a ritual point of view he continues, reading a newspaper – and we might add watching a television programme, attending the cinema, or playing a computer game – is less about gaining information and more like 'attending a mass, a situation in which nothing new is learned but in which a particular view of the world is portrayed and confirmed' (ibid: 20).

Certainly during times of emergency both cinema and television have been requisitioned by the state, and capitalism has long understood that stories of national heroism make good box office both during war and in peacetime. What is new, however, is the idea that the actors within the MIME-Net are now losing their relative autonomy and are combining in one networked system. As John Burston argues, it is the 'ubiquity, sophistication and complexity' (2003: 168) of this network that sets new priorities for academic research. For Burston, the recent NBC TV movie *Asteroid* is a perfect example. In his synopsis the film is about an end-of-the-world scenario prevented by an airborne laser owned by the US military. He notes that the weapon is not entirely fictional given that it is in development, in part funded by General Electric (GE). GE, he continues, is also the parent company of NBC. The result is that 'everybody inside the militainment nexus gets to do a deal and then go home happy. The film's producers agree to certain script recommendations from a Pentagon media liaison and, as reward, are granted full access to air force personnel, bases and aircraft for their shoot. At the same time, both the Pentagon and GE get the right kind of exposure for a new component of the still highly controversial "Star Wars" weapon system' (ibid: 168).

How computer games 'teach an appreciation of war'

For Der Derian, the formation of the MIME-Net in the particular synergistic, hybrid and cybernetic form it takes today was first intimated by the appropriation of Doom II software for training purposes. As Rob Riddell (1997) reported for *Wired* magazine, in 1995 following a decision made at the Annual Officers Symposium, the US Army were tasked, according to Lieutenant Colonel Rick Eisiminger, 'with looking at commercial off-the-shelf computer games that might teach an appreciation of the art and science of war' (ibid: 117). One year later such usage of advances made in modelling and simulation technology by the entertainment industry was to become military doctrine. A US National Research Council report published in 1996, entitled *Modelling and Simulation: Linking Entertainment and Defense*, argued that the 'common interests suggest that the entertainment industry and the DoD may be able to more efficiently achieve their individual goals by working together to advance the technology base for modelling and simulation. Such co-operation could take many forms, including collaborative research and development projects, sharing research results, or co-ordinating ongoing research programs to avoid unnecessary duplication of effort' (in Burston 2003: 163). The result was the formation of the Institute for Creative Technologies (ICT) at the University of Southern California 'where technologies of the spectacular are being simultaneously developed as entertainment technology and as cutting edge military technology' (Burston, 2003: 166).[5]

Returning to the ritualist nature of MIME-Net communication and the representation of an underlying order of things, this also permits us to think how the operation might be thought in terms of propaganda. In Jacques Ellul's (1976) famous study he offers a four-fold account of its workings and differentiates between political and sociological; agitative and integrative; vertical and horizontal; and rational and irrational propaganda. In the first instance, the ritual communication of the MIME-Net is akin to Ellul's conception of sociological propaganda. As opposed to political propaganda, which involves attempts by a government or party to influence behavior, sociological propaganda is understood as a situation in which 'existing economic, political and sociological factors progressively allow an ideology to penetrate individuals or masses' (ibid: 63). I would argue that the ideological impact of the MIME-Net as the organization of a particular socio-economic grouping, together with the vectors of mimesis it supports is best understood through this sociological analysis.

We can also understand it as integrative. Unlike agitative propaganda that is 'most often subversive and has the stamp of opposition [seeking] to destroy the government or the established order' (ibid: 71), integrative propaganda promotes conformity and 'total adherence to a society's truths and behavioral patterns' (ibid: 75). In this regard it follows closely the defining trait of the mimetic impulse, which is to act according to the laws of one's cultural milieu. But while the MIME-Net displays elements of vertical propaganda, that is, it can be seen to descend from above, it is primarily a form of networked power and is thus better understood as horizontal propaganda, where 'each individual helps to form the opinion of the group, but the group helps each individual to discover the correct line' (ibid: 81). The end product is voluntary rather than mechanical adherence and this fits perfectly with the ideology of choice through which the products of the MIME-Net are consumed. Finally, the irrationality of the propaganda takes the shape of the consumption of myth.

Amidst all the supposedly factual data and information made available through the various MIME-Net outlets, it is the mythology of abstract enmity and the state of permanent emergency that is the MIME-Net's guiding message. However, the current situation is far from the 'complete environment' that Ellul described (ibid: 18). Due to the fact that the products of the MIME-Net are textual, and that communication is never simply a case of transmission but always requires complex processes of interpretation, means that the MIME-Net can never produce and make fixed simple acts of imitation at home and cannot prevent acts of inversion and appropriation of this mimetic logic abroad. In other words, the MIME-Net lays itself open to incursions by the enemy. In a similar way to the problem of auto-immunity whereby the military are 'injured' by their weapon of choice, namely digital technology, so the MIME-Net takes 'hits' through subversive acts of mimesis that function as agitative propaganda.

Aberrant mimesis

While Burston calls for the reassessment of research priorities in media studies in relation to this 'militainment nexus' and Der Derian speaks of the 'mimetic codes of technoscientific authorities and media elites' (2001: 209) that are yet to be mapped, they both fail to address the moments of what I would like to call *aberrant mimesis* that also need analyzing. If Der Derian is right that the future of war will be a 'contest of signs' (ibid: 118), and from what has been discussed so far I think there is ample evidence to support this claim, then we need to remembered that the sign itself is always already a point of contest. As Roland Barthes wrote in *The Rhetoric of the Image*, 'all images are polysemous; they imply, underlying their signifiers, a "floating chain" of signifieds, the reader able to choose some and ignore others' (1977: 38-9). It is for these reasons, Barthes notes, that every image today seems to be accompanied by a linguistic message to halt this floating chain and 'anchor' the meaning to that which is preferred. Consequently, while the spectacle may have become 'the model of socially dominant life '(Debord 1987: 6) this does not mean that it is 'the sun that never sets over the empire of human passivity' (ibid: 13): in fact, quite the contrary.

The spectacle of images and signs through which the MIME-Net operates is also a site of resistance, refusal and subversion both at home and abroad. As Stuart Hall demonstrated in his influential essay Encoding/decoding, the 'audience is both "source" and "receiver"' of a message (1980: 130). This means that the receiver is active in the process of communication and that if communication is to be successful the receiver, or decoder must share the encoder's 'frameworks of knowledge' (ibid). This activity on behalf of the receiver is only hidden because the codes, or frameworks, have been naturalized over time. For Hall, three possible types of reading are possible. Where there is symmetry between encoder and decoder the dominant or preferred reading is taken. Where there is asymmetry, a negotiated, or oppositional reading is taken, dependent upon the degree of this asymmetry. It is these oppositional readings that I am interested in, preferring to call them *aberrant*, so as not to suggest that they operate outside the system.

Examples of aberrant mimesis include the appropriation and use of the digital technology deployed by the MIME-Net. One example is the short video entitled *Mujahideen World Cup* in which the viewer is asked to choose between the more beautiful goal, with the first goal being a clip of a footballer scoring a goal from a free kick, while the second goal is a film of a US armoured jeep driving over and detonating a road-side bomb. Videos like these emerge on jihadist websites and soon find their way into more mainstream sites such as MySpace and YouTube. Produced by the Global Islamic Media Front (GIMF) it represents an increased sophistication in the use of cyberspace. This sophistication is evident in another GIMF production, a first person 'shoot-'em-up' computer game called Night of Bush Capturing in which the player kills hundreds of US soldiers before being given the opportunity to go after Bush. The game is free to download and is said to be an adaptation of an older game entitled Quest for Saddam. As the computer game America's Army is both a recruitment and training tool, Night of Bush Capturing is its 'perverse' twin.

Other examples of aberrant mimesis are more specifically tied to the appropriation and oppositional use of Hollywood images by groups regarded by the West as terrorist. One such example is a recruitment video used by the group al Muhajiroun who feel that

Hollywood can do much to assist their own cause and who employ its images to visualize the destruction of America. The video includes the famous shot of the White House being blown up in *Independence Day* and the tidal wave crashing into and destroying New York in *Deep Impact*, a film which amongst many of its promotional tags included the phrase 'Heaven and Earth are about to collide'. Thus, images that originally signified America as the global saviour and epitome of unshrinking human spirit are now used to support fantasies of the ultimate suicide bomb and offer visualizations of the wrath of God against the infidel.

The inability to secure semiotic closure is especially acute in the appropriation by the same Islamic group of television footage of 9/11. The attempt to present a univocal account of the event as the ultimate crime, never to be repeated, is starkly undermined by its appearance in the al Muhajiroun video in which the collapse of the twin towers functions in the same way as the appropriated Hollywood image of the White House. The fact that the actual and the fictional are treated and deployed in a similar way is also very telling. One especially interesting example of the use of 9/11 images is in the 'music video' produced by the Union of Islamic Students in Iran entitled *The World without America* in which images of the planes crashing into the twin towers preface the voice of Ayatollah Khomeini who implores the 'distracted ones' to wake up and recognize 'the world is not safe from the hunter'.

The images and Khomeini's voice are all set to the accompaniment of sombre and what is no doubt supposed to be stirring music. The video is a bite-sized, consumable for the media-saturated, networked world.[6] But perhaps the most stark example of an aberrant reading being taken of the images of 11 September 2001 is the act of 'mimetic identification' (Weber 2003: 196) carried out by a young American boy, aged 15, from Palm Harbour, Florida called Charles Bishara Bishop who committed suicide by crashing a single-engined plane into the Bank of America building in Tampa, to create his own piece of 9/11 *homage* in a salute to Osama Bin Laden. According to Cynthia Weber, this event received little media attention, but when it did the aberrant nature of the act was reclaimed for the dominant mimetic discourse by pathologizing his actions, suggesting that his Arabness (middle name Bishara) had become 'a conduit for...evil influences to infiltrate America' (ibid: 195).

To call this 'attack' on the Bank of America a copy is to forget that the original 9/11 was also an act of aberrant mimesis. In the first place we have Osama Bin Laden's intriguing disclosure in his speech on the eve of the 2004 US presidential election, that he was inspired to consider destroying the Twin Towers of the World Trade Center when he witnessed 'those destroyed towers in Lebanon'. Most interpretations of what Bin Laden meant here believe he was referring to the US-supported attack on the Lebanon in 1982 and the bombing of Beirut, with its coastline of high-rise buildings. But in a prescient passage from *Virtuous War,* Der Derian intimates a more disturbing mimetic action for the attacks that emerges from the increased synergy of the MIME-Net. 'In the context of industrial accidents,' he writes, 'organizational theorists have already identified a "negative synergism" in complex systems that can produce unpredictable, worst-case failures. In the technological drive to map the future – to deter known threats through their simulation – are we unknowingly constructing new, more catastrophic dangers?' (2001: 96).

How the terrorist functions at the level of the symbolic

Jean Baudrillard's analysis of the spirit of terrorism witnessed on that day is framed precisely in terms of this 'negative synergism'. The destruction of the World Trade Center, the attack on the Pentagon and the third flight, which is assumed to have been heading for the White House, are all operations of aberrant mimesis within the society of the spectacle. As the dominant maintains itself increasingly through the deployment of information and the power of the image, so the terrorist functions at the level of the symbolic too. For Baudrillard, the collapse of the towers was 'an additional *frisson*' (2002: 29) added as 'a bonus of terror' to the primary target which was that of the icon, the symbol of American invincibility. In Baudrillard's terms, the 'negative synergy' of this event would be the mutual implication or reciprocity of domination and terror. Terrorism is a 'double agent' (ibid: 10) of the global 'technocratic machinery' (ibid: 9), double in the sense that it also deploys and appropriates the weapons of that machinery: 'Money and stock-market speculation, computer technology and aeronautics, spectacle and the media networks – they have assimilated everything of modernity and globalism, without changing their goal, which is to destroy that power' (ibid: 19).

It is mimetic because it fights 'terror with terror' (ibid: 9) and deploys the very machinery of globalized modernity against which it fights. It is also mimetic because it adopts 'the banality of American everyday life as its cover and camouflage, sleeping in their suburbs, reading and studying with their families' (ibid: 19). This particular aspect of the aberrant mimesis of the new global terror sets in play a 'reversibility that is [its] true victory' (ibid: 31). After 11 September 2001 there is no possible distinction between the 'crime' and the crackdown' (ibid), we are continually reminded by Bush and Blair that the terrorists hate our freedom and despise democracy, but the states 'under attack' then proceed to role back democracy to a far greater extent than the terrorists ever could. It is the Bush administration and the Blair government, caught up as they are in the economy of mimesis, that proceed to do the work of those who supposedly hate freedom. Mimesis is thus contagious. The touch of terrorism sets in place semi-autonomous, mimetic acts of violence. In response to terror, civil liberties become civil restraints, the open society becomes the surveillance society and freedom becomes regulation.[7]

Applying the concept of mimesis to Baudrillard's reading of the events of 11 September 2001, it is necessary go beyond the notion of aberrant mimesis towards what I would call *negative mimesis*, because what is so compelling about global terrorism is its capacity, according to Baudrillard, to 'defy the system by a gift to which it cannot respond' (ibid: 17), that is, the gift of death as an absolute, symbolic event. Central to the RMA is the deployment of information, simulation and virtuality to increase lethality and reduce, if not eradicate, its own mortality. The RMA is a risk-averse system seeking to eliminate its own death. The Counter-RMA that is global terror thus deploys death against a system for which death is unthinkable. The Counter-RMA deploys death against those that deal death but who, for themselves, can only countenance life.

The PSYOPs of the Counter-RMA is to declare: 'We want death more than you want life.' It is a negative mimesis that appropriates and inverts the logic of cyberwar while also removing the possibility of deterrence (cyber or otherwise), for every deterrent must assume the universality of a life instinct. And so this negative mimesis structures the entire metaphysics of the war against terror. Facing each other, George W.

Bush and Osama Bin Laden deploy all the technologies of the spectacle to play out the drama of Good and Evil. In a symbolic exchange of negative mimesis each casts themselves as the messenger of light and the other as the angel of darkness, a relation of mutuality that is in both their interests and from which both draw their power. A critique of this mimetic structure would, therefore, require the mapping and exposure of the MIME-Net in all its corporate complexity, the moments of aberrant mimesis that shadow and subvert this network, as well as the negative mimesis that organizes its metaphysics.

Notes

[1] For an interesting insight into the British government's production of fake news as propaganda see Miller (2006)

[2] At this point Graham and Luke refer to 'The military in the movies' documentary transcript. www.cdi.org/adm/Transcripts/1020/

[3] Der Derian borrows the concept of mimesis from Benjamin's essay On the Mimetic Faculty. There 'mimesis is understood as a capacity for producing similarities [and a] powerful compulsion [...] to become and behave like something else' (Benjamin, 1979: 160). But the concept is also important because of two related issues that are of particular significance when thinking how the entertainment industries and the military are becoming increasingly symbiotic. Der Derian notes how Benjamin believed that '"the school" for mimetic development is "play"' (1999: 58) and that mimesis, as Benjamin discusses in the essay 'On Aesthetics' is closely related to violence

[4] Further synergies between the worlds of news and entertainment include the 24-hour news channels' increasing dependency on the entertainment industries for ratings-grabbing content in the form of 'infotainment', as indicated in the hyphenated name of the corporate giant CNN-AOL-Time-Warner. Der Derian pointedly reminds us that when war is conducted as politics and politics is conducted as business the only question is which business should provide the model of best practice? Der Derian's answer is the 'prime-time, real-time, all-the-time hyphenated hydras' (2001: 161)

[5] As Burston points out, however, the ICT does not only collaborate with Hollywood ('Silliwood') engineers, but also calls on the entertainment industry to expand its rhetorical and story-telling capabilities. At an event at the ICT shortly after 11 September 2001, *Die Hard* screenwriter Steven E. De Souza, television writer David Engelbach (*MacGyver*), and directors Joseph Zito (*Delta Force One, Invasion U.S.A* and *Missing in Action*), Spike Jonze (*Being John Malkovich*) and David Fincher (*Fight Club, Seven*) were invited to 'brainstorm narrative scenarios in the service of future US-sponsored counter-terrorism efforts' (167). Burston also explains how this marriage with Hollywood is very good for the public image of the US military and helps break the stereotype of homophobic, conservative, WASP organization, giving it much wider appeal that helps bolster recruitment. Details of ICT projects and publications can be found at www.ict.usc.edu/disp.php

[6] Clips of this video, along with the *Mujahideen World Cup* and *Night of Bush Capturing* are available to view at MEMRI TV, www.memritv.org

[7] As Downey and Murdock have argued, the campaign of global terrorism brings about a process requiring 'information to be gathered from every available location [dismantling] the protective walls that have separated the military from civil society' (2003: 79)

References

Barthes, Roland (1977) *Image, Music, Text*, London: Fontana Press
Baudrillard, Jean (2002) *The Spirit of Terrorism*, London, Verso
Benjamin, Walter (1979) *One-Way Street*, London: Verso
Boose, Lynda E. (1993) Techno-Muscularity and the 'Boy Eternal': From the Quagmire to the Gulf, in Cooke, M. and Woollacott, A. (eds) *Gendering War Talk*, Princeton: Princeton University Press
Brown, John (2006) Our Indian Wars are Not Yet Over, TomDispatch.Com. Available online at www.tompdispatch.com/indexprint.mhtml?pid=50043, accessed 14 October 2006
Burston, John (2003) War and the Entertainment Industries: New research Priorities in an Era of Cyber-Patriotism, in Thussu, D. and Freeedman, D. (eds) *War and the Media*, London: Sage Publications pp 163-175
Carey, James (1992) *Communication as Culture: Essays on Media and Society*, London: Routledge
Debord, Guy. (1987) *Society of the Spectacle*, Rebel Press
Der Derian, James (2001) *Virtuous War: Mapping the Military-Industrial-Media-Entertainment Network*, Boulder: Westview Press
— (1999) A Virtual Theory of Global Politics, Mimetic War, and the Spectral State, *Angelaki*, Vol. 4, No. 2 pp 53-67
Downey, John and Murdock, Graham. (2003) The Counter-Revolution in Military Affairs: The Globalization of Guerrilla Warfare, in Thussu, D. and Freedman, D. (eds) *War and the Media*, London: Sage Publications pp 70-86
Ellul, Jacques (1973) *Propaganda: The Formation of Men's Attitudes*, New York: Vinatage Books
Graham, Philip and Luke, Allan (2003) Militarizing the Body Politic: New Mediations as Weapons of Mass Instruction, *Body and Society*, Vol. 9, No. 4 pp 149-168
Hall, Stuart. (1980) Encoding/decoding, in Hall, S et al (eds) *Culture, Media, Language*, London: Hutchinson
Mattelart, Armand (1994) *Mapping World Communication: War, Progress, Culture*, Minneapolis: University of Minnesota Press
Miller, David. (2006) The propaganda we pass off as news around the world, *Guardian*, 15 February
Monbiot, George (2002) Both Saviour and Victim, *Guardian*, 29 January
Mumford, Lewis (1964) *The Pentagon of Power: The Myth of the Machine*, New York: Harcourt Press
Riddell, Rob (1997) Doom Goes to War, *Wired*, April
Thussu, Daya Kishan (2003) Live TV and Bloodless Deaths: War, Infotainment and 24/7 News, in Thussu, D. and Freedman, D. (eds) *War and the Media*, London: Sage Publications pp 177-132
Virilio, Paul (1989) *War and Cinema: The Logistics of Perception*, London: Verso
Weber, Cynthia (2003) The Media, the 'War on Terrorism', and the Circulation of Non-Knowledge, in Thussu, D. and Freedman, D. (eds) *War and the Media*, London: Sage Publications pp 190-199

CHAPTER SIXTEEN

THE NECESSARY SPECTACULAR 'VICTORIES': NEW MILITARISM, THE MAINSTREAM MEDIA AND THE MANUFACTURE OF THE TWO GULF CONFLICTS 1991 AND 2003

RICHARD KEEBLE

The 'war' myth

There were no Gulf 'wars' in 1991 and 2003. The US/UK forces faced no credible enemies. With the massive ranks of the 'allied' armies facing the rag-tag ranks of Iraqi conscripts and no-hopers, the outcomes of the conflicts were never in doubt. Both 'wars' were over in a matter of days. While thousands of Iraqi soldiers and civilians were slaughtered, US/UK forces suffered relatively few casualties.

In 1991 the Iraqi army was constantly represented in the media as 1 million-strong, the fourth-largest in the world, full of battle-hardened fanatics led by global monster Saddam Hussein. As thousands of Iraqi conscripts deserted in January and February 1991, Fleet Street still predicted the 'largest ground battles since the Second World War'. In the end there was nothing but a rapid rout: a barbaric slaughter buried under the fiction of heroic, necessary warfare.

As Noam Chomsky commented (1992: 54): '…from August 1990 through July 1991 there was little that could qualify as "war". Rather there was a brutal Iraqi takeover of Kuwait followed by various forms of slaughter and state terrorism, the scale corresponding roughly to the means of violence in the hands of the perpetrators and to their impunity.' In 2003, the US/UK invasion was supposedly over Iraq's weapons of mass destruction – but these claims were all lies. The official US report of 6 October 2004, which concluded an intensive 15-month search by 1,200 inspectors of the Iraq Survey Group, found Iraq had destroyed all its weapons of mass destruction following the 1991 conflict.

US/UK jets had been bombing Iraqi targets regularly since the end of the 1991 conflict so there was no clear start to the conflict. And with the president of the defeated state melting away into thin air there was no clear end. Casualties on both sides mounted as hostilities continued after the end of the so-called war. Thus the bombing of Baghdad on 19 March 2003 became the manufactured 'start' of the 'war' narrative; and there were two contrived endings: the symbolic toppling of the Saddam statue before the world's media on 9 April and the statement by President Bush before a gathering of US troops on 1 May that the 'major combat operations' were over.

Significantly, on the 2003 conflict, defence expert John Keegan reported in the *Daily Telegraph* of 8 April: 'In truth, there has been almost no check to the unimpeded onrush of the coalition, particularly the dramatic American advance to Baghdad: nor have there been any major battles. This has been a collapse, not a war.' AFP photographer Cris Reeves, with the US marines, saw hardly any action at all. 'It was like two weeks of camping for me with 20-year-old marines. I was 48 so I was exhausted' (Guillot 2003).

But this does not make the 'wars' of 1991 and 2003 massive elite conspiracies. Rather, the origins of the war myth and the New Militarism which has emerged in the US and UK since 1980 lie deep within complex military, historical, economic, ideological and political forces which it is crucial to identify. And the myth has such potency because it is based on widely held assumptions, beliefs and ideologies. Moreover, while the similarities between the two conflicts are particularly striking, New Militarism is not static and so there are important differences to be highlighted in the media coverage of them.

From militarism to New Militarism

The traditional militarism of the First and Second World Wars, in which the mass of the population participated in the war efforts either as soldiers or civilians, is constantly the subject of nostalgic, patriotic celebration in the mainstream media in the UK. Yet both wars threw up serious problems for Western elites. Throughout the West, the old elites were discredited by appeasement and collaboration with the Nazis. Trade union militancy flourished in Britain and 2,194 strikes were recorded in 1944 – up to then the highest ever (Harris 1984: 66). Mass employment encouraged the further emancipation of women while on the continent a 'transnational revolutionary mood' emerged between 1943 and 1947 (Gunn 1989: 7-8).

Since 1945, the democratic problems posed by mass conscription have been resolved in a number of ways. National service has ended while military strategy emphasizes low intensity operations away from the media glare or spectacular adventures against manufactured enemies (Curtis 1998 and 2003; Newsinger 2002; Pilger 2002). And following the secret launch of the UK nuclear weapons programme in the late 1940s, the emphasis has shifted to nuclear 'deterrence'.

Democratic advances were also witnessed in the United States during the world wars. Unions gained in strength and workers struggled for higher wages. Significantly mass conscription during the Vietnam War (though not a total war for the US) was also accompanied by substantial social dislocation with the emergence of student, black and feminist radicalism – and urban riots. Up until 2003, the emphasis had been on avoiding Vietnam-type confrontations. With a shift to an all-volunteer army in the 1970s, technical development became the army's top priority. So men (and the occasional woman) have given way on the 'battle front' to the computerized machine.

But while the two world wars provided the UK with enduring myths of patriotic glory, Vietnam threatened to destroy the beliefs in victory and triumph which are so central to America's national identity. As Tom Engelhardt comments (1995: 15): 'It is hardly surprising that, after 1975, the basic impulse of America's political and military leaders (as well as of many other Americans) was not to forge a new relationship to the world but to reconstruct a lost identity of triumph.' New Militarism, in effect, provided the solution, manufacturing conflicts in which the US could gain its necessary 'victories' and so 'kick the Vietnam syndrome'.

In addition, the enormous political and economic power exerted by the military/industrial complexes in the US and UK means that militarism has become a core, defining reality for these societies. Warfare has become a technological imperative as the US aims to assert its capitalistic, worldwide hegemony (Boyd-Barrett op cit: 36-38). At the same time, it provides the crucial testing ground for professional soldiers (desperate for 'a piece of the action') and new weapons systems (Keeble 2003a).

Yet most of US/UK imperialism advances essentially in secret. Both countries have deployed forces virtually every year since 1945 – most of them away from the glare of the media (Peak 1992). But at various moments the US/UK chooses to fight overt, manufactured 'wars'. We, the viewers and readers, have to see the spectacle. It has to appear 'real'. In this process the permanent war economy is both legitimized and celebrated.

MacKenzie (1984) has described the 'spectacular theatre' of 19th century British militarism when press representations of heroic imperialist adventures in far-way colonies had a considerable entertainment element. Moreover, the Victorian 'small' wars of imperial expansion in Africa and India were glorified for a doting public by correspondents such as William Howard Russell, G.A. Henty, Archibald Forbes and H.M.Stanley (Featherstone 1993; 1993a). But Victorian newspapers and magazines did not have social penetration of today's mass media. And Victorian militarism was reinforced through a wide range of social activities and institutions such as the Salvation Army, Church Army and uniformed youth organisations, rifle clubs and drill units in factories.

By the 1980s, this institutional and social militarism had given way to a new mediacentric, consumerist, entertainment militarism in which the mass media, ideologically tied to a strong and increasingly secretive state, had assumed a dominant ideological role. Thus, instead of active participation in wars, people are mobilized for New Militarism through their consumption of heavily censored media (much of the censorship self-imposed by the journalists) whose job is to manufacture the spectacle of war as entertainment.

The birth of New Militarism

The military adventures of the UK in the Falklands (1982), and the US in Grenada (1983), Libya (1986) and Panama (1989) all bore the hallmarks of the New Militarism.

They were all quickie attacks. The Libya bombings lasted just 11 minutes. All the others were over within days.

They were all largely risk-free and fought from the air. All resulted in appalling civilian casualties. Yet the propaganda – in Orwellian style – claimed the raids were for essentially peaceful purposes. Casualty figures were covered up and the military hardware was constantly represented as 'precise', 'surgical', 'modern' and 'clean'. Diseases and deaths amongst 'enemy' civilians and 'allied' troops resulting from the use of depleted uranium in artillery shells and Tomohawk missiles were largely covered up (Boyd-Barrett op cit: 35-36).

Media and military strategies were closely integrated. With journalists denied access to planes, the massacres were hidden behind the military's media manipulation and misinformation. Moreover, mainstream journalists' links with the secret state (the massively over-resourced MI5, MI6 and GCHQ, the Cheltenham-based signals spying centre, secret armies and undercover police units) grew closer during the 1980s and 1990s (see Dorril 2000). By 1991, a military, intelligence, media system was in place which meant a conflict under the glare of 24-hour media gaze could be fought in secret.

Following the end of the Cold War and the collapse of the Soviet Union, the military/industrial complex needed the manufacture of 'big' enemies to legitimize the massive expenditure on the weapons of war. Thus the threats posed to US/Western interests, in all these military adventures, were either grossly exaggerated or non-existent.

Central to the new strategies was the demonization of the leaders of the 'enemy' states. In the case of Grenada, they were 'communists'. Colonel Gadaffi, of Libya, was demonized in the US and UK mainstream media throughout the early 1980s as a 'terrorist warlord' and his supposed links with the Soviet Union were constantly stressed (Chomsky 1986). Immediately before the raids President Reagan dubbed him a 'mad dog'. Over the Panama invasion, the propaganda constantly focused on the demonized personality of 'drug-trafficker' Noriega (Dickson 1994).

All the invasions were celebrated in ecstatic language throughout the mainstream media. The editorial consensus remained firmly behind the military attacks. Administration lies were rarely challenged just as the global protests against the actions were largely ignored. Significantly James Combs commented on the UK's Falklands campaign and the US invasion of Grenada the following year in this way (1993: 277):

> It is a new kind of war: war as performance. It is war in which the attention of the *auteurs* is not the conduct of the war but also the communication of the war. With their political and military power to command, coerce and co-opt the mass, the national security elite can make the military event go according to script, omit bad scenes and discouraging words and bring about a military performance that is both spectacular and satisfying.

The manufactured Gulf War of the 1991

Despite the appearance of 24-hour saturation coverage of the Gulf War of 1991, it was, in fact, a conflict entirely shrouded in secrecy. Journalists were the real prisoners of war, trapped behind the barbed wire of reporting curbs, according to William Boot (1991: 24). Very few journalists were allowed to travel with the troops; little actual combat was observed since reporters were denied access to planes; most were confined to hotels in Saudi Arabia. Colin Powell, in his account of the conflict (1995) estimated that 250,000 Iraqi soldiers had been eliminated. And yet the media celebrated the allied strikes as 'clean', 'surgical', 'precise' and 'humanitarian'. Shots from video cameras on missiles heading towards their targets (shown on television and reproduced in the press) meant that spectators actually 'became' the weapons.

As Robins and Levidow argued (1991: 324): 'The remote technology served to portray as heroic 'combat' what was mainly a series of massacres.' According to Cummings (1992: 121) the 1991 conflict appeared not as 'blood and guts spilled in living colour on the living room rug' but through a 'radically distanced, technically controlled eminently "cool" postmodern optic'. Kellner (1992: 386) described it ironically as 'the perfect war'. Indeed, out of the 353 'allied' deaths only 46 were killed in combat. Of those, 24 (52 per cent) were caused by so-called 'friendly fire' (military jargon that has slipped so effortlessly into the lexicon of contemporary conflict).

We now know that 1,600 people, mostly women and children, perished when the Ameriyya shelter in Baghdad was bombed by an American Stealth jet during the Gulf massacres of 1991 (Petley 2003). Yet at the time most of Fleet Street blamed 'Saddam', described it as a propaganda coup for the Iraqi leader or claimed it was inevitable (Keeble 1997: 166-172). All of this was part of a strategy to deflect blame for the atrocity away from its perpetrators. Phillip Knightley commented (2000: 494-495): '...one reason for this almost hysterical reaction was that the reporting of the Ameriyya bombing threatened the most important element in the military's propaganda strategy – an attempt to change public perception of the nature of war itself, to convince everyone that new technology has removed a lot of war's horror...The picture that was painted was of a war almost without death.'

From a military standpoint many soldiers amongst the thousands sent to the Gulf were irrelevant. As part of an attempt to revive the heroic images of the Second World War and as a symbolic assertion of the heroic possibilities of major warfare, they were essential. Most crucially, the manufactured conflict provided a theater in which the US could win a 'big' war and 'kick the Vietnam syndrome'. The Iraqi army could never pose a threat to the mightiest army ever assembled. Inevitably then, the emphasis by the media, military and politicians on the demonized Saddam Hussein as a 'global monster', the 'new Hitler' and 'evil madman' was the crucial ingredient in the manufacture of the 'big' war (Keeble 1998; Smith 1999: 210).

Argentina, Grenada, Libya and Panama were all puny under-developed countries while the US/UK's low-intensity military adventures and the assassinations of enemy leaders were deliberately conducted in secret beyond the gaze of the media throughout the 1980s and 1990s. Now in 1991 with the 24-hour media coverage (though reporters, kept well away from any action, ended up interviewing other journalists) the 'big' war could crucially be seen.

All the editors, safe in their Fleet Street bunkers, backed the Desert Storm assaults on Iraq as did the vast majority of commentators. And so the New Militarist consensus held firm. As early as 3 August 1990, immediately after the Iraqi invasion of Kuwait, virtually all of Fleet Street had gone on a war footing calling for strikes against the new-found monster 'Saddam'. Only the *Guardian* expressed a certain scepticism throughout.

The New Militarist wars of the 1990s

During the 1990s, Iraq became the focus of regular manufactured crises (Carapico 1998). In January and June 1993, September 1996 and December 1998, US jets attacked sites in Iraq during rapid, risk-free actions and only an 11th-hour intervention by UN secretary general Kofi Annan prevented strikes after a media-hyped crisis exploded in January-February 1998. Throughout 1999 and 2000, regular attacks on Iraq by US and UK jets had become institutionalized, gaining hardly any mention in the media.

Predictably, the US/UK-led attacks on Yugoslavia in 1999 'turned out to be the most secret campaign in living memory', according to historian Alistair Horne (cited in Knightley 2000: 501). They were risk-free and conducted entirely from the air (as were Nato's earlier strikes against Bosnian Serbs in 1995). Celebrated as 'humanitarian' and 'precise', thousands, in fact, died during the Kosovo attacks; many more were traumatised and military sites, broadcast stations, hospitals, homes were bombed (Ali 2000; Chomsky 1999). Hundreds of thousands were left jobless. Neil Clark reports (2004) on the 1999 bombing of Serbia: 'Nato only destroyed 14 tanks but 372 industrial facilities were hit – including the Zastava car plant at Kragujevac, leaving hundreds of thousands jobless. Not one foreign or privately owned factory was bombed.'

The attacks were part of a desperate attempt by a newly-enlarged Nato to celebrate its 50 years' anniversary with a symbolic victory in a manufactured, spectacular 'war' (Keeble 1999: 16; Johnstone 2000: 8-9). Significantly, the Kosovo theater of war was transformed into a no-go area for the international media. The state systems of Yugoslavia and US/UK both found it in their interests to deny media access to the front line.

The New Militarist consensus fractured on Fleet Street during the 1990s with the *Express*, *Independent* and *Guardian* all expressing criticisms of the attacks on Iraq. Then, with the Kosovo crisis the consensus re-emerged with virtually all the editorials backing air strikes and even calling immediately after hostilities began for a ground assault against the new monster 'Milosevic'. Not even the generals dared adopt this battle plan of Fleet Street's armchair strategists. There was just one exception to the pro-war consensus, the *Independent on Sunday* – and its editor, Kim Fletcher, was sacked just days after the strikes were halted. Newspaper columns, however, were opened up to debate on an unprecedented scale. Out of 99 prominent columnists I surveyed, 33 spoke out against the US-led attacks (Keeble 2000a; Keeble 2000b). For the 2001 attacks on Afghanistan and the toppling of the Taliban, the whole of Fleet Street backed the action – but again there was a wide-ranging debate amongst columnists and letter writers (Keeble 2001).

The manufactured responses to September 11

Within this context, it can be seen that the US/UK responses to the 11 September atrocities, with the launch of the endless 'war on terrorism', the assaults on Afghanistan in 2001 and Iraq in 2003 and the threats to the 'rogue' states, Syria, Iran and North Korea, are not distinctly new strategies but accelerating long-standing strategies of military imperial adventurism (Curtis 2003; Boyd-Barrett op cit: 36-38).

Al Qaeda, blamed for the 11 September atrocities and a series of later attacks on Western interests, is a shadowy grouping. As Burke comments (2003: 6): '…even when at its most organized in late 2001, it is important to avoid seeing "Al Qaeda" as a coherent and structured terrorist organization with cells everywhere, or to imagine it had subsumed all other groups within its network.' Certainly against such an elusive threat, traditional, war fighting strategies (involving major battle confrontations) are inappropriate. The attack on Afghanistan in 2001 produced the necessary risk-free 'victory' against a quickly manufactured 'enemy' but they remained largely invisible with journalists kept well away from the 'frontlines' as the US proxy forces, the Northern Alliance, advanced on Kabul. More than 800 Afghan civilians were killed in the US airstrikes, though many tens of thousands died through hunger, disease and exposure (ibid: 324). And in the end, Al Qaeda leaders Osama Bin Laden and Mullah Omar escaped into the void.

With image and entertainment the dominant concerns in New Militarist adventures against hopelessly overwhelmed 'enemies', soldiers end up becoming actors. As Philip

Hammond comments (2003: 27): 'The US special forces who went into Kandahar in October 2001 were essentially actors, staging a stunt and videotaping their exploits for the world's media.' The operation was of dubious military value, Hammond argues, since army pathfinders had already gone in beforehand to make sure the area was secure. So the US/UK are left having to manufacture once again in 2003 a necessary spectacle of traditional 'warfare'. As US novelist Don DeLillo commented on the Iraq invasion: 'I'm almost prepared to believe that the secret drive behind out eagerness to enter this war is technology itself – that has a will to be realized. And that the administration is essentially a Cold War administration looking for a clearly defined enemy which was not the case after 11 September. Now there is a territorial entity with borders and soldiers in uniform' (see Campbell 2003).

Hammond (op cit: 23) also sees the 'war on terrorism' primarily as a war of images. 'Just as the 11 September attacks were calculated not simply to wreak terrible destruction but to create a global media spectacle by targeting symbols of American prestige and power, so too the response of the US and UK governments has been highly image-conscious. Particularly in those aspects of the war on terrorism which have involved actual war fighting, producing the right image appears to be at least as important as any tangible results achieved on the ground.'

The 2003 invasion of Iraq and the crucial 'big' lies over WMD

The invention of 'Saddam's weapons of mass destruction by the US/UK elites to legitimize the invasion of Iraq in 2003 (and dutifully reported throughout the mainstream media) was the inevitable culmination of the demonization process begun in 1990 by the US/UK elites desperate to manufacture a credible enemy to fight a 'big' war. Predictably the disinformation about Iraq's WMD was spread by dodgy intelligence sources via gullible journalists (Keeble 2004). Thus, to take just one example, Michael Evans, *The Times* defence correspondent, reported on 29 November 2002: 'Saddam Hussein has ordered hundred of his officials to conceal weapons of mass destruction components in their homes to evade the prying eyes of the United Nations inspectors.' The source of these 'revelations' was said to be 'intelligence picked up from within Iraq'.

Early in 2004, as the battle for control of Iraq continued with mounting casualties on both sides, it was revealed that many of the lies about Saddam Hussein's supposed WMD had been fed to sympathetic journalists in the US, Britain and Australia by the exile group, the Iraqi National Congress (Landay and Wells 2004). Amongst the 108 articles listed between October 2001 and May 2002 were those in *The Sunday Times*, the *Observer, Daily Telegraph, Guardian*, the *Economist, Birmingham Post, Daily Express, Western Mail*. The most sensational assertion – that Iraq could deploy WMD in 45 minutes – had come from Iraq's Prime Minister-designate, Iyad Allawi (a man with close ties to the CIA and MI6: see Cockburn 2004). Alawi, according to the leaks, was also the source of allegations that Saddam Hussein and the leader of the 9/11 hijackers, Mohamed Atta, were working together (Beaumont, Harding, Harris and Hinsliff 2004).

Significantly, on 26 May 2004, *The New York Times* carried a 1,200-word editorial admitting it had been duped in its coverage of WMD in the lead-up to the invasion by dubious Iraqi defectors, informants and exiles (though it failed to lay any blame on the US President: see Greenslade 2004). Chief among *The Times*'s dodgy informants was

Ahmad Chalabi, leader of the Iraqi National Congress and Pentagon favourite before his Baghdad house was raided by US forces on 20 May.

Then, in the *Observer* of 30 May 2004, David Rose admitted he had been the victim of 'calculated set-up' devised to foster the propaganda case for war. 'In the 18 months before the invasion of March 2003, I dealt regularly with Chalabi and the INC and published stories based on interviews with men they said were defectors from Saddam's regime.' He concluded: 'The information fog is thicker than in any previous war, as I know now from bitter personal experience. To any journalist being offered apparently sensational disclosures, especially from an anonymous intelligence source, I offer two words of advice: *caveat emptor*.'

Since then no British newspaper has apologized for being so easily duped over the WMD. But in the United States, on 12 August 2004, the *Washington Post* followed the *NYT*'s lead and admitted underplaying reports critical of the push for the invasion while promoting prominently the government's case for war. The coverage had 'looked strikingly one-sided at times'.

Hiding the horror of war

Central to the manufacture of New Militarist warfare has been the constant propaganda focus on precise, clean weapons. War is a civilized, humanitarian business – that's the essential message. And people don't die in them, massacres never happen – unless through mistakes or through the fault of the 'enemy'. During the 1991 massacres descriptions applied to the weapons of the US-led forces were always positive: sophisticated, super, spectacular, awesome, stunning, brilliant, smart, precise, accurate, amazing, incredible.

For the enemy the descriptions were the opposite: dirty, crude, primitive (the Iraqi supergun was an exception – but that was being constructed by British firms). Allied onslaughts always provoked superlatives – such as the 'greatest aerial bombardment in history' – behind which all the terrible human suffering was hidden, silenced. Throughout the Iraqi crisis from the invasion of Kuwait in August 1990 until the formal start of Desert Storm onslaught on 17 January the military monopolized the agenda and the language in which it was articulated – the glorification of military technology was the inevitable consequence (Keeble 1997: 139-159).

Up to 10,000 civilians died during the Iraq invasion of 2003 (Pilger 2004: xxiii). As J.K Galbraith comments (2004): 'We are accepting programmed death for the young and random slaughter for men and women of all ages. So it was in the first and second world wars and is still so in Iraq. Civilized life, as it is called, is a great white tower celebrating human achievement, but at the top there is permanently a large black cloud. Human progress dominated by unimaginable cruelty and death.'

Thus the essential function of the mainstream media in New Militarist wars is no longer to naturalize and humanize the possibility of nuclear holocaust as during the Cold War but to acclimatize the public to the acceptability of mass slaughters of the nameless 'enemy'. *New York Times* reporter Chris Hedges writes (2004): 'War is made palatable. It is sanitized. We are allowed to taste war's perverse thrill but usually spared from seeing its consequences. The wounded and dead are swiftly carted offstage. The maimed are carefully hidden in the wings while the band plays the majestic march.'

All the mainstream media highlighted the use of 2,000 precision missiles in the US's 'shock and awe' opening attacks on Baghdad on 20 March 2003. Notice how the *Guardian* highlighted the precision claims on 19 March. Under the headline: 'US microwave bomb to make debut in most hi-tech battlefield campaign ever' the new bomb is celebrated as 'new and devastatingly effective'. Reporter Stuart Millar continues:

> The so-called high-powered microwave (HPW) weapon, or ebomb, will be the most sophisticated new weapon to get its operational debut in Iraq during a campaign that promises to be the most hi-tech ever fought. The last Gulf war may have marked the introduction of space age weapons – from laser-guided bombs to cruise missiles 'smart' enough to know which set of traffic lights to turn left at – but as collateral damage figures later proved, the technologies were still in their infancy.

Let's examine closely this text since it shows how the *Guardian*, one of the most outspoken in its criticisms of the US/UK rush to conflict, still promotes various dominant discourses that ultimately serve to legitimize the attack on Iraq. Note the use of the phrase 'most sophisticated' in relation to the weapon – with all its positive associations of intelligence and efficiency. And the reference to turning left at the traffic lights is such an extraordinary phrase reducing the horror of mass slaughter to the level of the familiar, ordinary discourse of the urban everyday. 'Collateral damage' is that heartless militaryspeak euphemism for civilian deaths while the reference to the 'infant technologies' of mass slaughter reduces the horror of military power to the innocence of a baby.

Or let's take this story in the pro-war tabloid *Sun* of 20 March as US jets began their attacks on Baghdad. Under the headlines: 'The first "clean" war' and 'Civilian deaths could be zero, MoD claims', it reported: 'The war in Iraq could have almost no civilian casualties, defence chiefs claimed last night.' It continued: 'A senior defence source said last night: "Great attention to precision-guided weapons means we could have a war with zero casualties. We are a lot closer towards that ideal. We may be entering an era where it is possible to prosecute a humanitarian war."' In other words, just as US/UK imperialism was reaching new levels of unnecessary aggression so the language used to legitimize it was reaching new heights of exaggeration.

The breakdown of the New Militarist consensus

In 2003, with significant opposition to the rush to war being expressed by politicians, lawyers, intelligence agents, celebrities, religious leaders, charities and human rights campaigners – together with massive street protests – both nationally and internationally, the breakdown in Fleet Street's consensus was inevitable. Yet still for the invasion of Iraq, the vast bulk of Fleet Street backed the action (though columnists and letter writers were divided). The *Independents*, carrying prominently the dissident views of foreign correspondent Robert Fisk, were the most hostile. Following the massive global street protests on 15 February, the *Independent on Sunday* editorialised: 'Millions show this is a war that mustn't happen.'

The *Guardian* did not criticize military action on principle but opposed the US/UK rush to war and promoted a wide range of critical opinions. The *Mirrors* were also 'anti' in the run up to the conflict (perhaps more for marketing reasons since the Murdoch press was always going to be firmly for the invasion) with the veteran dissident campaigning journalists John Pilger and Paul Foot given prominent coverage. But then, after editor in chief Piers Morgan claimed his papers' stance attracted thousands of protesting letters from readers, their opposition softened. And the *Mail*'s managed to stand on the fence mixing both criticism of the rush to military action with fervent patriotic support for the troops during the conflict.

A major survey by researchers at the universities of Manchester, Liverpool and Leeds, published in December 2006, found that in considering the 'humanitarian' rationale for the invasion, more than 80 per cent of mainstream media coverage mirrored the government position while less than 12 per cent challenged it (Robinson et al 2006). 'Most reports (54 per cent TV and 61 per cent press) making substantial reference to the WMD rationale for war reflected and reinforced the coalition argument by, for example, relaying the coalition's claims in unproblematic terms.'

The contradictions of New Militarism

A few months before his death, Edward Said (2003) identified the way in which the dominant discourse in the US/UK before the invasion of Iraq fabricated an 'arid landscape ready for American power to construct there an ersatz model of free market "democracy"'. But he concluded with typical optimism: 'Critical thought does not submit to commands to join in the ranks marching against another approved enemy. Rather than the manufactured clash of civilisations we need to concentrate on the slow-working together of cultures that overlap, borrow from each other and live together.'

Indeed, while US/UK militarism appears out of control it is clear from this analysis that it is built on lies, misinformation and myth. In Iraq and Afghanistan today the struggle against the occupying US and UK forces continues and a global movement for peace gathers strength. From 1976 to January 2004 as few as 900 US service people died overseas due to hostile action, about 38 per cent occurring in Iraq during the ten-month period 19 March to January 2004 (Conetta op cit: 13). Since then US and UK casualties (including scores of journalists) have been mounting along with appalling Iraqi death tolls.

New Militarism was built essentially on the premise of risk-free, rapid interventions as a response to the Vietnam trauma and as a way of legitimizing the permanent war economy. With US/UK forces now bogged down in Afghanistan and Iraq, Fleet Street's New Militarism consensus has broken down and voices calling for international co-operation and understanding are increasing. There are reasons to be cheerful: the US/UK military juggernaut can be halted.

References

Ali, Tariq (ed.) (2000) *Masters of the Universe? Nato's Balkan Crusade*, London: Verso

Anderson, Alison (2003) Communication, Conflict and Risk in the 21st Century: Critical issues for Sociology, *Sociological Research Online*, Vol. 8 No. 4. Available online at http://www.socresonline.org.uk/8/4/anderson.html, accessed on 11 September 2004

Beaumont, Peter; Harding, Luke; Harris, Paul and Hinsliff, Gaby (2004) UN sidelined in choice of Iraqi leader, the *Observer*, 30 May

Boot, William (1991) The press stands alone, *Columbia Journalism Review*, New York; March/April pp 23-24

Boyd-Barrett, Oliver (2004) Understanding the second casualty, in Allan, Stuart and Zelizer, Barbie (eds) *Reporting War: Journalism in Wartime*, London: Routledge pp 25-42

Burke, Jason (2003) *Al Qaeda: The True Story of Radical Islam*, London: Penguin

Chomsky, Noam (1986) *Pirates and Emperors*, Montreal/New York: Black Rose Books

— (1999) Lessons from Kosovo: The new military humanism, London: Pluto

Carapico, Sheila (1998) Legalism and realism in the Gulf, *Middle East Report*, No. 206 pp 3-6

Campbell, Duncan (2003) Notes from New York, a profile of DeLillo, the *Observer*, 4 May

Chomsky, Noam (1992) The media and the war: What war?, in Mowlana, Hamid, Gerner, George and Schiller, Herbert I (eds), *Triumph of the Image*, Boulder, Colorado: Westview Press pp 51-63

Clark, Neil (2004) The spoils of another war, the *Guardian*, 21 September

Cockburn, Patrick (2004) Exiled Allawi was responsible for 45-minute WMD claim, the *Independent*, 29 May

Collins, John M. (1991) *America's small wars*, Washington/London: Brasseys (US)

Combs, James (1993) From the Great War to the Gulf War: Popular entertainment and the legitimation of warfare, in Denton, Robert (ed.) *The media and the Persion Gulf War*, Westport CT: Praeger pp 257-284

Conetta, Carl (2004) Disappearing the Dead: Iraq, Afghanistan and the Idea of 'New Warfare', Project on Defense Alternative Research Monograph 9, 18 February. Available at http://www.comw.org/pda/0402rmp.html, accessed on 19 February 2004

Cummings, Bruce (1992) *War and television*, London: Verso

Curtis, Mark (1998) *The Great Deception: Anglo American Power and World Order*, London: Pluto Press

— (2003) *Web of Deceit: Britain's Real Role in the World*, London: Vintage

Dickson, Sandra H. (1994) Understanding media bias: The press and the US invasion of Panama, *Journalism Quarterly*, Vol. 71, No. 4 pp 809-819

Dorril, Stephen (2000) *MI6: Fifty Years of Special Operations*, London: Fourth Estate

Engelhardt, Tom (1995) *The end of victory culture: Cold War America and the Disillusionment of a Generation*, Amherst: University of Massachusetts Press

Featherstone, Donald (1993) *Victorian Colonial Warfare: Africa*, London: Blandford

— (1993a) *Victorian Colonial Warfare: India*, London: Blandford

Galbraith, J.K. (2004) A cloud over civilisation, the *Guardian*, 15 July

Guillot, Clare (2003) Nassiriya: le soldat Reeves face à la foule en colère, *Le Monde*, 17 April

Gunn, Simon ((1989) *Revolution of the Right*, London: Pluto Press with the Transnational Institute

Greenslade, Roy (2004) Saying sorry isn't enough, the *Guardian*, 31 May

Hammond, Philip (2003) The media war on terrorism, *Journal for Crime, Conflict and Media*, Vol. 1, No.1 pp 23-36

Harris, Laurence (1984) State and economy in the Second World War, in McLennan, George, Held, David and Hall, Stuart (eds) *State and society in contemporary Britain: A critical introduction*; Polity Press: Cambridge pp 50-76

Johnstone, Diana (2002) *Fools' Crusade: Yugoslavia, Nato and Western Delusions*, New York/London; Monthly Review Press/Pluto Press. Introduction available online at: http://www.swans.com/library/art9/dianaj01.html, accessed on 26 September 2004

Keeble, Richard (1997) *Secret State, Silent Press: New Militarism, the Gulf and the modern image of warfare*, Luton: John Libbey

— (1998) The myth of Saddam Hussein: New Militarism and the propaganda function of the human interest story, in Kieran, Matthew (ed.) *Media Ethics*, London: Routledge pp 66-81

— (1999) A Balkan Birthday for Nato, *British Journalism Review*, Vol. 10, No 2 pp 16-20

— (2000a) New Militarism and the Manufacture of Warfare, in Hammond, Philip and Herman, Edward S. (eds) *Degraded Capability: The Media and the Kosovo Crisis*, London: Pluto Press pp 59-59

— (2000b) Hiding the horror of 'humanitarian' warfare, *The Public*, Vol. 7, No. 2 pp 87-98

— (2001) The media's battle cry, *Press Gazette*, October 5.

— (2003a) Making the conflict seem unreal, *Lincolnshire Echo*, April 19

— (2003b) We see more and more of the conflict but we know as little as ever; *Independent on Sunday*, March 30

— (2004) Agents of the press, Press Gazette, August 27

Kellner, Douglas (1992) *The Persian Gulf TV War*, Boulder/San Francisco/Oxford: Westview Press

Knightley, Phillip (2000) *The First Casualty: The War Correspondent as Hero and Myth-Maker From the Crimea to Kosovo*, London: Prion

— (2003) Turning the tanks on the reporters; the *Observer*, 15 June

Landay, Jonathan S and Wells, Tish (2004) Iraqi group fed false information to news media. Available online at: http://www.realcities.com/mld/krwashington/8194211.htm, accessed on 16 March 2006

MacArthur, Brian (2003) Changing pace of war, *The Times*, 27 June

MacKenzie, John (1984) *Propaganda and Empire: The manipulation of British public opinion 1880-1960*, Manchester: Manchester University Press

Massing, Michael (2003) The high price of an unforgiving war, *Columbia Journalism Review*, May/June

Newsinger, John (2002) *British counter-insurgency: From Palestine to Northern Ireland*, Houndmills, Basingstoke, Hampshire: Palgrave

Peak, Steve (1982) Britain's military adventures, the *Pacifist*, Vol. 20 p.10

Petley, Julian (2003) War without death: Responses to distant suffering, *Journal for Crime, Conflict and Media*, Vol. 1, No. 1 pp 72-85. Available online at: www.jc2m.co.uk, accessed 13 March 2006

Pilger, John (2002) *The New Rulers of the World*, London/New York: Verso

— (2004) *Tell me no lies: Investigative Journalism and its Triumphs*, London: Jonathan Cape

Powell, Colin (1995) *Soldier's Way*, London: Hutchinson (with Joseph Persico)

Robins, Kevin and Levidow, Les (1991) The eye of the Storm, *Screen*; London: Vol. 32, No. 3; Autumn pp 324-328

Robinson, Piers et al. (2006) Media Wars: News Performance and Media Management During the 2003 Iraq War. Available online at: www.esrctoday.ac.uk, accessed on 26 January 2007
Said, Edward (2003) A window on the world, *Guardian Review*, August 2
Smith, Jeffery A. (1999) *War and Press Freedom: The problem of Prerogative Power*, Oxford and New York: Oxford University Press

INDEX

ABC 25, 31, 179
Abu Ghraib prison 3, 37, 70, 72, 138, 188
Afghanistan 2, 38, 46, 50, 51, 64, 71, 77, 92, 94, 96, 97, 135, 139, 143, 177, 182, 185, 192, 205, 209
African
    conflicts/wars 8, 10, 42-51, 58, 60
    correspondents 46
    states 8, 10, 43
Al Jazeera 3, 72, 82, 83, 130, 138
Al Qaeda 9, 34, 35, 51, 64, 98, 130, 131, 134, 139, 140, 205
Anglo-American
    Corporation 49
    journalism 36, 55, 91
    military power 163, 165
Angola 10, 42-50
anti-American 34, 90
anti-war 5, 11, 71, 73, 83, 112, 117-126, 177, 190
anti-terrorism 51, 192
Arab
    governments 167,
    language 36, 95, 166, 169-170
    media 3, 12, 164, 168, 174, 175
atrocities 23, 24, 71, 130, 131, 134, 154, 204, 205
audiences 20, 21, 24, 26, 27, 36, 43, 45, 46, 49, 55, 65, 69, 71, 72, 79, 80, 81, 86, 106, 119, 133, 135
    news audiences 80, 90-99
    perception 141-146
    target audience 12, 46, 141-146, 151-153, 156,157

BBC 22, 32, 43, 45, 70, 72, 77, 87, 99, 110
    correspondents 45, 47, 78, 79, 87
    news 42, 47, 78, 79, 87
    Radio 4 32, 42, 46, 80, 126
    World Service 45, 46
Bin Laden, Osama 30, 96, 97, 130, 131, 139, 192, 196, 198, 205
Blair, Tony 49, 98, 112, 121, 125, 132, 135, 173, 175, 197
blogging 71-87
Bosnia 6, 23-24, 43, 99, 123, 136, 204
Burundi 43, 47
Bush, George 2, 30, 31, 35, 36, 71, 83, 103, 106, 112, 125, 130-135, 165, 173, 186, 175, 181, 184, 190, 192, 195, 198, 201
    Bush administration 159, 177, 197

casualties 44, 64, 164, 208
    civilian 3, 55, 64, 136-137, 139, 149, 180, 202
    'collateral damage' 136, 148, 208
    military 19, 55, 125, 136, 200, 206
censorship 4, 5, 51, 55, 56, 57, 68, 105, 111, 112, 167, 179, 180, 202
    self-censorship 57
Chad 8, 43
CIA (Central Intelligence Agency) 30-37, 90, 93, 94, 96, 97, 99, 206
citizens
    citizen journalism 1, 71, 75, 77, 83
    mobilization of 3, 117
civil liberties 197
civil war 43, 48, 55, 58
Chechyna 7, 98, 135
CNN 21, 72, 77, 79, 108, 165, 166, 179, 180. 191
Cold War 2, 9, 13, 34, 50, 131, 133, 156, 178, 180, 203, 206, 207
command and control 3, 12, 146, 149
Congo (Belgium) 56
Congo (Democratic Republic of) 8, 10, 42, 44, 48, 49, 58
correspondents
    freelance 45
    foreign 45, 46, 48, 66, 81, 86
    frontline 66-72
    war 67, 85, 88
counter-
    claims 72,
    hegemony 112, 164, 166, 169
    insurgency 94, 132, 139
    propaganda 105, 189
    terrorism 51

Daily Express 33, 205
Daily Mail 32
Daily Telegraph 31, 38, 85, 206
Defense
    Ministry of 141
    Secretary of 62, 110, 125, 148
    Staff 147, 208
    US Department of 165, 193
Democratic Republic of Congo (DRC) 8, 44, 48, 49, 58
democracy
    democratization 85, 87
    liberal democracy 2, 124
    Western democracy 36
discourse theory 11, 103, 104
disinformation 4, 13, 68, 156, 174, 206

extradition 42
embedding 4, 69, 108, 170

foreign policy 97, 179, 181, 192
Former Yugoslavia 43, 63, 98, 147, 204, 205
Fox News 109, 179, 191, 192
'friendly fire' 5, 12, 67, 109, 204
fundamentalism 2, 4, 5, 7, 63-64, 106

genocide 9, 54, 58
global
    media 106, 134, 135, 139, 163, 64, 174, 200, 204, 206, 209
    politics 8, 132, 138, 203
    survelliance 12, 132, 140, 164, 192, 196, 208
    terrorism 9, 134, 138, 197
globalization 6, 7, 8, 62, 64, 65, 66, 167
Guantanamo Bay 37, 171
Guardian, the 31, 32, 34, 36, 46, 67, 68, 69, 78, 83, 85, 98, 119, 204, 205, 206, 208
guerrilla tactics 6, 96
Gulf War (1991) 158, 160, 163, 165, 166, 174, 177, 179, 180, 181, 190, 203,

Hizbollah 154, 159
Holocaust 22-23, 56, 58, 207
hegemony 93, 103-106, 112, 169, 202
hegemonic discourse 11, 103, 105, 112, 164, 166, 167
human rights 1, 29, 32, 33, 34, 35, 37, 66, 83, 136, 138, 139, 208
humanitarian
    agencies/organizations 5, 42
    crisis 8
    intervention 91, 132
Hussein, Saddam 9, 21, 72, 83, 104, 106, 107, 109, 131, 136, 154, 156, 159, 164, 180, 192, 200, 204, 206, 218

imperialism 13, 202, 205, 208
Independent, the 32, 33, 34, 122, 125, 208
information
    campaign 141, 149
    environment 11, 62, 71, 72, 188
    Technology 3, 179, 180
    War 63-72
    Warfare 2, 7
Internet 3, 12, 36, 32, 65, 67, 70, 72, 80, 84, 112, 133, 159, 164, 165, 167, 189, 191
intervention
    media 24, 25, 133
    state/military 1, 8, 19, 76, 132, 141, 190, 204, 209

Iraq
    regime 5, 80, 131, 156, 163, 164, 165, 174
    War (1991) see Gulf War
    War (2003) 2, 3, 4, 11, 13, 19, 67, 71, 138, 159 160
Iran 94, 97, 107, 196, 205
Islamic
    audiences 166, 167
    terrorism 97, 99, 110, 131, 134, 135, 137, 138, 139, 159
Israel 48, 98, 135, 152-159, 165
ITN 5, 67

journalism
    investigative 10, 29-38, 211
    war 5, 6, 11

kidnap video 163-175
Korea 64, 205
Kosovo 3, 8, 65, 99, 132, 138, 205

media
    management 4, 5, 106, 108, 111, 112, 133, 203
    representations of war 4, 9, 11, 19, 43, 86, 112, 182
mediation 26, 69, 70, 112, 165, 179
memory 10, 18-27, 47, 91, 111, 204
military
    military-industrial complex 13, 91, 178, 179,
    military-industrial-media-entertainment (MIME) 12, 189-198
    military-media complex 12, 177-186
    military-media relations 4
    US military 5, 12, 95, 125, 138, 139, 163, 178, 181, 189, 190, 191, 193, 206
militarism 13, 136, 138, 190, 200-209
    New Militarism 13, 201, 202, 209
misinformation 64, 111, 158, 177, 182, 203, 209
Ministry of Defense 141
mobilization
    of population/civilians 3, 65, 95, 117, 126, 132-133, 153, 202
myth
    of war 13, 183, 194, 200-209

NATO 1, 6, 65, 138, 205
NBC 25, 80, 193,
newsworthy 7, 8, 9, 14, 69, 70, 110, 125, 126, 167, 168 191
New York Times 57, 96, 206, 207, 200

objectivity (of journalism) 5, 68, 72, 82, 99, 110, 111, 113
Observer, the 32, 34, 98, 206, 207

Palestinian 48, 135, 152, 155, 165
patriotism 6, 57, 77, 174, 178, 179, 182, 183, 185, 201, 209
peacekeeping 1, 6, 8, 42
peace movement 73, 117
Pentagon 69, 95, 96, 111, 177, 180, 181, 193, 197, 207
Persian Gulf War see Gulf War (1991)
private security firms/contractors 6, 93,
propaganda 3, 5, 7, 11, 12, 13, 68, 69, 72, 87, 94, 97, 99, 105, 106, 108, 109, 112
protest 11, 112, 117- 127, 179, 203, 208, 209
public
    opinion 120, 126, 138, 158, 159, 166
    relations (PR) 165, 166, 178, 191
    sphere 3, 4, 8, 72, 73, 106, 112, 170, 174, 178, 182
psychological
    warfare 12, 151-167
    operations (psyop) 151-167, 197

radio 25, 26, 57, 156, 157, 160
real time news 62, 69, 160, 180
rendition 10, 29-38
Reuters 5, 47, 77, 82, 85
Revolution in Military Affairs (RMA) 2, 188, 189, 197
Rwanda 58

Scotland on Sunday 120, 122, 123, 125, 126
Sierra Leone 8, 142, 143
Sky News 67
Somalia 3, 8, 43, 46, 50, 51, 190
spectacle 72, 87, 126, 189, 190, 195, 197, 198, 202, 206
spectators 65, 168, 173, 203
Stalin, Josef 56, 66, 149
Sudan 30, 43, 46, 47, 48, 51
Sunday Express 120, 125
Sunday Herald 120, 122, 124, 125
Sunday Mail 120, 123, 124, 125
Sunday Mirror 121, 122, 123, 124, 125
Sunday Telegraph 121, 123, 124, 125
Sunday Times, The 32, 34, 98, 123, 125, 206
survelliance 12, 98, 132-139, 168, 179, 188, 197
symbolic power 31, 32, 164, 165, 167, 169

Taliban 9, 136, 205
television
    news 18, 21, 25, 26, 27, 80
terrorism
    coverage of terrorism 6, 9, 97, 106
    global terrorism 9, 134, 197
    war and terrorism 1, 2, 7, 10, 11, 12, 91, 106, 132
    'war on terror' 2, 12, 20, 33, 6, 47, 48, 65, 76, 92, 130, 131, 132, 139, 165, 191, 205, 206
terrorist
    acts 2, 6, 7, 12, 25, 26, 34, 64, 95, 97, 98, 118, 131, 136, 138, 143, 192
    groups 7, 65, 96, 97, 130
    suspects 31
    warfare 7, 12, 130-151, 203
Times, The 32, 33, 36, 57, 66, 69, 206

UN 1, 6, 33, 44, 49, 51, 53, 204
    Convention Against Torture 31

Vietnam War 19, 64, 68, 71, 92, 93, 112, 117, 118, 136, 148, 155, 158, 177, 179, 181, 190, 201, 202, 204, 209
virtuality 191, 197

WMD (weapons of mass destruction) 2, 106, 107, 110, 111, 126, 206, 207, 209

www.ingramcontent.com/pod-product-compliance
Ingram Content Group UK Ltd.
Pitfield, Milton Keynes, MK11 3LW, UK
UKHW021319180426
11947UKWH00015B/1317